ONTOLOGICAL
REDUCTION

ONTOLOGICAL
REDUCTION

by Reinhardt Grossmann

INDIANA UNIVERSITY PRESS

BLOOMINGTON · LONDON 1973

Published in Canada by Fitzhenry & Whiteside, Ltd., Don Mills, Ontario
Library of Congress Catalog Card No. 72-85604 ISBN 0-253-34246-5

This volume is No. 72 in the Indiana University Humanities Series.

MANUFACTURED IN THE UNITED STATES OF AMERICA

CONTENTS

Preface   1

Introduction: A Principle of Acquaintance

1. Perceiving and Sensing   3
2. Intuition and Judgment   10
3. Atomic and Molecular Facts   17

Part One: Numbers and Quantifiers

4. Abbreviations   29
5. Identity and Equivalence   36
6. Descriptions and Leibniz's Law   47
7. Recursive Definitions   55
8. Definition by Abstraction   61
9. Existence and the Quantifiers   69
10. Necessity   78
11. Possible Entities   89
12. Implicit Definitions   93
13. Constructional Definitions   101

Part Two: Properties and Classes

14. Contextual Definitions   109

CONTENTS

15. Property Abstraction 116
16. Sets versus Classes 122
17. Impredicative Definitions 130

Part Three: Individuals and Structures

18. Wholes and Parts 141
19. A Problem of Perception 149
20. Bundles of Properties 153
21. Spatial versus Ontological Analysis 162
22. Emergent Properties 167

Conclusion: A List of Categories 177

Notes 191

Index 207

PREFACE

The structure of this book requires a brief explanation. The philosophical inquiry proceeds simultaneously, as it were, on three different levels. First and foremost, there is the problem of the nature of ontological reduction. What reduction devices and methods have been proposed? How does one go about showing that a given ontological kind can be reduced to another? What kinds of definitions are important from a strictly ontological point of view? These and similar questions arise in connection with the main topic of this book. I shall contend that most kinds of definitions have no reductive power whatsoever. On the positive side, I maintain that there are only two ways of showing that what is alleged to be an ontological kind reduces in reality to another kind. First, it may be discovered that two expressions which apparently represent different entities or different kinds of entities refer in truth to the very same entity or kind of entity. In most instances, one of the two expressions will then be an abbreviation of the other. Second, it may be discovered that a certain informative identity statement is true. In this case, either a description describes the same entity or kind of entity for which there is also a label, or two different descriptions describe the very same entity or kind of entity.

On the second level there are comments about the status and nature of a selected group of categories. Here the main topics are indicated by the five main parts of this book. The first part consists of some introductory remarks about the so-called principle of acquaintance. The second part deals with numbers and quantifiers in general. In the third part, the discussion turns to properties and classes. The fourth part is concerned with individuals and structures. The fifth part contains a summary of the most important results and a list of categories.

A discussion of the nature of ontological reduction has to be illustrated by examples. Numbers (and quantifiers in general), properties, classes, individuals, and structures are the five categories selected here as examples. In regard to numbers, it is argued (1) that they cannot be reduced to properties or classes, (2) that they form a subcategory of their own, and (3) that they belong to the main category of quantifiers. In regard to properties, the main contentions are (1) that there are no complex properties—that is, no properties represented by complex propositional forms—and (2) that there are properties which do not determine classes. Classes, I shall affirm, need not be determined by properties. The fourth section consists of essays about four particular problems which arise because there are structures and, in particular, spatio-temporal structures.

On the third and last level of inquiry, an attempt is made to formulate a complete list of the main categories. But while the problem of ontological reduction is rather thoroughly discussed, and while there is also a fair amount of talk about particular categories, discussion of the hierarchy of categories is admittedly rather sketchy. Nevertheless, a glimpse at the whole system of ontology seemed to me better than no glimpse at all.

Thus, with the three levels of inquiry in mind, you may think of this book in rather old-fashioned terms, as "A discussion of ontological reduction, with special reference to the status of selected categories and culminating in the outline of a list of categories."

Professors Paul Eisenberg and Michael Dunn read the manuscript and made a number of helpful suggestions; I am very grateful to them.

Bloomington, Indiana   R. Grossmann
November, 1970

A Principle of Acquaintance

1 PERCEIVING AND SENSING

What are the categories of the world, and how do they hang together? How do we find out what the categories are and that they hang together in certain ways? To ask the first question is not to ask the second. Ontology is not epistemology; it is not even the theory of how we know categories. Yet these two questions are inseparable. If one proposes to list the categories, one must give some thought to the question of how these categories are known. This book deals primarily with ontological problems, but in the first three chapters I shall also say a few things about the epistemological issue.

We know that something exists because we are acquainted either with it or with something else from which we can infer its existence. There is no other way of knowing. Hence whenever we claim to know that a certain thing exists, we must be prepared to show either that we are acquainted with it or that we are acquainted with something else from which we can infer its existence. I understand these assertions to state the essence of what some philosophers call *the principle of acquaintance*. It is a very general principle, indeed. Like all such extremely general theses, it has its share of ambiguity. To accept the principle, as I do, is to accept it in a more distinct form. What is meant by acquaintance? What shall we understand by inference?

In the present context we do not need to concern ourselves with the second question. The categories to be discussed are not inferred from what we are acquainted with; they are acquaintances of ours. Thus the problem reduces itself to how we can defend the view that we are acquainted, not only with such mundane individual things as trees, pains, and thoughts, but also with such extraordinary entities as properties, classes, connectives, and numbers, to mention just a few. The heart of this defense consists of an explication of what it means to be acquainted with something.

Acquaintance consists of mental acts. There are many kinds of mental acts and hence many ways in which one can be acquainted with something. The most obvious examples of mental acts are acts of perception. Among these, visual perception, or seeing, stands out and may therefore serve in the following discussion as our paradigm of acquaintance. We know that certain entities exist, because we have seen them. For example, we know that there are tigers, because we have seen some. But we also know that there are colors—properties of a certain kind rather than individual things of a certain kind—because we have seen them. Do we also know that there are numbers, because we have seen them? I shall argue that we do. I shall argue that we see numbers in precisely the same way in which we see colors and colored individual things. This does not mean, of course, that numbers are like colors and individual things. They are very different kinds of entities. Numbers and colors, in my view, belong to entirely different categories. Nonetheless, we are acquainted with both kinds in visual perception. What holds for numbers, I shall also maintain, holds equally for other categories. They, too, are presented in acts of perception.*

Do we see numbers? Well, we do not see, say, the number 3 all by itself in isolated numerical splendor. That much is clear. But neither do we see, say, the color saffron all by itself, separated from everything else. Yet who doubts that we can see it? To see something, therefore, does not mean to see it isolated from everything else; it does not mean to see it by itself. We see the color saffron when we see a saffron-colored robe. Similarly, to see the number 3, it suffices to see three robes. Do we see, then, a *number* of things in the way that we see colored things? If we can show that we do, then we see numbers in the only sense relevant to our discussion, and we have proved our point.

Few philosophers would be happy with this comparison between colors and numbers. The root of their uneasiness, I suspect, is the belief that while there are such things as color sensations, there are no

---

* Ultimately I wish to hold, of course, that not only the entities belonging to such categories as that of number are presented, but that the categorial property of being a number and other such categories are also presented.

corresponding number sensations. The seeing of numbers, they would wish to maintain, must be a seeing of quite a different sort from the seeing of colors; for colors are really and truly presented to us in color sensations, while numbers do not come through the senses in this fashion.* The seeing of numbers must be a matter of judgment rather than of sensibility. It may perhaps be compared with the "seeing" that someone is a thief, but not with the seeing that something has the color saffron. Frege, for example, describes this difference in the following way. While there is a sensible impression that corresponds to the word 'triangular' when we look at a triangle, there is no similar sensible impression that corresponds to the word 'three' when we look at its angles (or sides). We do not see the number 3 directly, but "see something upon which can fasten an intellectual activity of ours leading to a judgment in which the number 3 occurs."[1]

Frege presents two arguments for his contention. First, if we assume that there is something sensible corresponding to the numeral '3,' then we should also find that same sensible thing in three concepts. Hence we should find something sensible, whatever corresponds to '3,' in something entirely nonsensible, such as three concepts. Second, how is it that we become acquainted with the number of figures of the syllogism as drawn up by Aristotle? Not with our eyes, for what we see is at most certain symbols for the syllogistic figures, not the figures themselves, and how can we see their number if the figures remain invisible?

Both of these arguments make the same point: that nothing sensible can correspond to the numeral '3,' because there are also nonsensible entities which are so numbered. But why does this latter fact refute the assumption that something sensible corresponds to '3'? After all, it is only the concepts which are granted to be nonsensible and not the (complex) referent—whatever that may be—of the expression 'three concepts'. Why, in other words, should it be assumed to be impossible for something sensible to occur together with

---

* The question is not whether numbers can come through several senses, as Aristotle seems to claim (*De Anima*, Book II, chaps. 6 and 7), while colors can only come through one, but rather whether numbers can come through any sense at all. I do hold that one cannot only see numbers by seeing, say, three robes, but that one can also hear them by hearing three tones, and that one can also feel them by feeling three pains.

something nonsensible, granting, of course, that something nonsensible cannot at the same time be sensible? Assume that there does indeed correspond something sensible to the numeral '3'. Now, when we are presented, say, with three lines, we may be said to be presented with two sensible things: the sensible entity corresponding to '3' and the sensible lines. On the other hand, when we are presented with three concepts, then we may be said to be presented with something sensible, the sensible entity 3, as well as with something nonsensible, namely, concepts. Frege seems to beg the question when he supposes that not only concepts, but also the (complex) referent of the expression 'three concepts' must be wholly nonsensible. We shall see presently why it may have seemed obvious to him that a sensible entity can never be presented together with something nonsensible in one and the same mental act.

For the sake of the argument, we assumed that concepts are nonsensible. But we can only hope to shed some real light on the issue if we take a closer look at what one could reasonably mean by a sensible entity in the present context. And we may hope to succeed if we start once again from the sensible entity which is a color.

Under normal circumstances, when we are in the presence of a blue perceptual object, we experience a blue sense impression.* This much I shall take for granted without further argument, even though there are a number of philosophers who deny the existence of sense impressions. To go into their arguments would lead us too far afield.[2] Frege, at any rate, would agree with this statement.[3] But at the next step in our analysis we part ways. Not only do we have a blue sense impression under normal circumstances, but the perceptual object also shares this very color with the sense impression. In other words, the color blue—this particular property—is exemplified both by the perceptual object before us and by the sense impression which we experience. It is my impression that Frege would disagree. According to him, we must distinguish between the sensation blue and the concept

---

* I do not mean to imply that we cannot be in the presence of a blue perceptual object, see that it is blue, and yet have a differently colored sense impression. The color of the sense impression may or may not be the same as that of the perceptual object before us; and we may or may not be "fooled" by the color of the sense impression we experience into seeing the object as having a color different from the one which it has.

blue. The former corresponds, roughly, to the blue sense impression; but the latter, the concept blue, is nothing visual or perceptual. It is, like all concepts, something wholly nonsensible.[4] Frege does not realize that the concept-object distinction applies to sense impressions just as much as to perceptual objects.[5] Had he seen this, he would have observed that to talk about a sense impression is to talk about an object, and not to talk about the referent of 'blue'. He would have further realized that to speak of a blue sense impression is to speak of an object as falling under the concept blue. And this in turn would have led him to see that the concept blue which is attributed to a perceptual object is one and the same entity with the referent of 'blue' attributed to a sense impression.*

But be that as it may, the perception of a blue object involves under normal conditions at least three entities that could be called sensible, namely, the perceptual object seen, the sense impression experienced which is caused (in part) by the perceptual object, and, most importantly, the color blue which is exemplified by both the perceptual object and the sense impression. To say that the number 3 is not a sensible entity could therefore mean several different things. Let us agree that 3 is neither a perceptual object, nor a sense impression, nor a property of sense impressions and perceptual objects. I am willing to grant all this, because I am convinced on other grounds that numbers are neither individual things, like perceptual objects and sense impressions, nor properties of such things, like colors. Hence numbers cannot be sensible entities, if sensible objects are exhausted by the three kinds of entities just mentioned. But is this the only reasonable explication of what it means for something to be sensible? Surely not; for otherwise, spatial *relations* would not be sensible entities. Yet it seems obvious that we can see that a perceptual object is to the left of another perceptual object just as clearly as we can see that both of them are blue.† We must approach the whole matter from the opposite direction. We must not try to pick out some kinds of entities which are obviously

* The reason for this mistake is Frege's view (which he shares with many philosophers) that the blue sense impression is really an "instance of blue," that is, it belongs to an ontological kind different from both objects and concepts. Compare the next chapter on this point.

† Sense impressions, too, stand in spatial relations to each other; but they do not stand in such relations to perceptual objects. One sense impression, for

sensible and then reject all other kinds of entities as nonsensible. Instead, we shall start out with mental acts of a certain kind, "sensible acts," and ask ourselves what kinds of entities can be presented by means of such mental acts.

Under normal circumstances, when we see a blue perceptual object, there occur among other things two mentals acts that matter for our discussion, namely, an act of *sensing* a blue sense impression and an act of *seeing* a blue perceptual object.* What else can one *see* and/or *sense*? It seems to me that one can see two blue perceptual objects and that one can sense two blue sense impressions. Hence, if we can be said to see the color blue when we see a blue object and to sense the color blue when we sense a blue sense impression, then we can with equal justification be said to see the number 2 when we see two blue perceptual objects and to sense the number 2 when we sense two blue sense impressions. Of course, numbers are neither perceptual objects (individuals), nor sensory objects (individuals); nor are they properties of these two kinds of individual things. But they are perceptual entities nevertheless. They are "sensible" entities, too; for they can be presented through mental acts of perception and sensing just as much as those other kinds of entities.

I have assumed, without defense, that there are sense impressions. Now I must add two further undefended assertions. For reasons quite independent of those we are considering at present, I believe that all mental acts are propositional.[6] This means that all mental acts intend states of affairs rather than, say, single individuals, single properties, single relations, single numbers, etc., in isolation. Linguistically speaking, every sentence which mentions a mental act and its intention could be rephrased so as to contain a "that clause" followed by a whole sentence. For example, although we say such things as that we have been thinking of Paris, there actually occurs a whole series of mental acts of imagining, wishing, remembering, etc., each one of which intends a state of affairs. For example, there may have occurred an

---

example, may be to the left of another, but it is not to the left of any perceptual object.

* When I speak here of seeing a blue perceptual object, I do not mean merely that there is such an object in front of a person, but that it is seen as being blue.

imagining that one was in Paris, a remembering that one had eaten in a certain restaurant, etc. When we are asked what we have seen, we may well reply, "A horse." However, according to the view adopted here, the intention of the mental act of seeing which actually occurred must have been of the sort *This is a horse* or *There is a horse over there* or *This is a beautiful horse*. The precise state of affairs is left open by the reply; nevertheless, there did occur a mental act which intended some such state of affairs.

We shall also maintain that a mental act of seeing does not consist of any other kinds of acts; and what holds for seeing holds as well for the other kinds of perceptual acts, namely, hearing, smelling, feeling (i.e. touching), and tasting. These acts must be distinguished from, among other things, acts of sensing, acts of remembering, acts of desiring, acts of imagining, and, most importantly, acts of judging. Seeing, according to this view, does not involve judging. Seeing and judging constitute two irreducible kinds of mental acts; one experiences them as distinct. When one sees that the moon is full, there occurs a mental act which "feels entirely different" from the mental act of judging that the moon is full. This felt difference, it is here claimed, is a difference between the acts themselves, not a difference in the rest of the conscious states of a person; it does not consist, for example, in a difference between the kinds of sense impressions that are sensed on those two occasions. In particular, seeing does not consist (as a very common philosophical view will have it) of sensing plus judging.

When we see two chairs, for example, there occurs—always under normal conditions—an act of seeing which intends some such state of affairs as the one represented by the sentence 'There are two chairs in that corner'. There also occurs an act of sensing two sense impressions of certain shapes and colors. Both facts, the state of affairs intended by the act of seeing and the state of affairs intended by the act of sensing, involve the number 2 in the very same sense in which two corresponding states of affairs involve the property blue. And since we are presented with every constituent of a state of affairs if we are presented through a mental act with the state of affairs, we are presented with the number 2 through an act of seeing as well as through an act of sensing, just as we are presented with the color blue both through an act of seeing and an act of sensing. We can now give a general answer to the question, What are the sensible entities which are presented in sensing and/or seeing? We must count as sensible entities all the constituents of those states of affairs which can be intended by acts of sensing or acts of seeing. Thus numbers are sensible entities; for one can see such a fact as that there are two chairs in the corner. It must be admitted that this explication of the notion of a sensible entity allows what most philosophers consider to be "abstract" entities to enter the circle of what is sensible. It clashes, therefore, with the traditional and even now widely accepted account of what the objects of sense and what the objects of reason are. A comparison between the traditional view and the position here defended may shed some further light on important issues not as yet discussed.

2 INTUITION AND JUDGMENT

According to the tradition, the mind has two eyes. One eye sees the sensible world, while the other contemplates what is not sensible: the ideas, the forms, the universals. Let us speak of two kinds of act, *intuition* and *conception*. To these two eyes of the mind there correspond two kinds of entities which are seen. Each one of these mental acts has its own appropriate kind of object. However, knowledge seems to reside neither in intuition nor in conception as such. We express knowledge, to put the matter linguistically, not in single words or descriptions, but in whole sentences. And sentences express neither intuitions nor conceptions; rather, they express *judgments*. Thus a third kind of mental act, judgments, is added.

What does the eye of judgment see? Does it, too, have its own kind of appropriate object? The traditional answers have, generally, been negative. Some philosophers, Kant, for example, thought of judgment as a kind of intuition; a kind that presents several ordinary objects of intuition in combination, so to speak.[1] Other philosophers, Brentano for one, defended the uniqueness of judgment as an irreducible kind of mental act distinct from intuitions. But they, too, denied that judgments had their special objects. Instead, they sought the uniqueness of judgment in the features of affirmation and denial.[2] There are some exceptions to the rule. Frege, for example, held that judgments intend thoughts, where by a thought he meant an objective

entity which differs both from an individual thing and a concept.[3] And
Meinong maintained that there are objectives in addition to objects.[4]
The history of Fregean thoughts and Meinongian objectives is the
history of the emancipation of states of affairs, facts, or propositions in
recent ontology.* The emergence of states of affairs as a separate
category of entities—on a par with individuals (substances) and
properties (modifications of substances)—marks the most decisive break
of modern philosophy with the Aristotelian heritage.

Intuition is the eye of the senses. Through it and it alone are we
acquainted with sensible entities. If we are acquainted with other
entities at all, then we must be acquainted with them through acts
other than intuitions. And if there are other kinds of mental acts, then
they must acquaint us with entities which are not sensible. This familiar
(I am tempted to say Kantian) theme clashes with our earlier assertion
that colors are sensible entities which are presented through the senses.
According to the traditional view, not even colors are really sensible
entities. But if not even colors are to be counted as sensible objects,
something must surely have gone wrong with this conception of
intuition as the only access to that which is sensible. This concept
combines two irreconcilable features, as it were. On the one hand,
intuition is supposed to be the one and only access to what is sensible.
On the other, it is also the mental eye whose only appropriate object is
the individual, the particular. Hence the sensible must be identified
with the particular. There can be no entities which are both sensible
and nonparticular. Properties, therefore, cannot be sensible. Colors, it
follows, cannot be sensible. But if even colors are not sensible entities,
what things are? Thus, if we insist that colors are sensible entities and
that they are therefore presented in intuition, then we must give up the
idea that intuition can acquaint us only with individuals. Moreover,
having made room for colors as objects of intuition, we open the gates
for other kinds of entities to slip in. Why should numbers, for example,

---

* This emancipation culminates in Russell's remark at the beginning of
The Philosophy of Logical Atomism: "The first thing I want to emphasize is that
the outer world—the world, so to speak, which knowledge is aiming at
knowing—is not completely described by a lot of 'particulars,' but that you must
also take account of these things that I call facts, which are the sort of things that
you express by a sentence, and that these, just as much as particular chairs and
tables, are part of the real world." *Logic and Knowledge,* ed. R. C. Marsh
(London, 1956), p. 183.

not be objects of intuitions? Do we not see with our eyes that there are two apples on the table just as clearly as we see that there are red apples on the table? The criterion of what is sensible has changed from what is individual to what comes through the senses, and that, surely, is as it should be.

The notion that intuition presents us with the particular and with nothing else is more powerfully reinforced by another theme. This one, too, is Kantian in flavor, if not in origin. Time and space, as the saying goes, are the forms of intuition. Accordingly, all the objects of intuition are localized in space and/or time.[5] What is so localized are individuals and only individuals. Hence, properties cannot possibly be objects of intuition, because they are localized neither in space nor in time. Nor, of course, can numbers be objects of intuition according to this view, since numbers are not localized in space and time either. So strong is the mutual support of the two theses (a) that intuition is the source of what is particular, and (b) that space and time are the forms of intuition, that even such a master of phenomenological analysis as Husserl succumbs to their influence. That color is something sensible, if anything deserves to be called sensible, is obvious. Yet, according to the dogma of localization, it cannot be an object of intuition. We know how Husserl tried to assure our knowledge of color in particular and of properties in general. In addition to sensory intuition, he maintains, there is also a different kind of mental act, eidetic intuition, which presents us not with the particular, but with the universal—not with the temporally and spatially localized, but with what is neither in time nor space.[6]

However, the addition of eidetic intuition to sensory intuition does not really remove the tension created by our commonsensical belief that color is a matter of the senses. Husserl tries to resolve this tension by inventing a new kind of entity, the perfect particular, the instance of some property, or what he calls, in the case of a red individual, the *Rot-Moment*. In addition to the property red, for example, there also exist then numerous individual reds as parts of the many red individuals. Since these property items, as I shall call them, are individuals, they can be objects of sensory intuition. At the same time, they have something to do with properties, they are instances of properties, and hence they are supposed to explain our belief that, say, colors are sensible.

Husserl's property items are ontological absurdities.[7] As individuals, they can at best *be* red, that is, have the property of being red. But if so, then the tension mentioned earlier is in fact not resolved; for what then comes through the senses is an individual which is somehow connected with the property red, but which does not by itself "contain anything of redness." Property items are absurd entities because they are conceived of as particular and yet not wholly particular, as universal and yet not wholly universal, as simple and yet also complex. They owe their dubious existence to an irresolvable tension between the dogma of localization, on the one hand, and the ordinary belief that colors are sensible entities, on the other. With the rejection of the dogma of localization, there disappears the ontological attraction of such entities.

The dogma of localization is false. Space and time are not forms of sensibility. Sensible entities do not have to be localized in space and/or time. They do not have to be particular. Properties, colors for instance, can be objects of sensory intuition. Nor do we have to stop at properties, as we saw earlier. But our criticism of the traditional view goes deeper. We must realize that the traditional image of a separate eye for each separate category is fundamentally mistaken. The mind has several eyes, it is true, but all these eyes see entities of the same category, namely, states of affairs. There are many kinds of mental acts—our version of mental eyes. There are acts of sensing, and these acts correspond roughly to what philosophical tradition calls sensory intuition. There are also acts of memory, acts of imagining, acts of desiring, etc. And there are, last but not least, perceptual acts. But the intentions of all these acts, according to our view, are states of affairs. And since a mental act presents us ipso facto with the constituents of the state of affairs which it intends, mental acts acquaint us with as many different categories of entities as there are categorically distinguished constituents of intended states of affairs. Perception, for example, presents us not only with the individuals perceived, but also with the properties which we perceive these individuals to have. It acquaints us not only with certain individuals and their properties, but also with the perceived number of individuals with such and such a property. Furthermore, perception presents us with spatial and temporal entities, that is, with durations and temporal relations as well as shapes and spatial relations. These kinds of properties and relations are also constituents of states of affairs which are intended by perceptual acts. Space and time, far from being the forms of sensibility, are simply two of many kinds of ontological ingredients with which the senses acquaint us.

We have seen that Frege distinguishes between the sense impression blue and the concept blue. Only the former is a sensible entity. We suspect that he, too, was influenced by the Kantian notion that sensible entities must be particular in nature. The blue sense impression which Frege has in mind is not an individual which is blue; it is not, in his terminology, an object which falls under the concept blue. Rather, it is a property item, a perfect particular. Thus there is an obvious parallel between Frege's and Husserl's distinctions. But there is also a difference. While both Frege and Husserl hold that there are entities other than individuals, properties for example, Frege holds that all these further nonsensible entities are presented in judgment, while Husserl's acts of eidetic intuition may acquaint us, so to speak, with a property in isolation.

According to Frege, all sensible entities are subjective. All objective entities are presented through acts of judging. Thus there are two eyes: the eye of intuition, which acquaints us only with what is sensible and hence subjective, and the eye of judgment, which presents us only with the nonsensible and hence with objective entities. We now clearly see why he could take for granted that a sensible entity cannot be presented in conjunction with a nonsensible entity in a single mental act, for such a mental act would have to be neither an intuition nor a judgment. In any case, it follows that all objective entities are presented to us within the context of a state of affairs, that is, within the context of what Frege later comes to call a "thought"; for the proper objects of judgments are not single individuals or single concepts, but are "thoughts" expressed by whole sentences. This, I submit, is the source of one of the three principles which Frege stresses at the beginning of the *Foundations of Arithmetic*, namely, "never to ask for the meaning of a word in isolation, but only in the context of a proposition."[8] Frege does not mean to say that "meaning is use." What he has in mind is that the referents of words are to be found within the contexts of "thoughts," because one can become acquainted with such a referent only through judgment.

If we do not heed this particular principle, Frege explains, "one is almost forced to take as the meanings of words mental pictures or acts of the individual mind."[9] Much later in his book, he claims that only by adhering to this principle can one "avoid a physical view of number without slipping into a psychological view of it."[10] What does he have in mind?

Recall the Kantian schema according to which there are, first, ideas and judgments, and second, two kinds of ideas, namely, sensory intuitions and concepts. Frege changes this division. He proposes to use the term 'idea' only for mental, subjective entities in order to avoid the idealistic tinge of Kant's terminology. Such ideas are the proper objects of the senses. But in addition to ideas, there are also objects and concepts which are objective entities. These two kinds of objective entities are not presented through the senses, but are given through another kind of mental act, namely, judgment. Now, if there are only these two kinds of basic mental acts, intuition and judgment, then it follows that the meanings of words will have to be subjective entities, unless we assume that they are presented in contexts, that is, judgments.

As for the second quotation from Frege, we must remember that Kantian sensory intuitions are particular, while concepts are general. This aspect of the Kantian distinction roughly agrees with Frege's dichotomy between objects and concepts. Furthermore, Frege insists, for well-known reasons, that numbers are objects rather than concepts. But this means, according to the Kantian framework, that they would be sensory intuitions rather than concepts. A Kantian could therefore claim that since numbers are not supposed to be concepts, they must be either "outer" or "inner" intuitions, that is, they must be either perceptual objects or mental pictures. Frege tries to prove that numbers are not perceptual objects. If he is right, then there remains only the possibility that they are mental, subjective pictures. By affirming the principle of contextual presentation, Frege tries to avoid the necessity of having to choose between these two equally unacceptable consequences. This explains why he thinks that only by holding that particular entities (objects) can be given in the contexts intended by judgments can one avoid the view that numbers are either something physical (perceptual objects) or something psychological (sense impressions or acts).

It is clear that in Frege's epistemology judgments play the role which perceptual acts play in ours. All acts are judgmental, according to our view, insofar as they all intend states of affairs. Yet we have also insisted, for example, that a perceptual act of seeing does not consist of a judgment plus something else. In this respect, we have much of the traditional epistemology against us; for seeing is usually analyzed into a sensory component, say, the sensing of sense impressions, and judgment. It is not conceived of as an irreducible kind of mental act, distinguished both from other irreducible kinds of perceptual acts, like hearing and smelling, as well as from judgments in a narrower sense. There are judgments, but these mental acts form a kind among other kinds; they are not ingredients of perceptual acts. The popularity of the view that perceptions consist at least in part of judgments can perhaps be explained by the fact that perceptual acts are indeed propositional. Since the tradition insists that every act whose intention could be expressed in a sentence is a judgment, one inevitably assumes that perception involves judgment.

Frege saw quite clearly that properties as well as numbers are not sense impressions. He saw, too, that they are both presented to us in the contexts of states of affairs. However, since he was influenced by the traditional division of mental acts, he distinguished between a nonpropositional act of sensing and a propositional act of judging, and held that properties and numbers are always presented through judgment and hence never presented through sensing. Would he have held that they can be presented in perception? We know that the answer depends on how he would have conceived of perception. Insofar as perceiving may be held to involve judging, it could present us, even on Frege's view, with such objective entities as properties and numbers. This fact points out that it is of small consequence for our purposes whether perceptual acts are propositional and indeed irreducible, as I have claimed, or whether they consist in part of judgments. What matters is, rather, that perceptual acts are propositional, either directly or through the judgments which they contain; for, as long as perceptual acts are propositional in either way, they present us with states of affairs and with the constituents of states of affairs. And if we are acquainted with states of affairs through perception, then we have turned aside the traditional and most powerful motive for denying that perception can present us with "abstract entities," that is, with entities other than individuals.

These considerations clearly do not amount to a proof that we perceive numbers. They are merely intended to show that there exists a widespread traditional prejudice against our claim that we perceive numbers, that this prejudice rests on certain philosophical assumptions, and that these assumptions are not sound.

3 ATOMIC AND MOLECULAR FACTS

We have distinguished between sensing and perceiving and have rid ourselves of the dogma of localization. But we are not out of the woods yet. We have to deal with the view that we can, at best, perceive atomic facts of such forms as *A is F* or *A stands in the relation R to B*, but that we cannot perceive any other kind of facts. This view is based, of course, on the conviction that only atomic facts and no others exist. If we can show that molecular facts cannot be "reduced" to atomic facts, then we have shown that a preference for atomic facts as objects of perception is not as well founded as one may believe. We are then free to let the phenomena speak, as it were, and can consult our perceptions themselves as to what kinds of facts they intend.

Whether or not all facts can be "reduced" to atomic facts depends, obviously, on what one means by ontological reduction. Most of this book from here on is concerned with that issue. At present, I shall merely hint at certain types of considerations that in my opinion do *not* show that atomic facts alone exist in order to indicate, first, that all claims to have reduced molecular facts to atomic facts are spurious and, second, to suggest what really would have to be done in order to justify such a claim.

As paradigms of molecular facts let us take (1) the negative fact *A is not F*, (2) the conjunctive fact *P and Q*, and (3) the general fact *All things which are F are also G*. I believe not only that there are such facts, but also that one can perceive them. How could one go about showing that such facts do not really exist? It is not enough to prove that all the usual connectives can be "reduced" to just one such connective, for example, the relation of *neither–nor*, and that the universal quantifier can similarly be "reduced" to negation and the existential quantifier. This kind of "reduction" still leaves us with one connective and one quantifier. It leaves us, ontologically speaking, with the two categories of connective and quantifier; and, from an ontological point of view, all that matters is how many categories one acknowledges rather than how many entities belong to these categories. To admit the existence of one lonesome connective is to admit the existence of the category of connective, and this is as momentous as admitting that there are one hundred different quantifiers. As far as molecular facts are concerned, one has merely "reduced" all molecular facts to molecular facts of a certain sort, and not to atomic facts.

But does not this "interdefinability" of the expressions for connectives and quantifiers show that they do not represent anything, and hence that, though there may be molecular sentences, there could be no molecular facts? Wittgenstein believes that it does.[1] He argues as follows. The fact that 'If *P*, then *Q*' can be "defined" in terms of 'not' and 'or,' and that 'or' in turn can be defined in terms of 'not' and 'if, then' proves that the expressions for connectives do not represent entities; for, if these expressions stood for entities, then what the sentence 'If *P*, then *Q*' represents would have to be different from what the sentence 'Not-*P* or *Q*' represents. But from the fact that the logical expressions are interdefinable, it follows that there is no such difference. Hence the logical words do not represent anything. Wittgenstein's point becomes even clearer in connection with negation. His argument states that if 'not' represented something, then '*P*' and 'not-not-*P*' would have to represent different entities, and since they do not represent different entities, it follows that 'not' cannot represent anything.

Wittgenstein's argument rests on a mistaken notion of what the interdefinability of the logical words amounts to. He assumes that the "definition" of 'if, then' in terms of 'not' and 'or' is a matter of mere abbreviation, so that a sentence of the form 'If *P*, then *Q*' is a mere abbreviation of a sentence of the form 'Not-*P* or *Q*'. (Of course, we may also look at the latter sentence as an abbreviation for the former.) Wittgenstein implies that these two sentences represent the very same state of affairs (entity); and he believes that the so-called definability of 'and' in terms of 'not' and 'or' proves that they do. But it does no such thing. What the "definition" of 'if, then' in terms of 'not' and 'or' really means is that all states of affairs of the form *If P, then Q* are equivalent to states of affairs of the form *Not-P or Q*. More precisely, we are dealing not with an abbreviation, or, more generally, with two expressions which happen to represent the same entity, but rather with a true equivalence between distinct states of affairs. Most succinctly, the alleged definition really flows from the truth of the following general equivalence statement: For all facts *p* and *q*, *if p, then q* is equivalent to *not-p or q*. Thus we know that two facts of these kinds are equivalent, but we do not know that they are the same. I shall argue later that they are not the same. If so, then Wittgenstein's argument breaks down.

We see that the claim that there are only atomic facts is equivalent to the claim that the logical words do not represent anything, i.e., to the claim that the logical words are mere syncategorematic expressions. What comes to mind is the common method of showing that a certain expression is syncategorematic by means of a contextual definition. In order to prove, in our specific case, that logical words are syncategorematic, one would have to replace expressions in which logical words occur by expressions having the same meaning without logical words. Is there any possibility that this sort of "reduction" can be achieved? I can think of only one faint possibility. It is sometimes claimed that the truth-tables "define" the connectives. Do truth-tables yield the required expressions devoid of logical words? To raise this question is to see not only that the possibility cannot be realized, but also that the conception of truth-tables as "definitions" of logical words is untenable. Consider, for example, the truth-table for 'and'. What the truth-table conveys can be expressed by the sentence: The statement *P and Q* is true if and only if both *P* is true and *Q* is true. In ontological terms: The state of affairs *P and Q* exists if and only if both *P* exists and *Q* exists. It is clear that this is a straightforward true sentence; it is not a definition in any "reductive" sense. This sentence formulates the truth that a conjunction is a truth-function of its conjuncts, but it does not "define," in the sense of reduce, a conjunction to something else. Put ontologically again, the truth-table conveys the information that the existence of a conjunctive fact is a function of the existence of its constituent facts, but it does not reduce a conjunctive fact to anything else. Truth-tables, in short, are not "definitions" at all, but are certain ways of stating general truths about the existence of molecular facts as a function of the existence of their constituent facts.

Is there any other way of getting rid of molecular facts? Consider a "world" consisting of the following four facts and no others: (1) *A is F*, (2) *A is G*, (3) *B is F*, (4) *B is H*.* One might try to argue as follows. The alleged negative fact (5) *A is not H* can be reduced to the facts of our list, since we know that (5) is the case by an inspection of our list of atomic facts. Similarly, the alleged molecular fact (6) *All things are F* can be reduced to our atomic facts, since we know that (6) is the case by merely inspecting our list of four atomic facts. But this argument will not suffice. How do we know that (5) is the case? We deduce (5) from the fact that *A is H* does *not* occur in the list. Thus we are really deducing the negative fact (5) from another negative, and hence molecular, fact. Similarly, we can deduce that all things are *F*, only if we assume the molecular premise that *A* and *B* are *all* the things in the "world" under study. In both cases, therefore, we do not really infer our conclusions from the atomic facts listed, but from facts about this list as well.

Granted this objection, what about the inference from (1) and (2) to the fact *that (1) and (2)*, or to the fact *that some thing is F*? Can we not deduce this conjunction and this existential statement from the facts in our list? And if so, do not at least these molecular facts "reduce" to atomic ones?[2] Since we have the corresponding "inference rules," we can indeed deduce the conjunction from the separate conjuncts and the existential statement from the relevant singular statement. But in what sense does this deduction justify any claim to have "reduced" the conclusions of these simple arguments to their premises? The inference rules under discussion are not arbitrary rules, comparable to those of a game. They rest on certain facts about the world, namely, on the fact (a) For all states of affairs p and q, if p exists and q exists, then p *and* q exists, and on the fact (b) For all properties f and for all entities e, if e is f then there is something which is f. We see that the notion of reduction here used comes down to what follows logically from what. According to this approach, P is reduced to Q, R, etc., if and only if P follows logically from Q, R, etc. But surely this is an unsatisfactory conception of reduction in any ontological

* It will become clear in a moment that such a world is an absurdity, since it would have to include many further facts, and could not consist entirely of the four facts listed.

context; it is at least as unsatisfactory a notion as the one in terms of logical equivalence which we critized earlier, if indeed it is not more unsatisfactory. Briefly, that a certain fact logically follows from another simply does not mean that the two facts are the same. Thus, even though it is true that we can infer *P or Q* from *P*, a molecular fact from an atomic one, this does not imply that the two facts are the same.

This last attempt at a reduction of molecular facts to atomic ones having come to nought, let us return to the general problem. Those who hold that only atomic facts exist or, equivalently, that logical signs do not represent quantifiers and connections must provide us with a "language" which does not contain logical words or equivalent devices, for example, spatial arrangement, and in which they nevertheless can say everything that we can express by means of our enriched language. Of course, the problem arises as to how we are supposed to decide the claim that two "languages" can or cannot say the same thing; for there is always the easy answer that whatever one of the two "languages" is accused of not being able to say is not really part of the world anyway. But the issue is relatively clear: either construct a language without logical words or similar devices, or prove that even though there are no logical connections between states of affairs and no quantifiers, no language—by the very nature of a language—is possible without such words or devices. This, then, is the challenge to those who hold that logical words are mere syncategorematic signs, mere linguistic artifacts. Unless they try to meet this challenge, all talk about the syncategorematic nature of logical words remains empty and unconvincing.

As I said before, to show that no one has as yet really reduced molecular to atomic facts is not the same, evidently, as showing that one is acquainted in perception with molecular facts. But it goes a long way to debunk the soundness of the inference that one cannot perceive molecular facts because there clearly are no such entities. Freed from the ontological prejudice against molecular facts, we can now consult our mental acts and try to determine what kinds of states of affairs they intend.

Let us start with negative facts, since they seem to be the most suspect kind of intentions. As Russell once remarked, "There is implanted in the human breast an almost unquenchable desire to find some way of avoiding the admission that negative facts are as ultimate

as those that are positive."[3] And what holds for their being ultimate
holds doubly for their being perceivable. Can we see, for example, that
this pen is not red? It is quite obvious to me—discarding, of course, all
ontological prejudice against negative facts—that we can. We can see
just as much and in the same sense of 'see' that the pen is not red as
that it is, say, black. Why would anyone want to deny this
phenomenon? We already mentioned the prejudice against molecular
facts in general and negative facts in particular. But it seems that this is
not the only reason. There seems to exist a deep-seated conviction that
what one can literally see in our situation is only that the pen is black.
One may also come to *know* that the pen is not red, but one cannot *see*
that it is not red. Hence one cannot see a negative fact. How does one
come to know, according to this view, that the pen is not red? The most
obvious answer is that one concludes that the pen is not red from the
two facts (a) that the pen is black and (b) that something's being black
excludes its being red. This sort of analysis of the situation involves two
basic ideas which can vary independently of each other. First, there
may be an attempt to reduce negative facts to positive facts involving
the opposition of states of affairs, in the spirit of, say, Demos' article.[4]
Second, there is the idea, more important to our present interest, that
the negative fact or its equivalent in terms of opposition is not a matter
of perception, but a matter of judgment; that it is not seen, but merely
inferred. The difficulties connected with the first idea, a reduction of
negation to opposition, are so well-known that I shall not list them
once more.[5] Nor, of course, would such a reduction indicate, if it could
be accomplished, how to get rid of other molecular facts. Quite to the
contrary, it adds to the ordinary molecular facts another molecular
fact, namely, that two states of affairs are opposites of each other.
What I wish to discuss is the second basic idea: that negative facts, in
one form or another, are not intentions of perceptions, but intentions
of judgments.

What happens when we think that we see that the pen is not red
is allegedly this. There occurs a mental act of seeing that this pen is
black. There also occurs a mental act of thinking (judging) that if
something is black, then it cannot be red. Finally, there occurs the act
of thinking (judging) that this pen is not red. There are some questions
about the precise state of affairs which is intended by the first act of
thinking. Is it a singular fact of the form *Property F excludes property*

G? Or is it perhaps a general fact of the form *Everything that is black is not red*? Depending on what kind of answer one gives, one might also entertain different views as to how this kind of fact can be known. For example, one may argue over whether or not the fact is arrived at by some kind of induction. Be that as it may, the end result is the same: the negative fact that the pen is not red is the intention of an act of judging—which follows a perception and a judgment—and not the intention of an act of seeing, as we have claimed.

Of course, we do not dispute that we may on certain occasions conclude rather than see that the pen is not red. Nor do we deny that, if we mean by a judgment any mental act which intends a state of affairs, then the fact that the pen is not red must be the intention of a judgment. But in this case, we would also insist that the fact that the pen is black must be judged and cannot be seen or, perhaps better, that it can be seen only insofar as it is being judged. Our view that we can see as well as judge that the pen is not red is based on a distinction between acts of seeing and acts of judging as two irreducible kinds of mental acts. What we maintain is that the very same kind of visual, perceptual act can intend the fact that the pen is not red as well as the fact that it is black; and also, of course, that the very same kind of nonvisual, nonperceptual act of judging can intend either one of these two kinds of facts. But if we can experience acts of seeing which intend negative facts, why is there such a univocal opposition to our view?

Perhaps, it is the case that one can never see a negative fact unless one has first seen a certain positive fact. It is perhaps impossible to see that the pen is not red, unless there occurs first a mental act of seeing that the pen is black. As a matter of phenomenal fact, it may be the case that one has to see first what color the pen has before one can see what color or colors it does not have. If so, then we could explain, at least in part, the widespread notion that a negative fact such as that the pen is not red is a matter of judgment rather than of perception. Since there occurs, first, a certain act of seeing, and since the negative fact follows logically from the intention of this act together with a general truth, one is led to believe that what actually takes place is an inference from a perception and a judgment to the negative fact. One comes to hold that the negative fact is a matter of inference, not of straightforward perception. But it is clear that there are other possible views. Assuming that there occurs, first, a mental act of seeing that the pen is black, there may occur immediately afterward, on certain occasions, a second act of perception which intends the negative fact that the pen is not red. The occurrence of this second mental act is caused in part by the occurrence of the first, but this second act is just as much an act of perceiving as the first. Our opponent may have made the mistake of confusing the logical relationship between the positive fact that the pen is black and the negative fact that it is not red, established by a third fact, with the causal relationship between various acts of perception, judgment, imagination, memory, etc. Although it may be true that there occurs first a mental act of seeing that the pen is black, and even though it is true that the negative fact that the pen is not red follows from this intention together with the fact that what is black cannot be red, it does not follow that there must occur two further acts of judging, having for their intentions the additional premise and the conclusion. In particular, no judgment concerning the exclusion of red by black need actually occur. And if this judgment need not occur, then the act of intending the negative state of affairs need not be a judgment either. In short, there can occur the perceptual act which intends the negative fact, in the wake of another perceptual act which intends the fact that the pen is black.

This is as much as I can say in defense of the view that perceptual acts intend negative facts. The opposite view may have arisen since we undoubtedly see positive facts and since negative facts can be inferred from positive facts in conjunction with other premises. Since they can be inferred, one might have been misled into believing that they must be so inferred.

Most of what has been said about negative facts holds also for other kinds of molecular facts. We hold, for example, that one can perceive quantified facts of the forms *All F are G* and *Some F are G*.[6] For example, I may see that all the pens on my desk are black or that some of the books on my desk are green. Again, these facts need not be the intentions of mere judgments, arrived at on the basis of the perception of a number of atomic facts. But again, it may be the case that other perceptions of atomic facts precede, as a matter of "occasion," or as a matter of necessity, the perception of a quantified fact. One can also perceive a special kind of quantified fact, namely, facts involving numbers. For example, I may see that there are three books on my desk. And I may see a conjunctive fact, say, that there are black pens on my desk and that there are green books on my desk. In each one of these cases, it is important to realize that the causal relationships between mental acts must not be confused with the deductive (or, perhaps, inductive) relationships between their intentions. The general fact that all the pens on my desk are black may be inferred on a certain occasion by induction, as the saying goes, from a number of singular facts presented in a series of perceptions. But it need not be so inferred; it can also be perceived. The fact that there are three books on my desk may, on a certain occasion, be deduced from a number of facts presented in perception, but it need not be so deduced; it can also be perceived. And so on.

For the following discussions I shall thus embrace a thesis as bold as it is general. Perception, but by no means perception alone, acquaints us with all the existing categorial kinds by presenting us with facts of the most startling variety and complexity. A thesis of this nature cannot be proved. In these first three chapters I have merely tried to make it more plausible by defending it against some main objections. I may not have succeeded even in this. But it should at least be clear to the reader what kind of answer I would give to the epistemological question of how we know that there are those categories which, for the remainder of this book, I shall mention and discuss.

PART I

Numbers and Quantifiers

4 ABBREVIATIONS

Frege is customarily credited with the first detailed and successful attempt to reduce arithmetic to logic.[1] Since his general viewpoint as well as his specific proposals show a far greater sensitivity to purely philosophical issues than the work of many later reductionists, I will begin by discussing Frege's position. But it should be understood that he serves merely as an example of one kind of reductionist attitude; therefore, I shall feel free to deal rather briefly with Frege's more idiosyncratic convictions. It should also be understood that frequent and lengthy diversions will be necessary in order to deal with important issues which are not directly or sufficiently discussed by Frege. In short, Frege's view will guide our investigation for the time being, but not too firmly.

According to the *Foundations of Arithmetic*, the philosophy of arithmetic consists of two main problems. The first problem concerns the nature of natural numbers; the second concerns the nature of arithmetical statements. To ask what numbers are is to ask, in a philosophical context, to what basic kind of entity or entities they belong. It is to ask, in the more traditional terminology, to what category numbers belong. Consequently, Frege divides the first main problem into two more specific ones. First, are numbers mental (subjective) or are they nonmental (objective) entities? Second, are they objects or are they functions? The second main problem derives from the traditional notion that arithmetic propositions are somehow akin to logical ones. Accordingly, Frege divides the problem into two more specific ones: First, are arithmetic statements analytic or are they synthetic? Second, are they known a priori or a posteriori?

Frege's answers to these four questions are now well-known. He holds that arithmetic propositions are analytic and known a priori. As for numbers, he thinks that they are objective rather than subjective entities. Their existence does in no way depend on there being minds. Since I agree with this answer, I shall take its truth for granted in the remainder of this book. Frege also thinks that numbers are objects. We recall that he distinguishes between two main categories of entities, namely, between saturated objects and unsaturated functions. Numbers, he holds, belong to a subcategory of objects. They are classes of a certain kind.[2] He describes them in the following way:

(F) The number of f's is the class determined by the property of being similar to f.*

It is not clear from the context whether (F) is to be understood as a general statement about all properties or as a general statement about all property expressions (of a given language). But I think that it is in the Fregean spirit to adopt the first of these two readings. According to this interpretation, Frege maintains that *for all properties* f, the number of f's is the class determined by the property of being similar to f. He does not say that *given any two property expressions ϕ and $\curlyvee$* (of English), the result of putting the property expression ϕ in the place of the blank in the expression 'the number of ____'s' is an expression which represents the same entity as the expression which results from putting the property expression $\curlyvee$ in the place of the blank in the expression 'the class determined by the property of being similar to ____'.

More important for our immediate purpose is the fact that Frege calls (F) a definition and speaks of defining the phrase 'the number of f's,' even though (F) is quite clearly a (general) identity statement. Does he mean to imply that definitions in general are identity statements? Or does he think of them as yielding identity statements. In short, what is his view on definitions?

There are quite a few remarks about the nature and importance of definitions in the *Foundations.* Yet no clear view emerges from these remarks. Frege seems to hold, on the one hand, that definitions are merely convenient abbreviations which are entirely expendable and

* I have taken the liberty to reformulate Frege's definition slightly, in order to avoid certain side issues and to unify the terminology.

governed solely by conventions.[3] However, on many occasions he also characterizes definitions as being informative, fruitful, and as having to prove their worth.[4] He seems to think of them as being somehow related to identity statements. And later, in his review of Husserl's *Philosophie der Arithmetik*, he explicitly maintains that every definition is an identity statement.[5] Let us see whether we can clarify the relationship between definitions and identity statements independently, so that we shall be in a better position to evaluate Frege's claim that numbers are a certain kind of class.

We are all familiar with abbreviation proposals. For example, the word 'similar' which occurs in (F) is usually introduced by the proposal to say for short that property F is similar to property G instead of that the entities which are F can be coordinated in a one-one fashion to the entities which are G. There may be reasons for rejecting a given abbreviation proposal, but it makes no sense to claim that the proposal is false. For example, one may criticize the proposal just mentioned, because the word 'similar' has already quite a different meaning in ordinary discourse. When we say that two properties are similar, we do not ordinarily have an isomorphism in mind. Hence one may argue that the new proposal is bound to invite confusion and that it would be far better to coin a new term for the purpose at hand.

Abbreviations, it is clear, are completely expendable.* Since they are introduced solely for the purpose of facilitating communication, their introduction does in no way contribute to our knowledge. If we eliminate all the abbreviations of a given language, we get a more cumbersome vehicle of communication, but we do not lose any descriptive power. Moreover, it is also clear that abbreviations represent neither more nor less than the corresponding abbreviated expressions. It is the essence of the notion of an abbreviation that it has the very same meaning—however we construe this meaning—as the expression for which it is an abbreviation. Hence, if one can show that a given expression is merely an abbreviation for another expression, then one can safely claim that the two expressions do not represent different entities. In this sense, the discovery that a certain expression is a mere abbreviation for another one can amount to a genuine ontological reduction.

* Most of what I say in the following paragraphs about abbreviations also holds, of course, whenever two expressions are said to represent the same entity.

The three connected notions of an abbreviation proposal, an abbreviation, and an abbreviated expression are quite clear and unproblematic. But whether or not a certain expression in a natural language is really an abbreviation for another one may turn out to be a difficult problem. There are a number of possibilities. We may, after considerable time, discover an explicit proposal which was accepted by a small or large group of people. Or we may have to be satisfied with a measure of circumstantial evidence, because we cannot find the actual proposal. Or, again, we may conclude from our investigation that there never was either an explicit or an implicit agreement to use the one expression as a mere abbreviation for the other. But whatever the case may be, we know in principle how to resolve any such problem: we must inquire into the tacit or expressed agreements among certain people or groups of people to use shorter expressions instead of longer ones. Whether or not we are confronted with an abbreviation is thus always a linguistic, historical problem.

We can distinguish between two related cases.[6] On the one hand, it may be a matter of introducing a completely new, shorter expression as an abbreviation for another well-established but longer one. On the other hand, we may be faced with an expression that has been in use for some time, and we have to determine whether or not it is in reality an abbreviation for another one. In the first case, we may make an abbreviation proposal; in the second, we may assert that a certain expression is in fact an abbreviation for another.

Identity statements are totally different from abbreviation proposals. They are not proposals or suggestions, but assertions to the effect that *something is the same as something.** The awkwardness of the italicized phrase reminds us that most identity sentences contain expressions for descriptions. If we assume that the respective language has at most one label for every entity, then every true identity sentence without definite description expressions states an instance of the general ontological law that everything is identical with itself.† All "interesting," all "informative" identity sentences in such a language

* I do not distinguish between sameness and identity, but use these two words interchangeably.

† I speak of labels rather than proper names, because I wish to hold that any thing whatsoever—not merely individual things—just as it can be described, can be labeled. According to this view, 'saffron,' for example, is a label for a certain color (property), while 'Paris' is a label for a certain city (individual thing).

contain at least one expression for a definite description.* Consider, then, an identity sentence with two different definite description expressions. Such a sentence states that an entity uniquely characterized by a certain property (or set of properties) is the same as an entity uniquely characterized by a different property (or set of properties). In order to grasp the inner structure of such a statement, one must realize that every definite description has two sides. One can and must always distinguish between *what* is described and *how* that entity is described; that is, one must distinguish between the entity described and its description. One and the same entity, for instance, may be described as the book on the desk in front of me and as my copy of Frege's *Foundations of Arithmetic.* To say that the one is the other is to say that the entity with the first property is the same as the entity with the second property. It is not to say that the first entity is self-identical or that the second entity is self-identical. Nor is it to say that the two properties are the same or that the two descriptions are the same.[7]

Informative identity statements may be either true or false; abbreviation suggestions are neither. The discovery of a true informative identity statement may greatly enlarge our knowledge about the world; the acceptance of an abbreviation proposal has no such effect. Informative identity statements, but not abbreviation proposals, may therefore be said to be "fruitful," to use one of Frege's expressions. Since informative identity statements may be false, it makes sense to hold—to speak once more like Frege—that they have to prove themselves.

But even though there are these flagrant differences between abbreviation proposals on the one hand and informative identity statements on the other, there is also a connection, as Frege points out. If we accept a certain abbreviation suggestion, then we can immediately formulate a true identity sentence based on the suggestion.[8] To be more precise, we can formulate such a true identity sentence if and only if the abbreviated expression represents something. For example,

* Even if a language contains more than one label for a thing, we must still distinguish between, say, 'Tully is the same as Cicero' and 'The man called Tully is the same as the man called Cicero'. Thus, it is sometimes said that John, for example, wishes to know whether Tully is Cicero when in reality John wishes to know some such thing as whether the man called Tully is the same as the man known to him as Cicero.

if we abbreviate the expression 'The f which is similar to the property of being square' by the letter 'Q,' and if we assume that the description expression represents something, then we can formulate the true identity sentence: 'Q is identical with the f which is similar to the property of being square'.* Or assume that the sentence '$2 + 2 = 4$' represents something, such as a state of affairs or a proposition, and that we abbreviate it by the letter 'P'. It follows then that P is identical with (the state of affairs that) $2 + 2 = 4$. I trust that the general principle is clear: The acceptance of an abbreviation proposal for an expression that represents something immediately yields an identity sentence which is true because the proposal has been accepted. But this fact must not be allowed to conceal the profound differences mentioned earlier between abbreviation proposals and identity statements. It calls, rather, for the following distinctions. First of all, there are identity sentences which contain abbreviations and which are true, because their expanded versions follow directly from the ontological law that every existent is identical with itself. Second, there are identity sentences with abbreviations which are true because their expanded versions are themselves true sentences, but not instances of the law of self-identity. In this latter case, we can further distinguish between expanded sentences consisting solely of labels and expanded sentences containing at least one description. If the expanded sentence contains two different labels for the same thing, then it is true by virtue of (a) there being these different labels in the given language and (b) the law of self-identity. These true identity sentences are, of course, as uninteresting and uninformative as those abbreviational identity sentences which reduce directly to instances of the law of self-identity. All informative identity sentences contain at least one description. Whenever we come across a true identity sentence, we may therefore ask ourselves whether or not it is an abbreviational truth, and if it is an abbreviational truth, whether or not it expands into an informative identity sentence with a description and a label or two different descriptions.

Similar considerations hold for sentences other than identity sentences. For example, if we consider the sentence "All whales are

* Eventually, I shall distinguish between what a description expression *represents* and what it *describes*. The present example presupposes this distinction.

mammals,' we may ask whether it is true merely because there exists some kind of linguistic convention according to which the word 'whale' abbreviates an expression involving the word 'mammal'. If there exists such an abbreviation agreement, then the truth of 'All whales are mammals' follows from this agreement together with some such logical law as: For all properties f, for all properties g, and for all entities e: if e is f and e is g, then e is f. The question under discussion is perfectly clear, but the correct answer may be hard to come by. The situation can become especially muddled whenever we deal with terms that have been "redefined" for technical purposes; for we are liable to confuse the ordinary term with its technical twin.[9] The average person, I take it, does not use the word 'whale' as an abbreviation for a certain expression that contains the term 'mammal'. When he utters the sentence 'All whales are mammals,' he does not mean to state an abbreviational truth. But we can imagine that zoologists think of whales as mammals "as a matter of definition." The point of this contrast should be as obvious as it is simple. We cannot decide whether a given string of marks or noises constitutes an abbreviational or a factual truth, unless we first find out what the marks or noises have been agreed on to represent. This does not mean, of course, that the difference between abbreviational and factual truths is a "subjective" one. Rather, it means that before we can answer the objective question of whether a given sentence is an abbreviational or a factual truth, we must know something about the words in it. Usually, we take for granted that words mean what we mean by them ordinarily. But there are occasions, as the example of the zoologists shows, when this assumption must be discarded.

An abbreviational truth, then, is a sentence which is true because (a) a certain abbreviation proposal has been accepted and (b) its expanded counterpart—with all abbreviations eliminated—is true (as a matter of fact).* A factual truth, on the other hand, is simply a true sentence devoid of abbreviations. Every abbreviational truth thus rests in part on a factual truth. Notice that this dichotomy uses a very wide notion of factual truth. For example, the earlier mentioned ontological

* In this connection we cannot avoid speaking of sentences as truths rather than as expressing or formulating truths; for sentences, of course, and not what they represent, contain abbreviations. But I trust that the reader will have no difficulty in reconciling this preliminary terminology with the ontological views expounded later.

law that all entities are self-identical is a factual truth; and so is the logical law mentioned in connection with the shifting status of the sentence 'All whales are mammals'. It is, therefore, partly a factual matter that, say, all bachelors are unmarried, even if we take it that the word 'bachelor' is an abbreviation; for if it were not a fact that every entity with the properties F, G, etc., has the property F, then it would not necessarily be true that all bachelors are unmarried. The sentence 'All bachelors are unmarried' may still turn out to be true, of course, but only because of some other factual truth, not because its expanded version happens to be an instance of the relevant logical law.

With these more or less obvious clarifications in mind, let us return to Frege's so-called definition of the expression 'the number of f's'. Is Frege's identity sentence an abbreviational or a factual truth? In the *Foundations*, there occurs no abbreviation proposal that would be relevant. Nor does Frege appeal in this context to common usage. On the contrary, his whole approach, as well as numerous remarks, suggests that he is trying to answer a factual rather than a linguistic question. I conclude, therefore, that his definition of numbers is a factual identity sentence. Is the sentence true? Are numbers really classes determined by certain properties? One thing is certain: if numbers are such classes, then Frege has succeeded in reducing numbers to classes in a sense relevant to ontology. We know then that there is no such category as the category of numbers.* But since the question just raised (though perfectly proper and intelligible in my view) is liable to arouse a fair measure of antipathy among antiontologists, it is necessary to provide some background by showing that this question is merely a special case of a more general question. In general, how do we decide whether or not a factual identity sentence is true, and how can we discover that, instead of two entities or two kinds of entities, there is only one?

5 IDENTITY AND EQUIVALENCE

A given identity statement may logically follow from several other true

---

* We know then that numbers form a subcategory of classes. The word 'number' is then merely short for an expression that characterizes this kind of class.

statements. In fact, there is a rather promising line of reasoning that seems to lead straight to Frege's conclusion that a number is a certain kind of class. If we stay with the somewhat abnormal use of 'similar,' it is clear that a property f is similar to a property g *if and only if* every property h is similar to f if and only if it is also similar to g. This means that f is similar to g *if and only if* a property h has the (relational) property of being similar to f if and only if it has the (relational) property of being similar to g. Hence f is similar to g *if and only if* the class determined by the (relational) property of being similar to f is the same as the class determined by the (relational) property of being similar to g. But it is also true that f is similar to g *if and only if* the number of f's is the same as the number of g's. Now, the left sides of the last two equivalence statements are the same; the two right sides are identity statements. One arrives at Frege's identity statement if one "identifies" the two left sides of the previously mentioned identity statements. Notice that I put the word 'identifies' in quotation marks. If that means nothing more than writing down the two appropriate expressions with an identity sign between them, then the question immediately arises whether or not the result of this "identification" expresses a true statement. The argument outlined above does not help us at this point; it does not lead to the conclusion that the number of f's is the same as the class determined by the (relational) property of being similar to f. Rather, what we may conclude is merely:

(1) For all properties f and for all properties g: the class determined by the (relational) property of being similar to f is the same as the class determined by the (relational) property of being similar to g *if and only if* the number of f's is the same as the number of g's.

It may be objected that Frege's identity statement follows after all, because the two sides of (1) "say the very same thing." It may be argued that they must have "the very same meaning," because they are equivalent. More precisely, it may be said that the left side of the first identity statement is identical with the left side of the second identity statement, because the two identity statements are logically equivalent. There are several things wrong with this objection, but, most importantly, it rests on a confusion between equivalence and identity. To say that a state of affairs is equivalent to another state of affairs is not to say that the two states of affairs are the same. It may help to keep the distinction in mind, if we avoid the expression 'equivalence' whenever possible and use the phrase 'if and only if' instead; for to say that something is the case if and only if something (else) is the case does not as readily lead to the conclusion that one is dealing with one and the same state of affairs in two linguistic disguises.

Equivalence, like identity, is a relation between entities.* Unlike identity, it does not hold between entities of all categories, but holds exclusively between states of affairs. As in the case of identity, we must of course distinguish between the relation of equivalence and the sign or signs used to represent this connection. Unfortunately, though, one often calls the sign for equivalence a connective and speaks of sentences as being equivalent. No doubt, this unfortunate custom rests on the prevailing conviction that the expressions for connectives are syncategorematic signs which do not represent anything. But it cannot be completely explained in this fashion; for even though there are also very few philosophers who admit that the relation of identity exists, most philosophers distinguish nevertheless between identity and a sign for identity. However, in my view equivalence is a relation between states of affairs, not a relation between expressions.

With this clarification in mind, let us return to the statement (1).[1] If we insist on stating this equivalence in terms of 'if and only if,' do we not imply that mere material equivalence rather than logical equivalence is involved? And does not logical equivalence, as distinguished from mere material equivalence, amount to sameness of meaning? And since the equivalence (1) is quite obviously logical, does not Frege's identity statement follow after all? I do not think so; and I shall try to show why by discussing the matter rather thoroughly.

First of all, we can strike another blow against the indiscriminate use of the term 'definition' by showing how this objection rests, among other things, on a confusion between logical truth and definitional, in the sense of abbreviational, truth. Start with a somewhat hazy notion of definitions as mere abbreviation proposals. An abbreviation, of course, represents whatever the abbreviated expression represents—nothing less and nothing more. Next, convince yourself that logical truths are true by definition. For example, consider the logical truth:

* It may become necessary, in the course of the ontological investigation, to distinguish among subcategories of relations. I will always use the term 'relation' for the category comprising everything that has been called a connection, relation, nexus, etc., by other philosophers.

(2) For all states of affairs p and q: the state of affairs p *or* q obtains *if and only if* the following state of affairs obtains: *it is not the case that both not-p and not-q obtain.*

Express this truth by saying that 'p or q' is equivalent to 'Not-(not-p and not-q)'. Since you believe that logical truths are true by definition, you may also believe that the two sides of this equivalence are equivalent by definition. Since you also think of definitions as mere abbreviation proposals, you may then conclude that the shorter side of the equivalence sentence is a mere abbreviation of the longer side. If so, you will maintain that the two sides of the equivalence sentence say the very same thing in two different ways.

But logical truths are not true by definition. They are no more matters of definition than the truths of chemistry, botany, or, for that matter, the truths of arithmetic. The logical truth (2) does not follow, as far as I can see, from a prior convention according to which sentences of the form 'Not-(not-P and not-Q)' are abbreviated by sentences of the form 'P or Q'. There exists no such abbreviation proposal. If we know what sentences of the form 'Not-P,' 'P or Q,' 'P and Q,' etc., represent, we also know what certain more complex sentences represent. As a consequence, we realize that a state of affairs P *or* Q obtains if and only if the quite different state of affairs *Not-(not-P and not-Q)* obtains.

But how do we know that the former state of affairs is not the same as the latter? To speak for once a jargon peculiar to some philosophers: "What is the criterion of sameness for states of affairs?" Presumably, so at least they claim, there is no criterion of this sort or, perhaps, no one has ever proposed a reasonably clear one. And since these philosophers also believe that the acceptability of an ontological kind depends somehow on there being a clear-cut criterion of identity for this kind, they conclude that states of affairs are suspect, to say the very least.

Is there a criterion for equivalence? Well, we say that two states of affairs are equivalent if and only if it is the case that if the one obtains, the other obtains, and conversely.* But this is merely an

---

* Entities divide into things and states of affairs. Correspondingly, I shall say that things *exist* or do not *exist*, while states of affairs *obtain* or do not *obtain.* But I do not wish to imply by this terminological distinction that there are two different modes of being. I do not know of any sufficiently convincing

abbreviational truth. It follows from our agreement to use the word 'equivalent' instead of a longer expression. Is there, then, a criterion that determines under what conditions a state of affairs obtains if and only if another state of affairs obtains? I cannot think of one. Nor would we be in a position to "define" equivalence if there were such a criterion; for any such criterion would itself have to be formulated in terms of the notion of equivalence. Such is the meaning of 'criterion' in our present context.

However, the situation is quite different for states of affairs. There is, first of all, the general criterion of identity which holds for all entities whatsoever, namely, Leibniz's principle, which states that two entities are the same if and only if they share all their properties (including relations). This law holds for states of affairs as well as for individual things, properties of individual things, classes, etc. But just as there exists a *second* criterion for the identity of classes in terms of the elements which they have, so there exists a second criterion of identity for states of affairs in terms of the constituents which they contain. This criterion has three parts. Two states of affairs are the same if and only if they contain (a) the same constituents, (b) in the same order, and (c) with the same number of occurrences. That the two states of affairs *P or Q* and *Not-(not-P and not-Q)* are not the same follows already from the fact that they do not contain the same constituents. The former, for example, contains the constituent *or*, the latter does not. On the other hand, the latter contains the constituents *not* and *and*, the former does not.

But this distinction in terms of constituents does not as yet suffice to differentiate among all different states of affairs. Take, for example, the two states of affairs *P or Q* and *Q or P*. They have the same constituents, yet they are merely equivalent, not identical. What distinguishes them is the fact that the orders of their ingredients are not the same. The heart of the matter is the ontological law that every relation has a direction or sense.* Every relation has a first place, a

---

argument to the effect that things must have a different ontological status from states of affairs.

* It goes without saying that relations are not classes of ordered couples, ordered triples, etc. Moreover, there is no ontological reduction of, say, an ordered couple to a class in the spirit of the Wiener-Kuratowski device. There exists an isomorphism between ordered couples on the one hand, and certain

second place, and so on. How many places it has depends, of course, on what kind of relation it is. Hence a state of affairs of the form $R(a, b)$ is never the same as a state of affairs of the form $R(b, a)$, regardless of what relation R may be. But, of course, the two states of affairs may be equivalent.[2]

If the respective states of affairs are equivalent for all entities for which the relation holds, then the relation is said to be symmetric. Thus to say that C is symmetric is merely a short way of saying that for all entities e_1 and e_2, C holds between e_1 and e_2 if and only if it holds between e_2 and e_1. But whether or not C fulfills this latter condition is not a linguistic matter, but a matter of fact. It depends on what relation C is, not on how we happen to talk or think about it. Thus we see in what sense it is a matter of language and in what sense it is not a matter of language to say that identity is a symmetric relation.

As to the third condition, it is necessary because two states of affairs may contain the same constituents in the same order and yet be different. Consider, for example, the two states of affairs P or P and P or P or P. Again, there is no doubt that the two states of affairs are equivalent. Even so, I think that they are different. What makes them different is neither a difference in constituents—both states of affairs contain precisely the same constituents, namely, P and or—nor a difference in the order of the constituents (at least in one obvious sense of this term), but the fact that the constituent P occurs only twice in the first state of affairs, but three times in the second, and that the constituent or occurs only once in the first, but twice in the second state of affairs.[3]

This, then, is the criterion for the identity of states of affairs, not counting Leibniz's principle. Accordingly, the state of affairs P or Q is not identical with the state of affairs Not-(not-P and not-Q): and in general, as shown by this criterion, equivalent states of affairs, even if they are equivalent as a matter of logic, are not identical.* Hence, even

---

classes on the other; but the existence of this isomorphism, as I shall later argue in detail (see Chapter 13), has no ontological bearing on the existence of the isomorphic entities.

    * Since logically equivalent states of affairs are in general not the same, the alleged paradox of confirmation is not really a paradox. If the state of affairs that all ravens are black were identical with the state of affairs that all nonblack things are nonravens, then it would indeed be paradoxical that a certain state of

if we assume for the moment that (1) is a logical equivalence, there is no reason to conclude that its two sides "say the very same thing," that is, represent the very same state of affairs.

But if we agree that logical truths in general and logical equivalences in particular are not abbreviational truths—are not true by definition, in one of the many meanings of this term—we seem to be faced with another problem; for we imply that there is no difference between so-called material equivalence and so-called logical equivalence. More accurately, we are implying that there exists just one such connection, called equivalence, and not two. And this corollary of our view, it may be said, is unacceptable. Hence our view is unacceptable. However, in my eyes, this consequence strengthens rather than weakens the view. I wish to deny explicitly the existence of a special kind of logical equivalence relation. There is only one equivalence relation between states of affairs, namely, the relation represented by 'if and only if'. The words 'material' and 'logical' do not indicate two kinds of relations, but, at best, can be said to indicate two kinds of states of affairs. If a particular state of affairs P is equivalent to another particular state of affairs Q, and this equivalence is not an instance of a general logical law, then we speak of material equivalence. On the other hand, (2) above is called a logical equivalence, because it is a general truth about any two states of affairs. Even though it is a logical truth, it contains the lowly material equivalence represented by 'if and only if' and not a peculiar logical kind of equivalence relation. From a linguistic point of view, the expression 'if and only if' represents the same relation regardless of whether it occurs between two English sentences or merely between two forms that are parts of an English sentence.

So far I have not questioned the assumption that (1) is a logical equivalence. I have merely tried to show that logical truths are not abbreviational truths and that logical equivalence is not the same as identity, so that it cannot be argued that the two sides of (1) represent the same state of affairs, if (1) is a logical truth. Now I shall explain why I do not think of (1) as a logical truth.

---

affairs confirms the latter but not the former; for identical entities share all their properties, relations, characteristics, and what have you, and hence must share the same "degree of confirmation." But since the two states of affairs are not identical, the paradox merely proves that logically equivalent states of affairs may behave differently in regard to confirmation.

How shall we use such words as 'logical' and 'logic' in the remainder of this book? I want to avoid certain philosophical misconceptions about the nature of logic and ontology; but, at the same time, I must pay attention to the more or less established notion of what logic is. It would be idiosyncratic, to say the least, to use these words with an entirely different and new meaning. On the other hand, I cannot hope to convey my views accurately while using the traditional, but for my purposes misleading, terminology. I think that the following explications do justice to both my philosophical intentions and the unreflected notion of logic.

There is, first of all, the traditional distinction between propositional logic and predicate or functional logic. The difference between these two fields, I believe, is very fundamental; as fundamental, for example, as the difference between predicate logic and set theory or the difference between set theory and arithmetic. It is, therefore, somewhat unfortunate that the term 'logic' usually covers both of these systems. But we can and shall, of course, distinguish between them. Only, I shall speak of the *general theory of states of affairs* and of the *general theory of properties and relations* instead of propositional logic and predicate logic. I shall further distinguish between the general theory of properties and the general theory of relations. Hence logic, as commonly understood, consists in my view of three rather distinct theories, namely, the general theory of states of affairs, the general theory of properties, and the general theory of relations.

The theory of states of affairs consists of all those laws which hold for states of affairs in general. (2) above is an example, and so is the law that for all states of affairs p, the state of affairs p *or not*–p obtains. Thus the theory of states of affairs consists simply of the laws of propositional logic. But my conception of it differs from the more common ones in the following important respects. First, as I see it, this theory is neither about truth values nor about propositions. Rather, it is about states of affairs. That truth values are not states of affairs is obvious; for there are only two truth values, while there are many different states of affairs. But the term 'proposition' may have been used to refer to what I call a state of affairs. So I must add that, as I use these two expressions, existent propositions—if there were such entities—would be correlated to false sentences as well as true ones, while only true sentences can be said to represent states of affairs which obtain.* In other words, if there were propositions, there would exist a proposition for every sentence, regardless of whether the sentence were true or false. States of affairs, though, obtain only for true sentences. Now, this is merely one difference between propositions and the states of affairs of my ontology, but it is an important one, and it may help to explain why I insisted above that the theory of states of affairs is not about propositions.[4]

However, it is an essential feature of the theory of states of affairs that its laws hold alike for states of affairs which obtain and for states of affairs which do not obtain. Consider, for example, the law that the state of affairs p *or not–p* obtains for all states of affairs p. According to this law, the state of affairs P *or not–P* obtains, even if P does not obtain. And this shows that the relation *or* can hold between a state of affairs which obtains and a state of affairs which does not obtain. It is this feature of the theory of states of affairs in general and of the connectives (including *not*) in particular which seems to be, at least in part, responsible for the ontological invention of propositions. Since either the state of affairs P obtains or the state of affairs $Not–P$ obtains, but not both, and since the state of affairs P *or not–P* obtains in either case, some philosophers seem to have reasoned that the connection *or* cannot hold between states of affairs, but must hold between propositions instead, where a proposition is supposed to be an entity that exists irrespective of whether the relevant sentence is true or false. In brief, I hold that the theory of states of affairs is about states of affairs, even about states of affairs which do not obtain, while the view I wish to reject holds that it is about propositions, that is, propositions connected with false as well as true sentences, but existent propositions in either case.

Second, the theory of states of affairs no less than predicate logic makes use of quantifiers. The law mentioned above holds for *all* states of affairs p; other laws hold for *all* states of affairs p, *all* states of affairs q, and so forth; and still others contain the existential quantifier *some*. Nor could it be otherwise; for how could there be a theory of states of affairs, that is, a body of laws, without quantifiers? This question points up another fact. Not only are the quantifiers not peculiar to

---

* States of affairs which obtain are often called facts.

predicate logic, since they occur in the theory of states of affairs as well, but they also occur in all other theories about any kind or kinds of entities. They are just as much part of, say, arithmetic and set theory, as they are part of the theory of states of affairs and property theory. They are even an indispensable part of chemistry and botany. Thus, they are not characteristic of logic at all, neither of propositional logic, nor of predicate logic, nor of the two fields thought of as combined. If they are characteristic of anything, then it is not of logic as such, but rather of theories in general that they are characteristic. In this sense, it is misleading to call the quantifiers logical quantifiers or, talking about their expressions, to call these expressions logical signs. Moreover, everything I have so far said about the quantifiers holds equally well for the connectives. They, too, are not characteristic of logic, even though they are most often called logical connectives. Rather, every theory that deserves the name, be it the theory of states of affairs, property theory, set theory, arithmetic, geometry, chemistry, etc., contains these connectives. What, then, is the distinguishing feature of, say, the theory of states of affairs that separates it from all other theories? The answer is as obvious as it is simple: what distinguishes the theory of states of affairs from all other theories is its subject matter, namely, that it is about states of affairs. While every theory worthy of the name contains quantifiers and connectives, only the theory of states of affairs deals with states of affairs in general. What distinguishes any two theories most essentially is their respective topics.

The general theory of states of affairs is about states of affairs. Its variables range over states of affairs and only over states of affairs. The general theory of properties is about properties in general. It has variables ranging over properties, as is to be expected, and also variables which range over entities other than properties insofar as these entities have properties. For example, the law: For all properties f and g and for all entities e: if e is f and e is g, then e is f does not hold only for individual things, but holds for all entities with properties whatsoever. Thus it would be more accurate to say that property theory is about entities with properties and about their properties. There is one additional constant, namely, the connection of exemplification which holds between any entity and a property which it has (exemplifies).

But property theory does not differ only in its subject matter from the general theory of states of affairs. There is another important difference. We saw that the theory of states of affairs holds for states of affairs which obtain as well as for states of affairs which do not obtain. This is not the case for property theory. The law of property theory mentioned in the last paragraph must be read more accurately as follows: For all *existent* properties *f* and *g* and for all entities *e*, etc. To put the matter differently, while we must let the variables of the theory of states of affairs range over states of affairs which do not obtain as well as states of affairs which obtain, we must restrict the property variables of property theory so that they range only over existents. The deeper reason for this difference consists in the fact that while states of affairs which obtain can be related by means of the connectives to states of affairs which do not obtain, the nexus of exemplification never holds between an entity and a property, unless the property exists. Entities do not exemplify nonexistent properties. In short, property theory, unlike the theory of states of affairs and like, say, chemistry, is about existent properties only.

It should be clear that property theory is not to be identified with quantification theory (predicate logic of *first order*) or with predicate logic of higher order, if the latter is confined to *individual things*, their properties and relations, properties of such properties, etc. It differs from the former, because it talks about all properties *f* and some properties *g*. All its "sentences" represent laws which either obtain or do not obtain. All its "sentences" are quantificationally closed. Nor could it be otherwise; for how could there be a general theory of properties without properties? It differs from the latter, because it is not restricted to individual things and the hierarchy of properties built upon such individual things. Rather, property theory deals with entities of whatever kind as long as these entities have properties. Similar and rather obvious differences hold between the theory of states of affairs, on the one hand, and the general theory of relations, on the other.

So much about the notion of logic. Now recall the statement (1). It mentions classes and numbers. Hence it could not possibly be a law of the general theory of states of affairs or a law of the general theory of properties and relations. But this means, as I use the word 'logic,' that (1) could not possibly be a logical truth. Nor is it a law of general set theory; for it mentions numbers. Nor, finally, is it a statement of arithmetic; for it talks about classes.* Rather, it is a "mixed" law, a law that establishes a connection between classes and numbers. I shall call these laws bridge laws. Whatever the precise status of such a law may be, and there are many like it, one thing is certain: it cannot be maintained that, since (1) is a logical truth, the two sides of (1) "say the same thing." Aside from the fact that the two sides of logical equivalences do not necessarily represent the same state of affairs, there is thus the further objection that (1) is simply not a logical truth to begin with.

But when ideas fail, a new word is often thought to do the trick. In this case, it is the term 'analytic'. The two sides of (1) "say the same thing," it may be argued, not because (1) is a logical truth in a narrower sense, but rather because it is analytic. Now it is not at all clear what this could mean, but whatever it may mean, the fact remains that (1) is not an abbreviational truth; and since it is not an abbreviational truth, we have no reason to believe that the two sides of (1) "say the same thing." For the rest, we do not only willingly admit but insist on the fact that (1), unlike statements of botany or chemistry, mentions the "abstract attributes" of being a class and of being a number, and that it contains quantification over properties. But I do not understand why that should make it analytic.

Frege's so-called definition of numbers, I conclude, does not follow from (1). This plain fact may, however, be overlooked if one confuses sameness with equivalence. In the present chapter, I have tried to dispel this confusion.

6 DESCRIPTIONS AND LEIBNIZ'S LAW

Perhaps we can prove Frege's identity sentence (F) directly, as it were. Let us fall back on Leibniz's law that entities are the same if and only if they share all properties (including relations). If we have any doubt that A is the same as B, we simply try to find a property which one of the two entities has but which the other lacks. The more certain we are that

* I anticipate, of course, one of our conclusions, namely, that numbers are not classes.

there is no such property, the more certain we can be that we are dealing with just one instead of two entities. This practice is familiar and common enough, but two comments are nevertheless appropriate: the first highlights Frege's circumspection, and the second uncovers still another misuse of the term 'definition'.

In the very context in which Frege proposes his definition of numbers, he also states that such a definition must prove itself, and that one way in which it may prove itself derives from Leibniz's definition of identity.[1] (This astute remark substantiates the view that Frege did not think of his crucial "definitions" as abbreviational truths, but conceived of them as true, informative, identity statements.) In the same context, Frege also calls Leibniz's law a definition. This is quite consistent with my earlier interpretation of Frege's view of definition. But it is not consistent, I submit, with the common view that definitions are abbreviation proposals. Leibniz's law is neither an abbreviation proposal nor an abbreviational truth. It seems to me that he did not conclude—after a fair amount of research, perhaps—that 'so-and-so is the same as such and such' (translated from the German) is merely short for 'so-and-so and such and such have all properties in common' (translated from the German). Rather, Leibniz discovered the general law that for any two entities e_1 and e_2, e_1 is the same as e_2 *if and only if* e_1 and e_2 have the same properties. In other words, he saw that two states of affairs are *equivalent*. Needless to say, this is no ordinary equivalence. It is not even a logical truth, unless one thinks of identity as being a matter of property theory. But since I see no reason not to, and since it seems to me that we are at a point where the terminological agreements become indeed largely arbitrary, I shall, from this point on, assign Leibniz's law to general property theory and hence to logic. However, even though it does not matter much whether we call Leibniz's law logical or ontological, something else does matter. We must beware never to confuse generality—even utmost generality—and intuitive obviousness with conventionality or arbitrariness. Just because Leibniz's law holds for all entities whatsoever—for individual things as well as for properties, for numbers as well as for connectives, for quantifiers as well as for states of affairs—this does not mean that it is "devoid of factual content," as some philosophers like to say. Similarly, just because the laws of the general theory of states of affairs hold for all kinds of states of affairs and the laws of general property theory hold for all kinds of entities and their properties, we must not carelessly imagine that they are "empty tautologies which say nothing about the world."*

Assuming that Leibniz's law is true as a matter of the logical structure of the world, we may proceed to test Frege's identity sentence (F). The question before us is this: Does each property (including relations) that belongs to the number of *F*'s also belong to the class determined by the property of being similar to *F*, and conversely? Or can we find at least one property or relation that belongs to the number, but not to the class, or that belongs to the class, but not to the number? In terms of substitutability, the crucial question is: Can one substitute the two expressions 'the number of *F*'s' and 'the class determined by the property of being similar to *F*' for each other in every context *salva veritate*? I think that the first formulation is to be preferred, because it does not introduce the vexing but irrelevant complication that two descriptions of the same entity may be different. After all, the question before us has absolutely nothing to do with how we talk about the respective entities; whether there is, say, more than one label for a given entity in the particular language, or whether most people happen to describe the given entity rather than label it in their language. But in order to see this clearly, we must take a look at definite descriptions.

Leibniz's law mentions all properties (including relations) of an entity. Accordingly, the substitution principle mentions all contexts. Nor is this surprising. An entity has all the properties it has, not a single property more, nor a single property less. Hence an entity could not possibly be the same as another entity, even if the former had a single, solitary property which the latter lacked. To talk about partial identity or degrees of identity makes absolutely no sense in this context. But it is nevertheless a strangely prevailing view that intentional and modal properties (as I shall say to be brief) are exceptions to Leibniz's law.†

---

* Philosophical confusions feed on each other. The mistaken view that logical truths are "true by definition" reinforces the mistaken belief that they "say nothing about the world," and conversely.

† I do not think that there are intentional properties like *being believed by P, being thought of by Q*, etc. But there are mental acts of believing and of thinking and these acts stand in a certain intentional relation to their objects. This intentional nexus is not truth functional like the connectives; hence the alleged

As far as I can see, this view rests on one crucial argument. Assuming that E_1 and E_2 are the same, one picks out an intentional or modal property I and tries to show that the sentence 'E_1 is I' is true (or may be true), while the sentence 'E_2 is I' is false (or may be false). Now, if E_1 is the same as E_2, and if the former sentence is, say, true, while the latter is false, then it follows of course that E_1 and E_2 do not share all properties, since they do not share I. And hence we have an exception to Leibniz's law. However, from this abstract point of view, the argument does not look very promising; for, if the two sentences really have different truth values, we might quite naturally conclude that E_1 and E_2—all earlier appearance to the contrary—are simply not identical. Or, if we start with the conviction that E_1 and E_2 are the same, we may conclude that the two sentences—all previous appearance to the contrary—do have the same truth value after all. But the argument becomes more convincing as soon as we turn to concrete cases, because then we are apt to use definite description expressions instead of 'E_1' and 'E_2'. Yet it is not sound. It is plausible only if one confuses an entity with a description of that entity.

Consider a less complicated case first. From the fact that the intentional property of being thought of by person P belongs to the fact that Scott wrote *Waverley,* we cannot conclude that it also belongs to the fact that Scott wrote *Ivanhoe,* even though—and this is important—these two facts concern the very same person, Scott. But it would not occur to us to complain that Leibniz's law does not hold in this case. Rather, we would insist that this law is not violated at all; for the fact that Scott wrote *Waverley* is not the same fact as the fact that Scott wrote *Ivanhoe*; hence the former may have properties which the latter lacks. And we would adhere to the belief that anything which is identical with the fact that Scott wrote *Waverley* must also have the intentional property of being thought of by P.

Let us now turn to definite descriptions. From the fact that P thinks of someone as the author of *Waverley*, it does not follow that he thinks of someone as the author of *Ivanhoe*, even though the two descriptions are descriptions of one and the same person, namely,

difficulty of substituting in intentional contexts. For details see Reinhardt Grossmann, *The Structure of Mind* (Madison and Milwaukee, 1965), and Gustav Bergmann, *Realism. A Critique of Brentano and Meinong* (Madison and Milwaukee, 1967).

Scott. Just as in the previous case, though, this does not show that there are exceptions to Leibniz's law. What it shows is that the description *the author of Waverley* is not the same entity as the description *the author of Ivanhoe,* even though the person described is the same in both cases. We must, therefore, distinguish between two entirely different identity statements. First, we may wish to assert that an entity described in a certain way is the same as an entity described in a quite different way. Second, we may wish to say that a certain description of an entity is the same as another description. The latter kind of statement is most naturally expressed by a sentence of the form 'Description$_1$ = Description$_2$'. Unfortunately, though, English sentences of this form are used to assert that the entities described in the two descriptions are the same, not that the descriptions are the same. To emphasize that it is not the descriptions but the entities described which are said to be identical, one should paraphrase (whenever it matters) and say, instead of 'The author of *Waverley* is the same as the author of *Ivanhoe*,' some such thing as 'One and the same person is the author of *Waverley* and the author of *Ivanhoe*'.*

Leibniz's law holds for intentional properties and modal properties as well as for "normal" ones.† But this fact is easily overlooked if one does not realize that what a definite description expression represents is a description and not the entity described. Consider the definite description *the author of Waverley.* There is no question what it is that is described as the author of *Waverley*; it is obviously a certain person, namely, Scott. But what does the description expression represent? What is it that is the same when we do not have two different descriptions of Scott but, rather, the same description in different linguistic guises? Frege was the first to raise this question and his answer is by now famous. He holds that description expressions express a sense in addition to referring to a referent. In my

---

* In a schema like *Principia Mathematica* the same effect is achieved, as is well known, by first applying Russell's so-called definition of definite descriptions to the English sentence 'The so-and-so is the such and such'.

† As for modal properties (or modal operators), I believe that there simply are no such entities. They do not belong to the furniture of the world, as I shall argue presently.

In regard to the alleged distinction between modality *de dicto* and modality *de re*, I have not the faintest idea what the latter could be, the recent rash of articles on the matter notwithstanding.

terminology, this means that a description expression represents a sense in addition to being used to describe an entity. Frege's answer, I believe, is wrong. It is wrong because there are no such entities as senses.[2] Definite descriptions, as I use the term, are not senses but states of affairs. Entities are described in states of affairs.

But description expressions like 'the author of *Waverley*' do not seem to represent states of affairs. They behave like terms rather than sentences. How does this fact of grammar agree with my claim that descriptions are states of affairs? The linguistic expressions we use do not always reflect the structure of the thoughts we express and the structure of the states of affairs we talk about in the most perspicuous way. Definite description expressions are a case in point. They behave like terms, grammatically speaking, but they do nevertheless represent states of affairs. The expression 'the author of *Waverley*,' for example, is merely short for 'the entity which is an author of *Waverley*,' and this latter expression represents the state of affairs that a single entity is an author of *Waverley*.[3] But when we use a description expression, we are not interested in the state of affairs which it represents. Rather, we are only interested in the entity described in the state of affairs, because we want to say something else about this object. This is the reason why a description expression never occurs alone. If we want to assert that the state of affairs represented by, say, 'the entity which is an author of *Waverley*' obtains, we have to change for grammatical reasons to a sentence like 'A single entity (person) is an author of *Waverley*' or 'Precisely one entity (person) is an author of *Waverley*'. The definite article and the word 'which' have the effect of drawing our attention away from the state of affairs which is asserted and to the entity described in the state of affairs; and they also prepare us for the predication yet to come. If description expressions, through an accident of linguistic development, looked more like sentences and less like terms, the problem of descriptions would reduce to nothing more than the question of how there can be two states of affairs (and hence two sentences) concerning one and the same subject.

Description expressions are not the only ones that have led philosophers away from the true ontological path. Just consider sentences of the forms 'All *F* and *G*' and 'Some *F* are *G*'. Here, too, the expressions 'All *F*' and 'Some *F*' look like terms, even though they really hide states of affairs. And think of all the views, logical as well as ontological, that were ingeniously invented in order to explain the behavior of these alleged terms until Frege gave the correct analysis of their meaning.* The only difference between definite description expressions and expressions of the forms 'All things which are F' and 'Some things which are F' consists in the fact that we can drop the 'which' in the latter two and get perfect grammatical sentences which represent the same states of affairs as the original sentences, while we do not get a normal expression if we drop the 'which' from 'The thing which is F'. In this case we have to paraphrase: 'Precisely one thing is F' or 'A single thing is F'.

Our considerations show that if one distinguishes properly between descriptions and what they describe, it becomes quite obvious that there are no exceptions to Leibniz's law. There is no property (or a relation), no matter how esoteric or abstract, that belongs to e_1 but not to e_2 if e_1 is the same as e_2. Now, consider the two description expressions 'the number of F's' and 'the class determined by the property of being similar to F'. The two descriptions, it is clear, are not the same. But what about the entities described? According to Leibniz's law, we merely have to find one single, solitary property of the number of F's which the corresponding class does not have in order to prove that the number is not the class. We do not have to cast around for long, because there are numerous such properties. Turning immediately to the general case, there are numerous properties which numbers have and classes lack, and conversely. The most essential feature of classes is that they have members.† To be more precise, classes stand in the *relation* of having members to entities. No number stands in this relation to anything. On the other hand, numbers are odd or even, divisible by N_1, the sum of N_2 and N_3, and so on. More precisely, numbers stand in various arithmetical *relations* to each other. No class stands in such a relation to anything.* It is obvious that there are many more examples. It follows that numbers are not classes. Hence they

---

   * It is rather surprising that Frege saw quite clearly that these "terms" had to be analyzed into contexts which include predication, and yet he never ceased to treat description expressions as terms. Put differently, it is surprising that he treated *all* and *some* as quantifiers, but not *the*.

   † Except, of course, the empty class if there is such an entity.

   * But a class may, of course, be said to have an odd or even *number of members*.

could not possibly be classes of the particular kind mentioned in
Frege's definition (F).

I have heard the objection that numbers have members after all
and that my view must therefore be false. They have members, it is
said, because they are identical with certain classes. But this objection
patently begs the question. Notice that I do not claim that numbers
have no members because they are not classes, but rather that since
they have no members they cannot be classes. How do I know that they
have no members? I cannot do better than to trust arithmetic, just as I
cannot do better than to trust physics when I want to know, for
instance, whether or not electrons have colors.* For the rest, I can only
challenge my opponent to name a single argument that speaks for
numbers having members—an argument other than that numbers are
classes, of course, and hence contrary to what we all commonly believe.
Such beliefs are not sacrosanct, but nobody can reasonably ask us to
give them up unless he has produced an argument against them.

Notice, in conclusion, one curious feature of our application of
Leibniz's law to numbers and classes. It was always understood that
two entities must share not only properties but also their relations to
other entities in order to be identical. In the case of numbers and
classes, all the examples mentioned involve relations, rather than
properties. To be sure, this is perfectly sufficient to establish that
numbers are not classes. But it raises the interesting question of
whether we could have listed instead properties of numbers which are
not shared by classes and properties of classes which are not shared by
numbers. More accurately, could we have listed such properties not
counting, of course, the properties of being a number and of being a
class? I must confess that I cannot think of such a property. All the
properties that come immediately to mind, like the property of being
odd, turn out to be, on second glance, relational and hence to be no
properties at all in the sense here intended.[4] If I were tempted to make
deep pronouncements in a calm manner, I would say that it is an
ontological feature of our world that individual things are characterized
primarily by the properties they have, while numbers and classes are

* The analogy is not perfect. While it takes indeed an expert to decide
whether or not electrons have colors, almost everyone can convince himself that,
say, the number 3 has no members, because we need no special apparatus or
complicated theory in order to *see* that there are three apples on the table.

primarily (or, perhaps, only) characterized by the relations numbers have to other numbers and classes have to other classes.

7 RECURSIVE DEFINITIONS

There is a traditional objection against our conclusion that numbers cannot be classes, since only numbers stand in arithmetic relations to each other. It is claimed that these airthmetic relations can be "defined" in terms of relations among classes. "The chief point to be observed" says Russell, "is that logical addition of classes is the fundamental notion, while the arithmetical addition of numbers is wholly subsequent."[1] Now, if this is true, then it follows that there really are no arithmetic relations, and hence our argument for the difference between numbers and classes breaks down. But we may have acquired by now a sagacious suspicion of any claim that certain entities do not exist because they can be defined in terms of other entities. We have become aware of the many meanings of the term 'definition'. This suspicion, as we shall presently see, is entirely justified.

Consider Russell's definition of addition:

(R) $m + n$ is the number of a class w which is the logical sum of two classes u and v which have no common term and of which one has m terms, the other has n terms.[2]

It is not clear how, precisely, (R) must be read, but there are at least two obvious possibilities. First, (R) may mean: The number which is the sum of m and n *is identical with* the number of the class w which is the logical sum of two classes u and v which have no common term and of which one has m terms, the other has n terms. Or it could mean: The number which is the sum of m and n is identical with the number of terms of a class w *if and only if* w is the logical sum of two classes u and v which have no common term and of which one has m terms, the other has n terms. According to the first interpretation, (R) is an identity statement with two descriptions. Numbers are described as sums of numbers and also as numbers of (the elements of) certain classes. In a given case, one and the same number is said to be the sum of two numbers and also the number of any class consisting of any two exclusive classes with certain numbers of members. There is no doubt that this identity sentence is true. The question is, is it true as a matter of mere abbreviation or not? Are not only the described entities the same but also the descriptions themselves?* In other words, is the description expression on the left side of the identity sign merely an abbreviation for the description expression on the right side? I do not think so. How could it be an abbreviation, since the description which it represents does not involve classes at all, while the description of the right-side expression does? I do not think , therefore, that this identity statement reduces to an instance of the law of self-identity. Rather, it is informative; it tells us that a number which stands in an arithmetic relation to two other numbers is the same entity as the number of elements of a class which stands to two other classes in a certain class relation. It tells us what the number of the members of a class will be in case the class is of a certain kind. If so, then there can be no doubt that (R) is an informative identity statement and that there exist arithmetic relations among numbers.

The same holds for the second interpretation of (R). It seems to me even more obvious, if anything, that the expression on the left side of the equivalence sign is not an abbreviation of the expression on the right side. The two sentences do not represent the same state of affairs. How could they, since the state of affairs represented on the left side contains the relation of identity, while the state of affairs of the right side does not? But if the two sentences represent different states of affairs, then one cannot claim to have shown that there is no such arithmetic relation as the sum relation.

So much about Russell's attempt to define arithmetic relations. The usual procedure is to "define" these relations by means of *recursive definitions.*[3] What is the *ontological* significance of such definitions?

First, a word of clarification. Usually, one speaks of recursive functions rather than recursive relations.[4] This raises the ontological question of whether or not there are functions. For reasons which I

---

* If one confuses the entity described with its description, one may be led to believe that in the case of a true informative identity sentence, not only the entities described, but also their descriptions are the same. Hence one may believe that one has not only "reduced" the entities described to just one entity but that one has also reduced the entities mentioned by the one description expression to the entities mentioned by the other.

shall not discuss in this book, I side on this matter with Russell rather than Frege.[5] While there are properties and relations, there are no functions. For example, an expression of the form 'the R of A' is merely short for an expression of the form 'the y which stands in (the relation) R to A'. Accordingly, the expression 'the sum of x and y' is merely short for 'the z which stands in the relation of sum to x and y'. Speaking quite generally but not very accurately, we may say that behind every function expression there lurks in reality a relation. But it will do no harm if I pretend occasionally that there are functions.

Dedekind, in his famous essay, proves a theorem of the following sort: Given the successor function for the natural numbers N and given a certain natural number w, there is one and only one function γ such that:

(a) $\gamma(1) = w$,
(b) γ (the successor of n) = the successor of $\gamma(n)$.*

If we assume that $w = 1$, then γ will be the identity function. In order to get a different function, we must select a number other than 1, say, the successor of m, where m is some number. Since the function γ will depend on this number m, we can call the value of the function for an arbitrary argument n the *sum of the numbers m and n*. This number is completely determined by two conditions:

(a) the sum of m and 1 = the successor of m,
(b) the sum of m and the successor of n = the successor of the sum of m and n.

Thus, what Dedekind proves, as far as our interests are concerned, is that there is one and only one function ϕ such that for all natural numbers m and n the following holds:

(1) $\phi(m, 1)$ = the successor of m,
(2) $\phi(m, \text{successor of } n)$ = the successor of $\phi(m, n)$.

It is not hard to guess what this function is; it is, of course, the function of addition. But to provide us with a clue as to what entity one has in mind is not to define this entity in the sense of reducing it to other entities. Dedekind proves that there is precisely one function which can

* Actually, the theorem of section 126 of Dedekind's work is much more general. But this makes no difference for our purposes.

be described as the function which fulfills conditions (1) and (2) above. If we look at these conditions carefully, we see that he has proved the existence of the sum function. He does not put it this way. Instead, he introduces the abbreviation 'sum of the numbers m and n' for 'the function which fulfills conditions (1) and (2)'. Of course e does not pick the term 'sum' out of thin air; after all, this term has a well-established meaning in ordinary discourse. But he acts as if he does. Now, there is no argument that we could use some other term in order to represent the function under discussion. And there is also no argument that we can pretend—for reasons of purity of exposition—that the term 'sum' has no previous meaning and that we introduce it solely as an abbreviation for a longer description. But even so, what we then call the sum function is in no way reduced to some other entity or entities.

Every recursive definition of a function (relation) is in reality a *description* of the function (relation). Hence the function which is recursively described is as little reduced to something else as Scott is when we describe him as the author of *Waverley*. But recursive descriptions, as I shall call them from now on, are of a peculiar sort. In one respect, they are quite different from "ordinary descriptions"; and it is this peculiarity, we may assume, which has led philosophers to ascribe to them ontological significance.

Consider condition (1) for a moment. It is an identity statement with two descriptions: The number x which is the sum of m and 1 is identical with the number y which is the successor of m. One and the same number is described in two different ways. Furthermore, this is a general identity statement which holds for all numbers m. Thus any description of the form *the number x which is the sum of M and 1* can be "replaced" by a description which involves the successor relation rather than the sum relation. It can be "replaced" by such a description in the sense that the description in terms of the successor relation will always describe the same number. Condition (2), similarly, makes it possible to replace a description of the form *the x which is the sum of M and N* by a description which does not involve the sum relation but contains the successor relation instead. In short, the two conditions allow us to "replace" any description of a number as the sum of two numbers by a description of the same number in terms of the successor relation. Any number that can be described as the sum of two numbers can also be described in terms of being a successor of some number. The recursive definition of the sum relation comes to this; for every description of a number in terms of the sum relation there is a description of that same number in terms of a different relation.*

We a[...]faced again with the following question: Given that, say, the number x which is the sum of M and 1 is identical with the number y which is the successor of M, do the two description expressions represent the same description? Only if we can show that the expression 'the number x which is the sum of M and 1' is just another expression for the description *the number y which is the successor of M* can we claim that there is no such entity as the sum relation in addition to the successor relation. Only then can we maintain that a genuine ontological reduction has taken place.

Again, I think that we do not deal with two expressions for one description, but rather with two descriptions of the same entity. If so, then there exist at least two relations for numbers, namely, the sum relation and the successor relation. Or rather, since I am convinced that there are these two relations, I am quite sure that we are dealing with different descriptions of the same entity rather than with the same description in two different linguistic guises.

We saw that the recursive description of the sum relation allows us to "replace" every description of the form *the number x which is the sum of M and N* where M and N are definite numbers, by a description in terms of the successor relation. Furthermore, to 'the number x which is the sum of m and N,' where 'm' is a variable and 'N' is a numeral, there correspond forms which mention the successor relation instead. But there is no such corresponding expression for the form 'the number x which is the sum of m and n,' where both 'm' and 'n' are variables. To get the corresponding expression, we can turn to the following identity statement: the number x which is the sum of m and n is *identical* with the number y which stands in the *nth iterate of the successor relation* to m.[6] We say for short 'R is the nth iterate of the successor relation' instead of 'R is the relation between two elements of a sequence h and k, where k is the first thing in the sequence, h is the nth thing in the

---

* A recursive relation, of course, is such that for every n-tuple of numbers it can be decided whether the relation holds for it or not. This is the feature that makes it so valuable to mathematicians and logicians.

sequence, and each succeeding thing in the sequence bears the successor relation to the thing before it'.* Details aside, we have again two different descriptions of the same number. From a slightly different point of view, we have the general equivalence that for all x, y, and z, the sum relation holds among x, y, and z *if and only if* the zth iterate of the successor relation holds between x and y. But this equivalence does not follow from the acceptance of an abbreviation proposal.

Let us take stock. I claimed originally that numbers cannot be classes, because only numbers stand in arithmetic relations to each other; classes do not. Russell would have objected that arithmetic relations can be reduced to relations among classes. But our analysis of Russell's alleged definition showed that it amounted merely to a true informative identity statement; one and the same number is described once as being related by an arithmetic relation to two other numbers, once as being the number of a certain class which is related in a certain way to two other classes. The two descriptions themselves are not the same. Then we took a look at so-called recursive definitions. Such definitions yield different definite descriptions for the same numbers. For example, any number which is related by the sum relation to two other numbers can also be described in terms of the successor relation between numbers. Again, there is no ontological reduction of one relation to the other. But notice that even if there were such a reduction, even if the two descriptions were the same and not just the numbers described, a further step would be necessary in order to refute my view that numbers are not classes. One would have to contend also that the successor relation (between numbers) is not confined to numbers. Put differently, one would have to maintain also that this successor relation (between numbers) can be defined in terms of (reduced to) a relation among classes; for the recursive description of the sum relation, even if it were ontologically significant, would merely reduce one arithmetic relation to another arithmetic relation. And even if the successor relation were the only relation which holds between numbers but not between classes, we would have a proof that numbers cannot be classes.

* Is there such a relation as the nth iterate of the successor relation? I do not think so, for reasons which I shall explain in detail in Chapter 15. But for the moment, I shall let the issue ride.

Does the successor relation hold between classes? It seems obvious to me that it does not. Of course, classes can be arranged in various ways by means of relations which are *isomorphic* to the successor relation, but all these relations are different from the successor relation between numbers. For example, consider the two progressions of classes: (a) Λ , $\{\Lambda\}$, $\{\{\Lambda\}\}$, ... and (b) Λ , $\{\Lambda\}$, $\{\Lambda,\{\Lambda\}\}$, ... The relations R_1 and R_2 which order these two progressions are isomorphic to the successor relation. Yet they are different from each other and not the same as the successor relation. R_1 is the relation between a class and its singleton; R_2 can perhaps best be described as the relation which an element has to the class which has exactly it and all its members as elements. Neither relation is the relation which a number has to the next following number.

I conclude, therefore, that numbers are not classes.

8 DEFINITION BY ABSTRACTION

If numbers are not classes, perhaps they are properties. Frege seems to mention this alternative in a footnote to his *Foundations of Arithmetic*,[1] in which he states that he could have written that the number of *f*'s is the same as the concept of being similar to *f*, rather than the same as the extension of this concept. But we must be cautious when we interpret this footnote; for it must be remembered that according to Frege, the expression 'the concept of being similar to *F*' refers to an object rather than a concept. Hence, if we take this idiosyncrasy seriously, Frege is not saying that numbers are concepts (properties), but rather that they are objects—but objects other than extensions (classes). Be that as it may, if one starts with the notion of similarity, one may hold that whenever two classes (or properties) are similar, they share a common property, and that this property is a number. In this fashion, numbers are said to be defined by abstraction.[2] Definition by abstraction, it goes without saying, is quite a different matter from abbreviation proposals, identity, equivalence, and recursive descriptions. But what, precisely, goes on when a property is defined by abstraction?

Frege, in search of a definition of numbers considers the judgment "line a is parallel to line b," and claims that it can be transformed into an identity statement or judgment.[3] If it is so transformed, we obtain the notion of *direction* and say: the direction of line a is identical with the direction of line b. Frege explains this step from 'parallel (a, b)' to 'direction of a = direction of b' as follows: "Thus we replace the symbol '//' by the more general symbol '=,' through removing what is specific in the content of the former and dividing it between a and b. We carve up the content in a way different from the original way, and this yields us a new concept." Hence, in order to get from the relation of parallelism to the notion of direction, one could try the following definition: 'direction of a = direction of b' is to mean the same as 'parallel (a, b)'. Similarly, one may try to obtain the notion of number on the basis of the notion of similarity: 'The number of F's = the number of G's' is to mean the same as 'similar (F, G)'.

But Frege raises three objections against this kind of attempt to define identity of numbers in terms of similarity. First, one may suspect that the definition does not so much define number as it defines identity of number, that is, a special kind of identity. Second, there is the possibility that the identity between the newly arrived at entities conflicts with identity as commonly understood. But these two objections can easily be met if we accept Leibniz's law and are able to show that substitution *salva veritate* works for the given case. Thus we would have to show, in order to justify the proposed definition, that the expression 'the number of F's' can be replaced by the expression 'the number of G's' in every context *salva veritate* if and only if F is similar to G.

The third objection, however, is more formidable. Even if we accept Leibniz's law, the definition does not decide whether the sentence 'The number of F's = Q' is true or false, unless 'Q' is given in the form 'the number of G's'. One may by tempted to "define" the notion of number as follows: 'Q is a number if and only if there is a concept G whose number Q is'. But this process of definition would be circular; for now we would have to know whether the sentence 'Q is identical with the number of G's' is true or false. And we cannot escape from the circle by proposing to conceive of Q as a number only if it has been introduced by the step from the similarity statement to the identity statement; for "then we should be treating the way in which the object Q is introduced as a property of Q, which it is not."[4]

The attempted "definition" does not allow us, therefore, to decide whether 'The number of F's $= Q$' is true or not, unless 'Q' is already in the form 'the number of G's'. Frege concludes that it does not yield a concept of number having sharp limits. He goes on to formulate his final "definition" of the number of F's in terms of the extension of the concept of being similar to the concept F.

Let us leave the historical context and look at definitions by abstraction from a systematic point of view. To be brief, we shall say that a relation R is an *equivalence relation* if it is both symmetric and transitive. Now, if R is an equivalence relation, then its field can be divided into mutually exclusive classes which fulfill the following two conditions: (1) R holds for each pair of entities in each one of these classes; (2) if an entity in one of these classes stands in the relation R to another entity, then the latter entity belongs to the same class as the former.[5] Let us say that a class C is an *equivalence class with respect to the relation R* whenever the two conditions just mentioned hold for C. Thus, if R is an equivalence relation, its field consists of equivalence classes.

Consider, for example, the relation of parallelism (P) between the lines of a fixed plane. P is an equivalence relation. Its field consists of equivalence classes. One may now reason as follows. The properties determined by these classes, properties which we may call directions, can be "defined" in terms of P; for directions are "defined" by the fact that two lines have the same direction if and only if they are parallel. Sameness of direction amounts thus to nothing more than parallelism. Moreover, this method of "definition" can be used for other groups of properties, even if the required equivalence relation is not so obviously at hand as is parallelism. Consider, for example, the family of properties consisting of the various shades of colors. These properties determine certain classes. Now think of these classes as equivalence classes with regard to a certain relation R. What is R? The answer seems to be easy: R is the relation in which two entities stand if and only if they have the same color; we may call it the relation of color-likeness. Starting with the relation of color-likeness, we can then reverse the process, as it were, and "define" the colors in the fashion outlined above. Thus it appears that any family of properties can be "defined by abstraction,"

that is, by means of an equivalence relation. Either the equivalence
relation is already given, as in the case of parallelism, or we introduce it
as a likeness-relation, as in the case of color-likeness.

However, this appearance is deceptive. Given an equivalence
relation like parallelism, it is indeed true that its field consists of
equivalence classes. But to assume that there must also be properties
which are determined by these classes is sheer superstition. Whether or
not there are such properties is a matter of fact which has to be
determined in each case separately. Of course, the members of a given
class, as one usually says, "have the property of being identical with a
or b or c or . . .," where a, b, c, etc., are the members of the class. But
this way of speaking is highly misleading. There is no such property as
that of being identical with 'a or b or c, etc.,' as I shall argue at length in
chapter 15. There are only the facts that each member of the class is
identical either with a or b or c, etc. Similarly, one also says that the
members of a given equivalence class with respect to R "have the
property of standing in the relation R to each other." But this, too, is
misleading. There is no such *property* as that of standing in the relation
R to each other (or to a given entity). But there are, of course, the *facts*
that, say, a stands in the relation R to z, b stands in the relation R to z,
etc. Assuming that there are no such properties as being identical with
something or the other and as standing in the relation R to something, I
maintain that the equivalence classes of an existing equivalence relation
need not determine properties. In each case, it has to be shown
separately that there correspond to the equivalence relation not only
equivalence classes, but also equivalence properties. On the other hand,
there is no reason to exclude the possibility that more than one
property corresponds to each one of the equivalence classes, so that the
question arises which of these properties a given equivalence relation
allegedly "defines."

Conversely, given a certain family of properties, it is indeed true
that these properties determine classes, but it is an open question
whether or not there also exists a corresponding equivalence relation.*
Hence it is not true that there always exists an equivalence relation to
which the family of properties can be "reduced." It will be objected

---

* This is not quite accurate. Not all properties determine classes, as shown
by Cantor's paradox. But for the moment I shall neglect this complication.

that we can always fall back on the respective likeness relation, say, color-likeness or pitch-likeness. But this objection rests on the false assumption that there is such an entity as the relation of having-the-same-color of the relation of having-the-same-pitch. As I have just said, I shall later explain and in great detail why I believe that there are no such relations.

Let us assume, for the sake of the argument, that there exist such properties as directions and that they are equivalence properties with regard to the (existing) relation of parallelism. In this case, the following statement is true: For all lines x and y: the direction of x = the direction of y *if and only if* parallel (x, y). Does this mean, as we so boldly put it earlier, that sameness of direction amounts to nothing more than parallelism? Of course not; for we assumed that there are directions as well as the relation of parallelism. The equivalence statement is just that—a mere equivalence. But now assume that we start out with a true equivalence of the kind just mentioned. Assume that we have before us the following true statement: For all properties f and g: the number of f's = the number of g's *if and only if* similar (f, g). How can we find out whether sameness of number is nothing else than similarity?* How can we find out whether in addition to the relation of similarity between properties there is also a family of properties called numbers? Just knowing that the above equivalence is true is not enough. It may be true as a matter of fact or it may be true as a matter of abbreviation. If it is true as a matter of fact, then there exist both numbers and similarity. Moreover, the statement that the number of F's is identical with the number of G's may not be the only identity statement that is equivalent to the statement that F is similar to G, so that the equivalence relation of similarity may "correspond" to other properties or relations.[6] For example, the following statement is also true: For all properties f and g: the sum of the number of f's and the number of h's, for any property h, is identical with the sum of the number of g's and the number of h's *if and only if* similar (f, g). Hence there is no reason to assume that the Fregean step from the judgment that F is similar to G to an identity statement must lead to just one such identity statement, namely, the statement that the number of F's is identical with the number of G's.

* I assume for the moment that the relation of similarity between properties exists.

If the equivalence is true as a matter of abbreviation, then the situation is quite different. The equivalence holds in this case, because to say that the number of F's is the same as the number of G's is just another way of saying that F is similar to G. We do not have two different though equivalent states of affairs, but merely one state of affairs, *similar (F, G)*, which is also represented—though hardly for reasons of abbreviation—by the sentence 'the number of F's is identical with the number of G's'. I cannot think of a single reason that speaks for this conception of the equivalence statement. But if it were acceptable, property abstraction would completely drop out of the picture. It would not be needed at all. One would simply claim that there are no numbers, since all sentences that purport to be about numbers are really about similarities. Thus, if we take it that the equivalence statement is not an abbreviational truth, then we may hold that numbers are properties of properties existing in their own right. If we believe that the equivalence is an abbreviational truth, then we may assert that there are no such entities as numbers, irrespective of whether we think of them as properties or in some other way.

But there is a third alternative. One may deny, on the one hand, that numbers are "straightforward, irreducible properties of properties" and also, on the other hand, that they are simply nothing, that they do not exist at all. Numbers, according to this view, are abstracted properties, but they are not "irreducible" properties. They are relational properties involving the relation of similarity.* One claims that the expression 'the number of F's' is just another expression for what the expression 'the property of being similar to F' represents. One maintains that there is the property of being similar to F and that this property is sometimes called the number of F's. One holds that it is this property which can be abstracted by means of the similarity relation. If so, then it would also follow that numbers do not form a separate category; they are merely "relational properties" based on the relation of similarity. But this guess as to what property accounts for the fact that different properties are exemplified by the same number of entities must be wrong. Properties, being what they are, may differ from each other even if the classes they determine are the same. If we assume that F and G are different properties, but that there are as many F's as there

* To repeat, I do not think that there are relational properties, but I shall pretend, for the sake of the present argument, that there are.

are G's, then the two relational properties of being similar to F and of being similar to G are different, even though the number of F's is the same as the number of G's. Hence it cannot be the case that the number of F's is the same as the property of being similar to F.[7] Essentially the same conclusion follows for the case in which the "abstracted property" is taken to be the property of being similar to the class determined by F. If we assume that F and G determine different classes with the same number of members, then the number of F's is the same as the number of G's, but the property of being similar to the class determined by F is different from the property of being similar to the class determined by G.

I said above that it is a mistake to hold that an equivalence relation must determine a family of properties by means of the equivalence classes. This mistaken view rests, most likely, on the assumption that there are such properties as that of standing in the equivalence relation R to a certain entity. But be that as it may, let us turn to the view that there actually exist certain equivalence properties with regard to similarity, called numbers. It is not a question of "reduction" any more; we are asking whether numbers are properties of properties or, perhaps, properties of classes.[8] No attempt is being made to "define" numbers in terms of the similarity relation. We are now asking whether or not numbers belong to the *category* of property.

One thing is certain: if numbers are properties, they must be type-indifferent properties. There are two possibilities. Either there are a great number of different 2s (for example, one for properties of individuals, another for properties of properties of individuals, and so on for each Russellian type), or else there is only one number 2 which can belong to properties irrespective of their type. In the first case, we would be forced to say that a number 2 belongs, say, to the property of being a green pencil on my desk, and that quite a different number 2 belongs to the property of being a color exemplified by a pencil on my desk. In the second case, we can speak of one and the same number 2 in both instances. The first alternative is clearly unacceptable; there is just one number 2, not a whole series of 2s. And this means that the number 2 must be quite a different entity from properties of individuals, properties of such properties, and so on up the type hierarchy; for the number 2 can belong to entities of different types, while each of these properties is exemplified by only one type of entity. Nor is this all. One and the same number 2 belongs not only to properties of individuals, properties of such properties, etc., but also belongs to properties which lie completely outside the hierarchy. Numbers also quantify members of classes, and classes, and classes of classes. They even belong to such categories as being an individual thing or being a property. In short, there is no property, no matter how esoteric or abstract, to which there does not belong a number. Thus if numbers are properties, they certainly are properties of a peculiar sort. They have to be type-indifferent properties which can belong to all properties whatsoever.

A moment's reflection shows that even the view that numbers are type-indifferent properties is not without its difficulties; for what could it possibly mean to say, for example, that the property F or the class determined by F has the property two. There is only one plausible answer: to say that F has the property two is, at best, short for saying that F has the property of being exemplified by two entities; to say that the corresponding class has the property two can mean, at best, that the class has the property of having two members.* If we sharply distinguish, as surely we must, between the number 2, on the one hand, and the property of being exemplified by two entities or the property of having two members, then the view that 2 is a property of properties or of classes loses all plausibility. Those who ostensibly embrace the latter view mean to hold, more likely than not, that properties can have the property of being exemplified by two entities and that classes may have the property of having two entities as members. They confuse with the number 2 the "relational properties" of being exemplified by two entities and of having two entities as members. These "relational properties" do not involve the relation of similarity; in this respect there is a difference between the view under discussion and the earlier mentioned position that numbers are nothing else but such relational properties as are similar to F, similar to G, etc. But they are relational nevertheless; the first involves the nexus of exemplification, the second that of class membership. The number 2 is merely one constituent of the whole property.[9]

If we realize that all talk about the property two derives its sense from talk about the properties of being exemplified by two entities and

---

* To say of a class that it is a couple is merely short for saying that it has two members.

of having two entities as members, then the question of which category the number 2 belongs to remains unanswered. I shall argue next that numbers are quantifiers.

9 EXISTENCE AND THE QUANTIFIERS

The alleged relational property of being exemplified by two entities bears a striking resemblance to the relational property of being exemplified by *some* entities and to the relational property of being exemplified by *all* entities. The only difference consists in the "definiteness" of the quantity mentioned: when we say that two entities have the property F, we mention a definite number; when we say that some entities have the property F, on the other hand, we leave the exact number open and state merely that more than one entity has the property F.* This similarity suggests that numbers belong to the same category as the entities *all* and *some*. If we agree to call this category *quantifiers*, then we can divide it into the two subcategories of general and of numerical quantifiers. Numbers are numerical quantifiers, while *all* and *some* are general quantifiers.† But whatever our terminology may be, the main insight is this: among the most general kinds of entities there is a category of quantifiers and the numbers as well as the entities *all* and *some* belong to this category. Quantifiers, as a category, take their place alongside such other categories as individual things, properties, relations, etc.

Let us return to the relational property of being exemplified by some entities. If there existed such a property, it would be a property of properties. It would be, in Frege's terms, a concept of second level. And if it existed, it would have to be distinguished both from the quantifier *some* and from *existence*. Frege, unfortunately, confuses it

---

* To say that 'some' shall be understood as 'at least one' is not to "define" the former; we merely make its meaning more precise; we make an arbitrary decision for those cases where the ordinary meaning of the word is somewhat fuzzy.

† I do not call *all* and *some* logical quantifiers for the reason mentioned earlier, namely, that they are no more intimately connected with logic than with any other theory.

with both of these other entities. Or, at least, he does not clearly distinguish them from each other. Nor is he the only one who does not make this distinction. Russell follows in his footsteps, and so do many contemporary philosophers. It will help to elucidate the category of quantifiers (and hence the nature of numbers) if we draw the proper distinctions at this point.

Frege's example is the sentence 'There is at least one square root of 4'.[1] He claims that by means of this sentence we assert something about the concept *square root of 4*, namely, that it falls under a higher concept. The Thought expressed by the sentence, according to Frege, can also be expressed by: 'The concept *square root of 4* is not empty' or 'The concept *square root of 4* is realized.'* Now, these two versions, especially the second one, reflect—presumably more perspicuously—the alleged structure of the underlying Thought because they mention the second-level concepts of being empty and of being realized, respectively. To be realized would be, in our terminology, a property of properties. This property replaces what is usually called the existential quantifier. The state of affairs commonly represented by 'Some entities are *F*' consists, according to this view, of the property *F* exemplifying the property of being realized; hence it would be more conspicuously mirrored by the sentence '*F* is realized'. This line of thought, I suggest, led Frege to think of what is usually called the existential quantifier as a second-level concept.

At the point of his argument where the example occurs, Frege is faced with a dilemma. He wants to show that concepts cannot but occur predicatively in Thoughts. On the other hand, he also thinks of the *so-called* existential quantifier as a concept of second level.† The problem is how to represent the Thought that there is a square root of 4 most adequately. We saw that the sentence '*F* is realized' agrees best with the notion that the so-called existential quantifier is a concept of second level. But if this sentence is the most perspicuous one, then there can be no talk of *F*'s occurring predicatively. The sentence does not at all show that *F* is predicated of something. On the other hand,

---

* I shall, whenever necessary, distinguish between thoughts and Fregean Thoughts.

† I speak of the so-called existential quantifier, because I shall argue that what the expression 'Some entities are' ('At least one entity is') represents is neither a quantifier nor anything having to do especially with existence.

Frege also maintains that the same Thought is represented by the sentence 'There is at least one entity which is a square root of 4'. If this sentence reflects the inner structure of the expressed Thought clearly, then it is quite obvious that the concept *square root of 4* occurs predicatively in the Thought; for the Thought is then of the form: There is at least one entity *which is F*. But then it also follows that the so-called existential quantifier is not a straightforward property of properties. The question of how to analyze it remains wide open. In sum, Frege's view that concepts always occur predicatively clashes with his conception of the so-called existential quantifier as a concept of second level.

Frege realizes that something must have gone wrong, because he presents two quite different sentences as the prime candidate for ontological conspicuousness. But he does not take the right measure to readjust his view. Instead, he claims that Thoughts can be split up in many different ways, "so that now one thing, now another, appears as subject or predicate. The Thought itself does not yet determine what is to be regarded as the subject."[2] But this claim contradicts his whole conception of a Thought. A Thought, according to Frege, is an objective entity that is what it is quite independently of us and our ways of representing it. It cannot be split up in different ways into subject and predicate for the simple reason that it is not a linguistic entity consisting of subject and predicate. Of course, we may express a Thought in different ways, but we can as little rearrange the constitutents of a Thought as we can rearrange the starry heavens.

What, then, is the proper way of representing the structure of the state of affairs under study? Frege, I believe, is correct when he claims that this Thought is very well expressed by the sentence 'There is at least one entity which is a square root of 4'. The property *square root of 4*—assuming for the moment that this is indeed a property—does occur, as Frege insists, predicatively in the state of affairs. There is no such property as *being realized*. To say that the concept *F* is realized is just another way of saying that some entities are *F*; and it is a rather misleading way at that. The existential quantifier is not a property of properties.

Granted that the existential quantifier is not a simple property like the property of being realized, why not conceive of it as a "relational property," namely, the property of being exemplified by some entities? If we do, we may be able to save both of Frege's contentions: that F occurs predicatively in the Thought that some entities are F, and that this Thought is of the form $\phi(F)$. But there are two considerations that speak against this way out of Frege's dilemma. First of all, if we want to safeguard the first contention, we must admit that relational properties in general, and the property of being exemplified by some entities in particular, are different from "ordinary simple" properties in being complex. We must admit that relational properties, as distinct from "ordinary simple" ones, have a structure, contain constituents, or however else we may want to express it. And if they are complex, then it stands to reason that they each contain, among other entities, a certain relation. But if they are complex, if they contain relations and other constituents, then it can only be misleading to say that a relational Thought or state of affairs is really of the form $\phi(F)$, where ϕ is a relational property; for nothing in the sentence '$\phi(F)$' reflects the admitted fact that ϕ is a complex entity containing as an essential ingredient a certain relation R. If we begin to take the notion of a relational property seriously, we are led back to the underlying relation and the fact that a relational state of affairs is of the form $R(a,b)$ rather than of the form $P(a)$.

Second, even if we clearly recognize that to talk about relational properties is to talk about relations, we cannot hold that being exemplified by some entity is a relational property. It is obvious what the underlying relation would have to be, if it were a relational property, namely, the nexus of exemplification. But what is the second term? To what is the property P related when it is exemplified by some entities? *Some entities*, of course. But what kind of entity is *some entities*?

It must be a complex entity. If we compare *some entities* with *all entities*, we see that they share a component and differ in another. Both contain (the plural of) the notion of entity; but the first contains the entity *some*, while the second contains the entity *all*. It may be argued that either one of these two quantifiers can be "defined" in terms of the other, so that our argument from the difference between *some* and *all* is spurious. The reader can probably anticipate our reply. It is true for all properties f that all entities e are f if and only if it is not the case that some entities e are not f. But this equivalence is true as a matter of logic. It is not the case that the sentence 'All entities are F' is an abbreviation of 'It is not the case that some entities are not F'.* If this is so, then *all* as well as *some* exist, and it makes sense to argue that what the expressions 'some entities' and 'all entities' represent must be complex.

Could we not also argue, in the same vein, that a comparison of *some individuals* with *some properties* shows that *some* is an entity in its own right? I do not think so. The expression 'some individuals,' it seems to me, is merely short for 'some entities which are individuals' and, similarly, 'some properties' is short for 'some entities which are properties,' 'some numbers' is short for 'some entities which are numbers,' etc. If this is true, then *some* (and also *all*) is always "attached" to *entities*, and a basic constituent of every state of affairs involving quantification is either the (complex) entity *some entities* or the (complex) entity *all entities*. We also see that what the expression 'some properties' represents has at least four constituents, namely, the quantifier *some*, the entity *entity*, the nexus of *exemplification* and the category *property*. What I call the quantifiers are only the entities *some* and *all* and not such complex entities as *some individuals* (are such that), all properties (are such that), etc. Whenever it becomes necessary to mention the latter, I shall continue to speak of the *so-called* existential and *so-called* universal quantifier.

Frege also claims that what is asserted about the concept *square root of 4* in the statement 'There is at least one square root of 4' can never be asserted about an object. He says: "I do not want to say that it is false to assert about an object what is asserted here about a concept; I want to say it is impossible, senseless, to do so. The sentence 'There is Julius Caesar' is neither true nor false but senseless."[3] Does Frege mean to say that it is nonsense to say that Caesar exists? Is he implying that one cannot intelligibly assert the existence of individual things? I am not sure, but I am inclined to believe that he does. Compare his statement with the following one by Russell: "So the individuals that there are in the world do not exist, or rather it is nonsense to say that they exist and nonsense to say that they do not exist."[4] Notice the change from Frege's '*There is* Julius Caesar' to Russell's 'Julius Caesar *exists*'. Does this difference really make a difference, or are they saying the same thing? It depends.

* Are there other nonnumerical quantifiers in addition to *all* and *some*? I am inclined to think that there are at least the three quantifiers *the, a,* and *no.*

Russell must be wrong. It is not only not nonsense to say that individual things exist, it is most certainly true that they exist. The book in front of me exists and Julius Caesar existed. Not only do individuals exist, every other thing exists as well. There is no thing that doesn't exist.* That makes existence a "property" of every thing and hence a rather queer property indeed.† So as not to confuse it with other, more "ordinary" properties, let us say that existence is a feature of every thing. In particular, it is a feature of individual things.

But in the context in which Russell announces that it is nonsense to say of an individual that it exists, he also claims that one can significantly say that an individual exists if the individual is described. This exception suggests that we may have misinterpreted Russell. His distinction between definite descriptions and logical proper names may be of importance. He may actually hold the following view. The sentence 'Julius Caesar exists' makes sense, but it makes sense only because 'Julius Caesar' is an abbreviation for a definite description. If we eliminate the abbreviation, we get a sentence like 'There is (exists) a man called Julius Caesar'; and this sentence is perfectly meaningful.[5] A sentence of the type 'A exists' is nonsense only if 'A' is a logical proper name, if it is neither a definite description expression nor an abbreviation for one.

Why should it be nonsense to say that A exists when 'A' is a label? Why should it make a difference when we say of something that it exists whether we merely label it or describe it? After all, according to Russell, there are many meaningful sentences that contain logical proper names; why should existence statements be exceptions? As far as I can make it out, Russell offers, at best, a single argument for his strange position. He says that 'Romulus' is not really a name but a sort of truncated description; for "if it were really a name, the question of

---

* This does not mean, of course, that one cannot *think* of things that do not exist, that one cannot imagine them, wish for them, etc. But things which one merely, say, imagines are not there, do not exist.

† The two features of being a thing and of being an existent are therefore coextensive. The same is not the case for the two notions of being a state of affairs and of obtaining; for some entities which do not obtain are nevertheless states of affairs, that is, do nevertheless exemplify the ontological property of being a state of affairs. In brief, I shall hold that while a nonexistent entity cannot be a thing, a nonexistent entity (an entity which does not obtain) may very well be a state of affairs.

existence could not arise, because a name has got to name something, or it is not a name."[6] What he has in mind seems to be this. Logical proper names are such that if one knows that a certain expression is a logical proper name, then one also knows that it represents something. Hence one learns nothing new if one is told that the referent of a logical proper name exists. Thus it is redundant to assert, for instance, that A exists when one has already asserted that 'A' is a logical proper name. But, obviously, if the sentence 'A exists' is redundant, it cannot be nonsense. What one implicitly understands cannot be nonsense, otherwise one could not understand it. Russell's argument, if it is an argument, does not prove his point. This suggests that there may be a deeper reason, a reason which has nothing to do with the distinction between labels and descriptions, for his view that it is nonsense to say of an individual that it exists.

Frege, we recall, maintains that one cannot assert of an object what one asserts of a concept when one says that *there is an F.* Assume that this is true. Assume also that 'F exists' is just another way of saying 'There is an F'. If so, then it follows that one cannot assert of an object that it exists. We arrive at the conclusion which both Frege and Russell seem to embrace. What may have misled them, I submit, is the idea that 'There is an F' means the same as 'F exists'.

'There is an F' is merely short for 'Some existing entity is F'; and this latter sentence says that some existing entity exemplifies (falls under) F. Now, consider the sentence 'There is Romulus'. If we think of this sentence as being short for 'Some entity is Romulus' in strict analogy to the case for F, we get the assertion that some existing entity exemplifies (falls under) Romulus. But Romulus, being an individual thing (an object), is the kind of entity which is never exemplified by anything (i.e., is the kind of entity under which nothing can fall). Since it is an ontological law that individuals are not exemplified, one might even say that it is nonsense to say of an individual that it is exemplified by something.* If one does, then it is nonsense to say 'There is Romulus,' while it is perfectly meaningful to assert 'There is an F'. Up to this point, the argument is sound. But now comes the mistaken

* In my view, it is not nonsense but merely false that individuals are exemplified by entities. But there is a tendency among philosophers to reject all those statements as nonsense which, as I look at it, are merely false as a matter of the *ontological laws* of the world.

identification of 'There is Romulus' with 'Romulus exists'. If the latter sentence says nothing more than the former, then it does indeed follow that 'Romulus exists' is nonsense; for what this sentence then says is that some entity exemplifies Romulus. But the sentence 'Romulus exists' does not assert that something exemplifies Romulus; and hence it does not follow that this sentence is nonsense. In general, it does not follow that it is nonsense to assert of individual things that they exist.

Russell, we saw, denies explicitly that the sentence 'Julius Caesar exists' makes sense. Frege, on the other hand, says merely that the sentence 'There is Julius Caesar' is nonsense. One may therefore argue on Frege's behalf that he never intended to go as far as Russell and to deny that it makes sense to say of individuals that they exist. What he has in mind, perhaps, is merely that it makes no sense to say of an individual that something falls under it. But this interpretation has to cope also with a remark like the following by Frege: "We must here keep well apart two wholly different cases that are easily confused, because we speak of existence in both cases. In one case the question is whether a proper name designates, names, something; in the other, whether a concept takes objects under itself. If we use the words 'there is a ____' we have the latter case."[7]

At any rate, is it really plausible to hold, as I do, that Russell and Frege may have confused existence with the nexus of falling under? If they were confused, then they were certainly not the first ones. Recall the Kantian notion that *exists* and *is* as they occur in *A exists* and *A is green* are one and the same thing. But while the Kantian assimilates the nexus of exemplification to the notion of existence, a Russellian may be tempted to do just the opposite.[8] Moore, for example, argues in "The Concept of Reality" as follows: (1) 'Lions are real' means the same as 'There are things which fall under the property of being a lion'. (2) Thus the expression 'real' does not stand here for any conception at all, because (3) the only conceptions which occur in the proposition 'Lions are real' are (a) the conception of being a lion, and (b) the conception of falling under something; and obviously 'real' does not stand for either of these two notions.[9] If Moore were correct, and if we think of 'Julius Caesar exists' as 'Julius Caesar is real,' we might conclude that 'Julius Caesar exists' must be nonsense, because the only conceptions which occur in this proposition are the conception of being Julius Caesar and the conception of falling under something, and it is nonsense to speak of something as falling under the property of being a Julius Caesar. But Moore's mistake is quite obvious. He overlooks two important ingredients of the proposition *There are things which fall under the property of being a lion*—namely, the notion of existence (there is) and the notion of a thing (entity). And since the proposition in reality contains this additional constituent of existence, it is very reasonable to argue that the expression 'real' stands for this very notion in 'Lions are real.' Thus 'Lions are real' means the same as 'Some *existing* entities are lions'.

I have argued that the quantifiers *some* and *all* must be distinguished from the so-called quantifiers some-individuals-are, all-properties-are, etc. I have also tried to show that they must be distinguished from the notion of existence. In particular, it is my contention that the so-called existential quantifier has no more to do with existence than the universal quantifier and that neither *some* nor *all* have anything to do with existence.

Now, the theory of states of affairs, I said earlier, deals with actual states of affairs (facts, states of affairs which obtain) as well as with merely possible states of affairs (states of affairs which do not obtain). The theory of properties, on the other hand, deals only with existing properties. The reason for this difference, as I said, consists in the fact that while a connection between two states of affairs can hold even if one of the states of affairs does not obtain, exemplification obtains only between an entity and an existing property. As a result, the quantifiers in the theory of states of affairs range over states of affairs which do not obtain as well as over states of affairs which obtain, while the property quantifiers of property theory range only over existing properties.

Take the law that for all states of affairs p, the state of affairs p *or not* p obtains. As one usually talks, the universal quantifier is represented by the expression 'all p (are such that)'. We already saw that this expression is merely short for 'all entities which are states of affairs (are such that)'; and we distinguished, among the entities represented by this expression, between the quantifier *all*, on the one hand, and such entities as being an entity, being a state of affairs, and exemplification, on the other. Now we see that this degree of complexity is not as yet sufficient to do full justice to the facts. The so-called quantifier is in this case represented even more perspicuously by the expression 'All entities which are states of affairs, whether or not they obtain, (are such that)'. Similarly, the so-called existential quantifier for properties in property theory is most perspicuously represented by the expression 'Some *existing* entities which are properties (are such that)'. In general, when we talk about all entities or about some entities, we may have in mind existing entities, entities which obtain, entities which do not obtain, or all three kinds, but the quantifiers *all* and *some* are not the same as the notion of existence or the notion of obtaining, nor does *some* have any greater affinity for existence or obtaining than does *all*.

It is, therefore, pointless to try to "define" existence in terms of the so-called existential quantifier. The usual proposal is to "define" the expression 'A exists' in terms of the expression $(\exists x)\ (x = A)$.'[10] But the latter expression is merely short for 'Some existing entity which is an individual is identical with A'. The state of affairs which it represents already contains existence. The proposed definition is, therefore, circular. However, the state of affairs that the individual A exists is, of course, equivalent to the state of affairs that some existing individual is identical with A. But existence has not been "defined." Nor can it be "defined," in the sense of ontologically reduced, in any other way.[11] Existence is an irreducible (sub)category. It differs from other subcategories and categories, though, in not being a property. I call it a feature. In brief, existence (and, perhaps, obtaining) is an irreducible category.

So much about the general quantifiers. If I have succeeded in throwing some light on their peculiar ontological position vis-à-vis such entities as existence, being a property, exemplification, and the like, I will also have illuminated the thesis with which we started this chapter, namely, the thesis that numbers belong to the category of quantifiers.

10 NECESSITY

If numbers are quantifiers, then the fact that there are three men in this room has the same ontological structure as the fact that there are some men in this room. But is it not also possible to number fictitious things? Do we not also speak of the three brothers Karamazov? If we distinguish between actual things and merely possible things, a large number of questions arise. What is the ontological status of the (alethic) modalities? What is the ontological status of possible entities? Are there, corresponding to the distinction between actual and merely possible things, two kinds of quantifiers, namely, quantifiers ranging over actual objects and quantifiers ranging over merely possible things.* If so, are there then also two kinds of numbers? Does the numeral '3' in '3 men are in this room' represent a different entity from the numeral '3' in 'The 3 brothers Karamazov hated their father'?

Modalities do not belong to the furniture of the world. There are no such entities as necessity and possibility. This is the basic thesis which I wish to defend in the present chapter. (In the next, I shall return to my main line of argument and discuss the possibility of special quantifiers). But it is impossible to deal thoroughly with the notion of necessity (and hence with that of possibility) in the short space of one chapter. I shall have to take many background considerations for granted; and I shall have to hint where detailed analyses would be in order in a different kind of book.

There are many notions of necessity, but two ideas play, in my opinion, the most central role in philosophical discussions. According to one notion, those and only those states of affairs are necessary where we cannot imagine any alternatives. According to the other idea, necessary states of affairs are lawful states of affairs.

Pursuing the first idea further, we may say that a necessary state of affairs is such, that we cannot even imagine what it would be like if it were not the case. Thus we can imagine that there are mermaids, but we cannot imagine what it would be like for something to be both red and blue (all over and at the same time). It is not necessary, therefore, that there are no mermaids, but it is necessary that nothing is both red and blue. What further kinds of truths are necessary in this sense? First of all, ontological truths must be counted as necessary; for it is impossible to imagine circumstances other than the prevailing ones in matters ontological. For example, it is impossible to imagine that individual things are exemplified by entities or that there are no properties whatsoever. Second, all logical truths—truths of the theories

* There are, of course, other ways of doing things. One sort of quantifier, for example, may be made to range over both actual and merely possible entities, while another ranges over actual (existing) entities only.

of states of affairs, properties, and relations—belong to the class of necessary truths. Third, the truths of arithmetic are necessary in the sense discussed here. Fourth, set-theoretical truths turn out to be necessary truths. Last but not least, there exists a group of facts which are neither ontological, nor logical, nor arithmetical, nor set-theoretical, but which have to be counted as necessary by our criterion. The fact that nothing is both red and blue is an example from this group; and so is the fact that round is a shape. It is this fifth and last group, I believe, which really gives rise to the present notion of necessity and constitutes the very core of necessary truths. This is, of course, the group of synthetic a priori truths.

Here, then, is our tentative explication of the illusive notion of the synthetic a priori: A synthetic a priori truth belongs (a) to those truths to which we cannot imagine alternatives, but does not belong (b) to ontology, logic, arithmetic, or set theory. It is indeed remarkable that there should be such facts; facts which do not belong to the "formal disciplines" mentioned and which are also distinguished from the facts of "ordinary science" by the criterion of imaginability.* These facts concern the "content" of the world rather than its "form." Yet they also differ from the common "scientific facts" about the world's "content." But as remarkable as it may be that there are such facts, their special status derives entirely from the scope and limit of human imagination. Such facts are remarkable from an epistemological point of view only. Ontologically speaking, they are just a group of facts among many such groups.

Can we describe the synthetic a priori truths without reference to the limits of human imagination? It seems to me that all such truths are about what I shall call the sensory dimensions.[1] In order to see what this means, let me list the most important kinds of synthetic a priori truths. (1) Certain facts constitute the various sensory dimensions. Examples are: Green is a color; round is a shape; of two pitches one is higher than the other; only a pitch is higher in pitch than anything else. Some of these facts are general, some are not.† (2) Other truths are about simple relations between two or more members of the same

* It may well be, however, that a large number of scientific facts, say, facts of physics, are not imaginable.

† I distinguish between quantified and unquantified facts. This distinction must not be confused with the one between atomic and molecular facts.

sensory dimension. Examples are: Midnight blue is darker than canary yellow: E is higher than C. (3) Still other facts concern relations which hold between the properties of a single dimension; for example: If the first of three pitches is higher than the second and the second is higher than the third, then the first is higher than the third. The facts of this group are all general. The most popular examples of synthetic a priori truths belong to the fourth and last group. (4) These general truths express how the members of two dimensions depend on each other and how the members of one or two dimensions exclude each other. Examples are: What has shape has color, and conversely; nothing has two pitches; nothing has both a color and a pitch.

I have remarked several times that some of these synthetic a priori truths are general. For instance, that nothing is both red and blue is a general fact of the form: For all individuals, if an individual is red, then it is not blue. It is not a fact of the form: Red excludes blue. There are no such facts of property inclusion and exclusion, I believe, because there are no such relations among properties (and, perhaps, facts) as inclusion and exclusion. Hence it is not possible to characterize necessary truths in general and synthetic a priori truths in particular in terms of these two relations.[2] According to this alternative explication, there exists not only the general fact concerning red and blue mentioned above, but also the unquantified fact that red excludes blue, and it is this latter fact which is truly known a priori. A proponent of this explication would object to our characterization of the general fact as being synthetic a priori; for a general fact, according to this line of objection, cannot possibly be known a priori. A general fact, unless it is deduced from other facts, can only be known by induction, and what is known by induction is not known a priori. From our point of view, the proponent of exclusion and inclusion invents these two relations in order to secure such facts as that red excludes blue. He needs such facts, structurally speaking, because he cannot rest with such general facts as that everything red is not blue. And he cannot rest with such general facts, because the very notion of knowledge a priori prohibits him from claiming that general facts can be known a priori.

Now it is certainly true that it is one important feature of the rather nebulous notion of a priori knowledge that such knowledge is not gained by induction.* Hence, if all general facts could be known

* I hold that there are no inductive relations between states of affairs. The

only by induction (unless they are deduced from other facts), then no general fact could be known a priori. Hence there could be no general synthetic a priori truths. But there seems to be another possibility. One could hold that certain general truths—like the truth that nothing red is blue—can be known, but known neither by deduction nor by induction. What may happen is this. Noticing that a certain object is red but not blue, we may entertain the general possibility that nothing red is also blue. Asking ourselves whether this general hypothesis holds or not, we try to imagine a counter instance; we try to imagine what it would be like for something to be both red and blue. We realize immediately that we cannot imagine such an object and therefore conclude that nothing could be both red and blue, that is, conclude that the general hypothesis does hold. We are convinced that the general fact obtains, in other words, not because we have observed numerous instances of red things which are not blue, but, rather, because we cannot imagine it to be otherwise. What is relevant for the notion of knowledge a priori is, not the distinction between facts which are general and facts which are not, if I may put it so, but the distinction between facts—be they general or not—for which we can imagine alternatives and facts for which we cannot. Even the general facts can be divided into two kinds by means of this criterion. We can imagine there to be a whale which is not a mammal and, hence, an exception to the law that all whales are mammals. But we cannot imagine there to be a red object which is also blue and, hence, an exception to the law that all red things are not blue.

What we can and cannot imagine is one thing; what we can and cannot conceive is quite a different thing. Our explication of a certain kind of necessity in general and of the synthetic a priori in particular rests on a very specific notion of imagination. In the spirit of this explication, we are quite literally invited to form visual, auditory, and other kinds of images in order to test whether or not a given state of affairs is necessary. What we can imagine in this narrow sense depends obviously on what our sense organs are. Small wonder that truths about sensory dimensions are the paradigms of this kind of necessity. It is also obvious that imagination in this narrow sense must be distinguished sharply from what we can and cannot conceive. While it is impossible,

only explication of induction is, therefore, psychological. To say that a certain law is known inductively is to say that we believe in its truth because we have observed some positive instances of it and know of no counterinstances.

for example, to imagine a red object which is also blue, we can easily conceive of such an object. We can even conceive of contradictory states of affairs. What would it be like, for example, for this book to be both red and not red? Well, it would be red and also not red; but, of course, I cannot imagine what it would have to look like. There are innumerable states of affairs of which we can conceive in this manner, but which we cannot imagine.* We can conceive that individuals are exemplified by other entities; we can conceive contradictions; we can conceive that $2 + 2 = 5$; we can conceive of alternative axioms for set theory; etc. How, otherwise, could we in matters of ontology, logic, arithmetic, and set-theory separate fact from fancy?

Necessity does not belong to the furniture of the world. I have tried to vindicate this thesis for one important notion of necessity. According to this notion, facts are divided into two groups, not by means of a special constituent, necessity, which the facts of the one group contain and the facts of the other group lack, but by means of a criterion in terms of the limits of human imagination.

The second main notion of necessity depends on that of lawfulness. The basic insight here is Frege's. He states it in the following way:

> The apodictic judgment differs from the assertoric in that it suggests the existence of universal judgments from which the proposition can be inferred, while in the case of the assertoric one such a suggestion is lacking. By saying that a proposition is necessary I give a hint about the grounds for my judgment. *But since this does not affect the conceptual content of the judgment, the form of the apodictic judgment has no significance for us.*

> If a proposition is advanced as possible, either the speaker is suspending judgment by suggesting that he knows no laws from which the negation of the proposition would follow or he says that the generalization of this negation is false.[3]

---

* If we explicate what is possible in terms of what is conceivable, even states of affairs which contradict laws of ontology—and which, therefore, are in one sense impossible—turn out to be possible.

I should like to put the matter this way. Sentences like 'Necessarily P' or 'It is necessary that P' are merely short for 'There are laws from which P follows'. To say 'P is possible' is to say either (a) 'There are no laws from which not-P follows' or (b) 'Not-P is not always the case'. Frege gives as examples for (a) and (b) the following two sentences: 'It is possible that the earth will at some time collide with another heavenly body,' and 'A cold can result in death'.[4] Furthermore, to say that P is impossible is to say, according to this explication, that there are laws which contradict P. The notion of *follows* used here is, of course, the logical one. It includes the law of universal instantiation, that is, the logical truth that what holds for all entities holds for some entities as well as for a particular entity. The notion of law is that of a quantified state of affairs. We can and must, of course, distinguish between states of affairs of varying degrees of generality as well as between states of affairs which are general in regard to quite different kinds of entities. But these details are unimportant for our present point.

What is possible, in one sense of the term, is what does not contradict any laws. An actual state of affairs, of course, does not contradict any laws and hence is possible. We must therefore distinguish between actual states of affairs which are possible and states of affairs which are possible but do not obtain. In the latter case, I shall speak of the merely possible. What is merely possible is thus possible but not actual.

We can and must, furthermore, distinguish between different kinds of necessity and possibility. There are as many kinds of necessity and possibility as there are kinds of laws. In this sense, we can, for example, distinguish between the laws of the theory of states of affairs and the laws of property theory. Now, consider an ontological law, for example, the law that individual things are not exemplified. It follows from this law that the pencil on my desk is not exemplified. It is, therefore, a necessary truth of ontology that the pencil on my desk is not exemplified. Put differently, it is an ontological necessity that the pencil on my desk is not exemplified. On the other hand, the pencil on my desk is not (now) both red (all over) and not red. But there is no law of ontology from which it follows that the pencil on my desk cannot be both red and not red. Hence it is an ontological (mere) possibility that the pencil on my desk is red and not red. That the pencil cannot be both red and not red follows, of course, from a law of logic. But this is an entirely different matter; for what is ontologically possible may not be logically possible. In our case, it is logically impossible for the pencil on my desk to be both red and not red, because there is a logical law from which the negation of this state of affairs follows. In short, instances of logical contradictions are logically impossible states of affairs, but they are nevertheless ontologically possible. The formation rules of artificial languages often reflect what is ontologically possible in our sense. These formation rules may admit expressions as well-formed which are not only false, but false as a matter of logic. For example, 'P and not-P' is usually considered to be well-formed, even though it represents a logically impossible state of affairs. But we must realize that the formation rules merely reflect the ontological laws which can and must in turn also be formulated. Given the formation rules of a certain artificial language, the sentence 'The individual A is exemplified by the property F' may be said to be ill-formed, but this does not mean that the sentence is nonsense. Far from it. Since this sentence is false, it could not possibly be nonsense. It represents an ontologically impossible state of affairs. If the laws of ontology were other than they are, then it could be an ontologically possible state of affairs that A is exemplified by a property.*

I have already mentioned logically possible and necessary states of affairs. But there are also arithmetical possibilities and necessities, set-theoretical possibilities and necessities, geometric possibilities and necessities, biological possibilities and necessities, and so on. How many different kinds we shall have to distinguish in the end will depend on how many independent fields of inquiry we shall come up with. I speak of independent fields in order to allow for the possibility of genuine ontological reductions of some fields of inquiry to others. In another sense of 'independent,' even ontologically independent kinds of entities may depend on each other because of the existence of bridge laws. Consider, for example, the two fields of psychology and physiology. Psychological laws, I shall assume for the sake of the example, are

---

* In the same vein, a merely possible world, for instance, is a nonexisting world composed of states of affairs which do not contradict the laws of the actual world. Here, too, we can distinguish between different kinds of possibilities. For example, a nonexisting world that is logically possible consists of states of affairs which do not contradict the logical laws of this world.

about mental entities like thoughts, perceptions, emotions, etc. Physiological laws, on the other hand, are about chemical and electric changes in the nervous system and other parts of the body. Let us further grant that mental entities are not identical with physiological ones. Let us assume that there is no ontological reduction of the mental to the physiological (or, ultimately, to the physical). Now, there is then a sense in which psychology will always be independent of physiology (or, ultimately, of physics). They will be independent of each other in the sense that they are not about the same states of affairs. Since they are not about the same states of affairs, we shall have to distinguish between what is psychologically possible and necessary and what is physiologically possible and necessary. But now assume also that there is a parallelism between mental and physiological states. Assume, in other words, that there are certain bridge laws which connect psychological and physiological states of affairs. In this case, what is, say, psychologically possible will also depend on what is physiologically possible, as long as we assume that the bridge laws hold. Given these bridge laws, for example, it cannot be the case that the mental state M_1 is psychologically impossible, while the parallel physiological state P_1 is physiologically possible. Thus certain purely mental states may be said to be physiologically possible or necessary, and conversely.

Since there are many bridge laws that connect states of affairs involving properties with states of affairs involving classes and either of these two kinds with states of affairs involving numbers, the notion of independence just explained is of great importance for our consider- ations. Recall, for example, the bridge law which holds that the class of properties which are similar to a property F is the same as the class of properties which are similar to G *if and only if* the number of F's is the same as the number of G's. Since this law holds, certain arithmetic possibilities and necessities will depend on there being or not being certain set-theoretical laws, and conversely. Therefore, it makes sense to say that a certain numerical state of affairs is set-theoretically impossible. Or consider the following bridge law connecting properties with classes: For all properties f and all entities e: e is f *if and only if* e is a member of the class determined by f.* Since there are laws of this

* I am assuming, falsely to be sure, that every property determines a class. Since this is not the case, the bridge law is more complicated.

kind, it makes sense to say that certain states of affairs involving classes are possible or necessary in regard to the laws of property theory, that is, are logically possible or necessary.

Thus, what is possible or necessary may depend not only on the laws that govern the respective subject matter, but also on laws about entirely different kinds of entities. This is always the case if there are bridge laws connecting two ontologically different fields. Of course, that there are such laws in a given case is a matter of fact; it is a matter of how the entities in the world are connected with each other, not a matter of how we happen to talk about them.

According to the second main notion of necessity, what is necessary is what is lawful. Recall our basic thesis, namely, that necessity (and possibility) is not a part of the furniture of the world. Does our explication really sustain this thesis? One may suspect that necessity has merely been transformed into a constituent of laws. This constituent, one may object, is precisely what distinguishes laws from other facts. Hence the shoe is really on the other foot, as it were; for, instead of explicating necessity in terms of lawfulness, one must explicate lawfulness in terms of necessity. Ontologically speaking, instead of being able to show that talk about necessity is merely talk about lawfulness, we are actually able to show that talk about lawfulness is talk about necessity.

The ontological issue is quite clear. Is there or is there not a common constituent which distinguishes laws from accidental generalities? If there is such a common ingredient, what ever it may be, then we may call it necessity, and it follows that necessity is part of the furniture of the world, namely, that part which distinguishes laws from all other facts. The answer I wish to give is equally clear. There is no ontological difference between accidental generalities and laws. What difference there is is to be explained in terms of further facts, such as that there are instances of the law, that there are other general facts which can be deduced from the law under consideration or from which the law under consideration can be deduced, etc.[5] The thrust of my reply is so familiar that I shall not bother to spell it out here in detail.[6]

To return to our explication of necessity, some philosophers identify the necessary with the analytic. Can we do justice to what they have in mind? We can to a certain point. The analytic-synthetic distinction plays no role whatsoever in my philosophy. What takes its place are the various distinctions between ontological facts and logical facts and set-theoretical facts, between logical truths and arithmetical truths, etc. Now, insofar as the notion of analyticity can be explicated in terms of any one or several of these distinctions jointly, the corresponding explication of necessity is at hand. For example, someone who identifies the necessary with the analytic and thinks of logical and only logical truths as analytic obviously holds, from our point of view, that what is necessary is what is true as a matter of logic. Similarly, someone may divide all theories up in such a way that ontology, logic, set theory, and arithmetic wind up on one side of the fence, while geometry, physics, chemistry, etc., find themselves on the other. He may call the former analytic truths and the latter, synthetic truths. And he may identify the analytic with the necessary and the synthetic with the (merely) contingent. We can describe his position perfectly well in terms of our distinctions.

But the analytic-synthetic dichotomy may also be said to be based on some such distinction as that between "empty tautologies" on the one hand and "informative statements about the world" on the other. There is then no corresponding dichotomy in our philosophy. But this is not a shortcoming; for it is simply not true that, say, the laws of logic are devoid of all information about the world. To be sure, they do not tell us what chemical elements there are or whether or not the sun shines right now in Bloomington, Indiana. But the chemical laws do not tell us the weather either, nor do the laws of chemistry tell us what statements are tautologies. The laws of logic, far from being uninformative about the "real world," tell us the most interesting things about it, namely, how states of affairs, properties, and relations behave.

Nor does it make any better sense to derive the analytic-synthetic dichotomy from the distinction between what is "absolutely certain" and what is "merely probable." Certainty, if there is such a thing, is a quality of beliefs, not a property of states of affairs; and we may feel more or less certain that a given state of affairs obtains, regardless of whether it concerns matters of biology, matters of arithmetic, matters of ontology, etc. I am fairly certain that there are no mermaids, as certain, at any rate, as I can be about many things in logic or arithmetic. On the other hand, I am not certain at all that the continuum hypothesis is true; I am as uncertain about this matter as I am about many things in the natural sciences.

Nor, finally, can the analytic-synthetic dichotomy be based on a distinction between what is true as "a matter of how we use language" and what is true as "a matter of fact." In an obvious sense, what we say depends on how we use words. But given that we mean certain things and not others by the noises and the marks we make, what we say about the world does not depend on language in any further interesting sense. And this holds for logic and ontology just as much as for biology and chemistry.

These remarks hardly amount to an argument. But they may indicate what kinds of arguments I would adduce in order to defend my explication of necessity in terms of what is unimaginable and what is lawful. They may help to explain why I treat here the analytic-synthetic distinction rather cavalierly.

11 POSSIBLE ENTITIES

A possible state of affairs is a state of affairs which does not contradict any laws. A merely possible state of affairs is a state of affairs which does not obtain, but which could obtain since its existence would not contradict any law. But what about possible individuals, possible properties, possible connectives, etc.? To speak of a possible individual thing for example, is to speak about a possible state of affairs, namely, the state of affairs that the individual exists. A merely possible individual does not exist, but it could exist. It would be an individual whose existence would not contradict any laws. The state of affairs that it exists would not contradict any laws. In short, to say that a thing is a mere possibility is to say that it does not exist, but that its existence does not contradict any laws. And here, too, we can and must distinguish between things that are logically possible, things that are physically possible, things that are ontologically possible, etc.

Similarly, a necessary thing, if there is such a being, is a thing whose existence is necessary, that is, whose existence follows from some laws. Again, what is necessary is not the thing, if I may put it so, but its existence. And again, we can and must distinguish between different kinds of necessities.

What ontological status do merely possible things have? They do not exist. Are there perhaps different levels of being, so that merely possible things, though they do not exist, participate in some other level of being, say, subsistence? I do not think so. Either a thing exists or it does not exist; there is no third possibility. There are no levels of being. Why, then, do so many philosophers go wrong so often and believe that there are different levels of being for things? I can offer a mere suggestion. Since there are indeed many different kinds of things and since these kinds differ in very fundamental ways, it may be that these differences among kinds of things have been mistaken for differences among levels of being. Differences among kinds of existents may have been mistaken for differences among kinds of existence. For example, a thing that exists "in space" and another thing that does not exist "in space" are not partaking in two different kinds of existence. Rather, both things exist plain and simple, but one has spatial properties and stands in spatial relations to other entities, while the other does not. Similarly, to exist in fiction is to exist in the imagination. And to exist in the imagination is not to exist at all but to be imagined. Hamlet does not have fictional existence as a kind of existence; Shakespeare imagined him and so do we when we read the play or hear him described to us. To talk about nonexistent things is not to talk, as Russell once maintained, about entities which do after all exist in some watered-down sense. Rather, it is to talk, as Brentano once held, about what we imagine there to be, what we mistakenly assume there to be, what we wish there to be, but what, alas, has not the slightest pinch of existence.

Merely possible things have no ontological status. Nor do they have any properties.* It is not true that Hamlet is indecisive. It is not true that Pegasus has wings. Rather, what is true is some such thing as that Shakespeare *thought of* Hamlet as being indecisive, that Shakespeare *described him* as being indecisive, that *we imagine* Pegasus to have wings. In brief, just as merely possible things do not exist but can be imagined to exist, so they do not have properties, but they can be

* Insofar as both Meinong's theory of objects and Husserl's phenomenology rest on the assumption that nonexistent things (other than states of affairs) have properties, both philosophies must be rejected.

believed to have properties, they can be imagined to have properties, etc.

At any rate, in the primary sense of 'merely possible,' only states of affairs are merely possible. Hence the questions of whether or not merely possible entities can have ontological status and can have properties reduce, from an ontological point of view, to the questions whether or not merely possible states of affairs have any kind of ontological status and whether or not they can have properties. As to the first question, I believe that merely possible states of affairs, just like merely possible things, have no ontological status whatsoever. A state of affairs either obtains or does not obtain. There is no other possibility. States of affairs which do not obtain do not have a watered-down form of being.

But I think that nonexistent states of affairs, unlike nonexistent things, have properties and stand in relations to other entities. The properties they have are not "ordinary ones." They are categorial properties. Every state of affairs, whether it obtains or not, is an entity—a something—and is a state of affairs. States of affairs which do not obtain exemplify, in my opinion, the two categorial properties of being an entity and of being a state of affairs. There are also (at least) two kinds of relations into which nonexistent states of affairs can enter, namely, an intentional nexus and the connectives.* Every mental act stands in the intentional relation to a state of affairs, irrespective of whether the state of affairs obtains or not. Every act, as I mentioned in the introduction, is in this sense propositional. Properly speaking, it is not Hamlet who stands in the intentional relation to a certain thought when someone, as we ordinarily say, thinks of Hamlet, but rather some state of affairs involving Hamlet; for example, the state of affairs that Hamlet is indecisive. The intentional nexus holds between a mental act—more accurately, between the content of a mental act—and a state of affairs. In this respect it differs from the second kind of relation in which nonexistent states of affairs can stand, namely, the connectives. These relations obtain between states of affairs only. By means of them, states of affairs which obtain can be connected with states of

---

* Not counting, of course, the nexus of exemplification which holds between every state of affairs which does not obtain and the two properties of being an entity and being a state of affairs.

affairs which do not obtain, as in the case where P *or* Q obtains, even though P does not obtain.

The relations of the world can therefore be divided into two groups, those that do and those that do not require that all their terms exist.* Perhaps one should not call the latter kind relations at all. Perhaps one should say that they are "relation-like." But these terminological matters are of secondary importance as long as we hold fast to the fact that there are entities that are like "ordinary" relations in some respects but differ from such relations in that not all their terms need to obtain.

The existence of these two kinds of relations suggests still another attempt to define existence.[1] Assuming, for the sake of generality, that all kinds of nonexistent entities, not just states of affairs, can enter into relations, and assuming further that there are also properties which can be exemplified by nonexisting entities, the proposed "definition" of existence runs as follows: 'E exists' means by definition 'E has some existence-property,' where an existence-property is a property or relation which only existents have. But it seems fairly obvious that this "definition" will not do. First, to say that E has some existence-property is to say, more perspicuously, that E has some *existing* existence-property. Hence, if we assume that there are no modes of being, the notion to be defined occurs already in the defining condition. Second, and more importantly, the very notion of an existence-property presupposes the notion of existence. One can only sort our existence-properties from other properties by asking whether or not the given property belongs solely to existents. And this shows that the sentence 'E exists' cannot be a mere abbreviation of the sentence 'E has some existence-property,' for the latter is short for 'E has some property which belongs to an entity U only if U exists'. To make the proposed "definition" work, one would have to show first that it is possible to specify existence-properties without relying on any knowledge as to whether or not only existents have these properties; and I do not think that this can be done.

In the primary sense of 'merely possible,' only states of affairs are merely possible. The theory of states of affairs, as I emphasized earlier,

* That there are two kinds of relations in this sense was at one time Brentano's view.

is about merely possible as well as about actual states of affairs. But it does not have two kinds of quantifiers, quantifiers for actual states of affairs and quantifiers for merely possible states of affairs. What 'some' and 'all' represent is the same in all true sentences of the theory. However, since all true sentences of the theory are about actual as well as about merely possible states of affairs, a more conspicuous way of reading, say, the law 'For all p, p or not-p' would be: 'All actual (obtaining) and merely possible states of affairs p are such that p or not-p (obtains)'. To talk about a merely possible state of affairs means in this context to talk about a state of affairs which does not obtain but whose being the case would not contradict any ontological laws. Nor do 'all' and 'some' represent something different when they occur in property theory, set theory, chemistry, etc. But in the case of property theory, for example, the phrase 'actual and merely possible . . .' is supplanted in the quantifier expression for properties by 'existing,' and we get laws like this one: 'All actual and merely possible entities e and all *existing* properties f and g are such that if e is f and g, then e is f.

We speak of the three brothers Karamazov. But this does not mean, as we now see, that there are three brothers Karamazov in some diluted sense of 'there are.' Rather, we imagine there to be three brothers Karamazov; and we imagine them to have all kinds of properties as well as relations to each other and to their father. Nor does it mean that we must distinguish between two numerical quantifiers, a number 3 that quantifies existing entities and a different number 3 that quantifies merely possible entities. Just as there is only one universal quantifier *all* and one particular quantifier *some*, so there is only one numerical quantifier '3'. And the same holds for all other numbers. But, of course, we can speak of three merely possible states of affairs just as we can talk about some merely possible states of affairs.

12 IMPLICIT DEFINITIONS

I could be fairly satisfied with the preceding discussion of definitions of numbers—and with my proposed categorization of numbers as quantifiers—were it not for a most popular method of eliminating numbers not yet touched upon. I mean the method of ontological reduction by model construction. This method has been effectively criticized in the past, for example, by Frege and Russell. Yet it is still with us. I can therefore hardly hope to do any better. But some criticism in philosophy bears frequent repeating.

Consider Dedekind's four "axioms" for a single infinite system: N:

(1) $\varphi(N)$ is a part of N.
(2) N is the intersection 1_0 of all those chains K to which the element 1 belongs. ·
(3) The element 1 is not contained in $\varphi(N)$.
(4) The mapping φ is one—one.[1]

These "axioms" contain, in addition to certain set-theoretical terms, the three expressions: 'N,' '1,' and 'φ'. Now if we interpret these expressions to mean *number, 1,* and *the immediate successor relation among natural numbers,* respectively, we get four true statements about the natural numbers. As long as we leave them uninterpreted, we merely have four forms and not as yet four sentences. This is the reason why I put the word axiom in quotation marks; for whether the expressions (1)–(4) are to be taken as axioms or merely as forms depends on whether we conceive of the three expressions 'N,' '1,' and 'φ' as names of certain entities, say, the property of being a natural number, the number 1, and the relation of immediate successor, respectively, or whether we conceive of them as mere variables ranging over certain kinds of entities. It is clear that we can complete the four forms in many different ways so as to get quite different groups of (true) axioms. For example, as N we could take the natural even numbers, as 1 the number 2, and as φ the immediate successor relation among even natural numbers. If we do, we get again four true statements, four axioms. But this time these statements are about natural even numbers, not about all natural numbers, and hence we have four axioms quite different from those we got from our first interpretation.

Now Dedekind claims that the four expressions (1)–(4) define the natural numbers. He writes: "If in the contemplation of a singly infinite system N, ordered by a mapping φ, we disregard entirely the peculiar nature of the elements, retaining only the possibility of distinguishing them, and consider only the relations in which they are placed by the ordering mapping φ, then these elements are called *natural numbers* or *ordinal numbers* or simply *numbers,* and the basic element 1 is called the *basic number* of the *number series N."*[2]

It is clear, I think, that Dedekind thinks of the four expressions (1)–(4) as forms rather than axioms. He does not identify the natural numbers with a certain definite progression, say, the progression of all even natural numbers. He is not saying that any group of entities which form a progression constitutes the class of natural numbers. He does not claim that the natural numbers are whatever "satisfies the axioms," as it is sometimes put. This becomes quite clear when he adds: "In regard to this liberation of the elements from any other content (abstraction) one can justifiedly call the number a free creation of the human mind."[3] According to Dedekind, the natural numbers are not to be identified with whatever "satisfies the axioms," with some progression or another, but, rather, are the product of a process of abstraction by means of which we obliterate all the distinguishing characteristics among particular progressions.

Dedekind's view seems to imply that the different entities which form progressions are in some sense complex and that they all share some common constituents called the natural numbers. But this is plainly not the case.[4] The progressions usually assumed to exist—like progressions of points, progressions of numbers, progressions of classes, etc.—consist of entities which have no common constituents. Of course, all progressions have in common that they are progressions. But, surely, the property of being a progression—assuming for the sake of the argument that there is such a property—is not the same as the natural numbers which have this property. "Moreover," as Russell remarks, "it is impossible that the ordinals should be, as Dedekind suggests, nothing but the terms of such relations as constitute progressions. If they are to be anything at all, they must be intrinsically something; they must differ from other entities as points from instants, or colors from sounds."[5]

Most importantly, by means of abstraction we may arrive at the notion of a domain of entities which form a progression, starting, say, from the notion of the progression of all natural even numbers. But the notion we arrive at in this fashion is not that of the class of natural numbers. What we get by the process of abstraction is a general property shared by various classes of entities; shared, for example, by the domain of natural even numbers and the domain of natural odd numbers.* We do not arrive at a domain of "indefinite" entities, called the natural numbers, but at a "definite" property of domains of "definite" entities.[6]

But so persuasive is the mistaken idea that axioms somehow define the terms they contain, that Hilbert, a few years after Dedekind, appealed to it when he presented his axioms for geometry.[7] In a series of articles, Frege describes the situation accurately and succinctly.[8] I shall here merely summarize his most important objections to Hilbert's method.

Axioms, as commonly understood, are true sentences. Definitions, on the other hand, are proposals to assign certain referents to arbitrary expressions. But we saw a moment ago that one can look at expressions called axioms in a different way. The crucial terms of the axioms are treated as variables rather than expressions with fixed referents. Or, more succinctly, the expressions in question are not treated as axioms at all but rather as forms. The expressions (1)–(4), for example, may be read straightforwardly as axioms of arithmetic; 'N' is then taken to represent the class of natural numbers, '1' the number 1, and 'φ' the successor relation among natural numbers. Or we may read these expressions as forms, in the way Dedekind does, with 'N' as a variable ranging over certain classes, '1' as a variable ranging over certain elements (individuals), and 'φ' as a variable ranging over relations. In this case, as Frege points out, the resulting forms resemble equations with three unknowns. But, and this is the crucial point, there are many values for the variables that turn the forms into true sentences. The forms do not determine uniquely any set of three values. A definition, on the other hand, assigns a definite referent to the defined expression. Therefore, it can only be misleading to call either the axioms or the corresponding forms definitions. It is misleading to claim that the four forms define the progression of natural numbers. It is, of course, equally misleading to maintain that they define the even natural numbers, the natural numbers divisible by 10, or any other progression. The situation is as described: starting from certain true sentences, one can get certain forms; and these forms have many interpretations

* Always assuming, for the sake of the present point, that there is such a property.

(models). The whole process has nothing whatsoever to do with definition. Nor does it make any more sense to call the axioms or the forms *implicit* definitions. To say that the four axioms implicitly define the natural numbers can at best mean that they are four true sentences about the natural numbers. And what does this fact have to do with definition? To say that the four forms implicitly define the natural numbers can at best mean that the three relevant notions yield one of many possible interpretations of the forms; and that amounts in the last analysis to nothing more enlightening than that Dedekind's axioms are true. But to know this much is neither to "define" numbers in the sense of reducing them to other entities, nor to "define" them in the sense of categorizing them, nor to "define" them in the sense of giving a meaning to a new expression. In brief, to say that axioms or forms are implicit definitions is a thoroughly confused and confusing way of saying that axioms are true statements about the entities they mention and that they yield forms which have different interpretations, forms for which there are several models.

As Frege clearly realized, there is still another, more formal, way of looking at Dedekind's and Hilbert's axiomatizations of arithmetic and geometry, respectively. We think of the axioms once more as containing the appropriate variables and hence as forms rather than axioms in the traditional sense. But we concentrate not on these forms as such, but rather on all those expressions which consist of axiom-forms as antecedents and theorem-forms (of the theory) as consequents. If we close these expressions in regard to the variables, we get a set of true sentences, namely, sentences of logic (property theory including the theory of relations). If these truths of logic are properly instantiated, we get true conditionals whose antecedents are the axioms of the theory, which can therefore be separated from the consequents. We thus deal with a set of logical truths, but from these logical truths we can get, say, geometrical truths if we properly instantiate and separate the antecedents from the consequents. Needless to say, the whole process has nothing whatsoever to do with definition.

After Frege's thorough discussion of the notion, one should have thought that implicit definitions had been laid to rest forever.[9] Quine, however, has recently tried to defend the notion once again.[10] He argues that the axiomatic development of every synthetic theory can be replaced by an axiomatic development of the same theory whose true statements follow from the truths of arithmetic. Then he claims that this alleged fact vindicates the view that axioms are implicit definitions.

Consider a set of chemical properties C_i of a certain theory of chemistry and let '$A(C_i)$' abbreviate the conjunction of all the axioms of this theory. Now it is well known that one can also give an arithmetic interpretation of the axiom-forms of this theory in terms of certain arithmetic properties K_i.[11] If we do, then we get the axioms '$A(K_i)$'. Quine now constructs a third interpretation in terms of properties F_i allegedly defined on the basis of both C_i and K_i. This construction proceeds in two steps.

First, the individual variables of the chemical and the arithmetic theories must be allowed to range over both physical objects as well as natural numbers. This is achieved by what Quine calls "hidden inflation."[12] We take an arbitrary element a of, say, the physical universe of discourse and extend the original interpretation of the chemical predicates to natural numbers by stipulating that the chemical properties belong to them if and only if they belong to a. Then we reinterpret the arithmetic predicates in a similar way.

Second, the predicates 'F_i' of the third interpretation are defined as follows: '$F_i(x)$' is short for '$(A(C_i)$ and $C_i(x))$ or (not-$A(C_i)$ and $K_i(x))$'* Now one can show that '$A(F_i)$' follows from the arithmetic truth '$A(K_i)$' alone. Hence it may be said that '$A(F_i)$' is true as a matter of arithmetic, that it is an arithmetic truth.* But, according to Quine, '$A(F_i)$' is still an axiomatization of chemistry. Hence chemical truths have been turned into arithmetic ones.

There are several things wrong with this construction and with Quine's conclusion. First of all, it makes absolutely no sense to stipulate that, for example, the inflated chemical predicates represent properties which belong to numbers if and only if they belong to an arbitrary physical object a. One cannot invent properties as one wishes; one cannot simply stipulate that there be certain properties. A contemplated property either exists or it does not exist. We can at best find out which is the case. There are certain chemical properties which

---

* I confine myself, for the sake of simplicity, to one-place predicates of the first level.

* Quine makes the point in terms of analyticity: if arithmetic is analytic, then '$A(F_i)$' turns out to be analytic. But I shall formulate the problem in my way, because it does not really matter.

may or may not belong to a. But these properties do not belong to natural numbers, and there is absolutely nothing we can do about it. At best we may find some properties—we would hardly call them chemical properties, however—which belong to physical objects and which also belong to natural numbers if and only if they belong to a given physical object a. But I have no idea what these properties could be and doubt that there are any.

As for the definition of the predicates 'F_i,' there are in turn several things wrong with it. As I shall argue presently in greater detail, there is no reason to assume that 'F_i' represents a property (or some properties) at all.[13] It certainly does not follow from the fact that we are willing to adopt a short way of writing a longer expression that the arbitrary sign 'F_i' is a predicate. Moreover, there is no guarantee whatsoever that the definiens represents a property (or properties). Quite to the contrary, since the definiens is a *form* it could not possibly represent a property, as I shall also argue at great length in one of the next chapters.[14] Leaving these two decisive objections aside, there is a further difficulty. Quine's definition assures that the properties F_i—assuming that there are such properties—are coextensive with the properties C_i. But these two sets of properties are not the same. If we hold, as seems reasonable, that two theories may be distinguished, among other things, by the properties they attribute to entities, then it follows that, contrary to Quine's assertion, '$A(C_i)$' is the axiomatic development of a chemical theory, but '$A(F_i)$' is not; for it mentions queer properties—if we continue to assume, for the sake of the argument, that there are such properties—which are not chemical properties but happen to be coextensive with chemical ones.

Furthermore, that F_i and C_i have the same extension is not a mere matter of abbreviation, as one may think from the definition given above. It depends on the chemical fact that '$A(C_i)$' happens to be true.[15] For if we assume that '$A(C_i)$' is false, F_i will have the same extension as K_i instead. Thus we have in 'F_i' a group of predicates representing properties whose extensions depend on whether or not a certain chemical theory is true. And this fact clearly distinguishes the properties C_i from the properties F_i.

But what does all this have to do with implicit definitions? It is not clear at all why Quine believes that the construction outlined above, even if it were otherwise unobjectionable, shows that implicit definitions are vindicated. Perhaps he reasoned as follows. To say that axioms are implicit definitions is to say, at least in part, that they are analytic, just like other kinds of definitions. By means of his construction, we can allegedly show that axioms can be turned into analytic statements. Hence a conception of axioms as a kind of definition is vindicated.

What the construction shows, if it shows that much, is that the "theory" '$A(F_i)$' can be deduced from '$A(K_i)$'. Thus, if '$A(F_i)$' were really a theory about certain entities and their properties, it would be true as a matter of arithmetic. Let us agree, for the sake of the argument, that it would be an arithmetic theory. But how does this show that '$A(C_i)$' is an arithmetic theory? It does not, of course, if we are right in concluding that, contrary to Quine's claim, the chemical properties C_i are not the same as the properties F_i. But even if we assume, contrary to fact, that '$A(F_i)$' is an axiomatization of the same theory as '$A(C_i)$,' this would merely mean that the chemical theory is true as a matter of arithmetic (whatever that may mean), but not that it is true as a matter of definition. Certain identity statements, we saw, are true by definition, that is, because we accept certain abbreviation proposals and because of the ontological law that everything is self-identical. The axioms '$A(F_i)$' are not in this sense true. Certain other statements, we further saw, are true by definition in the sense that they are true because we accept certain abbreviation proposals and because there are certain (factual) laws including laws of logic, laws of arithmetic, laws of biology, etc. Again, the axioms '$A(F_i)$' are not in this sense true. Since these are the only two possibilities, it follows that they are not true by definition at all. Rather, they are comparable to arithmetic truths that follow from other arithmetic truths.

Even if Quine's construction were sound, the desired analogy between axioms and definitions can be drawn, it seems to me, only if one uses an undifferentiated notion of analyticity as a verbal bridge. Statements true by definition are called analytic truths. Statements of arithmetic, those deducible from arithmetic truths, are also called analytic. Since both kinds of statements are analytic truths, they are supposed to have something in common. It is maintained that axioms are like statements which are true by definition in that they, too, are analytic. Thus one concludes that one may justifiably call them implicit definitions. How confused and confusing this type of argument is should be obvious in the light of the distinction we have drawn between abbreviational truth, on the one hand, and the truths of logic, arithmetic, set-theory, etc., on the other.

13 CONSTRUCTIONAL DEFINITIONS

Dedekind's forms do not in any reasonable sense implicitly define the natural numbers. Nor are the natural numbers arrived at by a process of abstraction which leads from a particular progression to the notion of a progression in general. But there exists still another attempt to read ontological significance into the construction of models for forms. According to this conception of ontology, one kind of entity is in an ontologically significant sense reduced to another kind of entity if both kinds yield isomorphic models for the same forms.[1]

Quine, one of the main proponents of this method, holds that ontological reduction has been achieved if one can specify a correlator between the individuals of the original theory and the individuals of the model such that all the properties (including relations) of the model are isomorphic to the properties (including relations) of the original theory. For arithmetic—as represented by Dedekind's axioms—there are many models that fulfill Quine's condition for ontological reduction. I have already mentioned the domain of even natural numbers and the domain of all natural numbers divisible by ten. But there are also certain classes that form progressions. For example, Frege's "definitions" of the numbers 0, 1, 2, etc. yield a progression. Two other famous progressions are mentioned by Zermelo and von Neumann, namely, the progressions Λ, $\{\Lambda\}$, $\{\{\Lambda\}\}$, ..., and Λ, $\{\Lambda\}$, $\{\Lambda, \{\Lambda\}\}$, ..., respectively.[2] It follows from Quine's conception of ontological reduction that the natural numbers can be reduced to Frege classes. But it also follows that they can be reduced to Zermelo classes or von Neumann classes. Indeed, it follows that they can be reduced to the even natural numbers or to all natural numbers divisible by ten. But, obviously, each of these progressions is different from all the others. We are dealing with completely different classes of entities. And the natural numbers could not possibly be identical with all of these quite different domains. If the natural numbers were really, say, Zermelo classes, then they could not also be Frege classes and even numbers and natural numbers divisible by ten, and so on. Yet, according to Quine's way of thinking, the natural numbers can be reduced to any one of these entirely different domains.

It appears that Quine's conception of ontology in general and of ontological reduction in particular differs fundamentally from ours and hence the traditional one. We do not just differ in our answer to the question of what numbers are; we do not even understand this question in the same way. If it is admitted that the different interpretations of the Dedekind forms constitute different domains of (different) entities, then, in my view, the question has been answered whether or not the natural numbers are one of these other kinds of entities. They are not. Hence, there can be no talk of reducing the natural numbers to any of the other kinds of entity. What one can show, though, is that very different kinds of entities yield models for the Dedekind forms. One cannot prove that, say, O is Λ, 1 is $\{\Lambda\}$, 2 is $\{\{\Lambda\}\}$, etc., but one can prove that the two classes of entities—natural numbers and Zermelo classes—can be so coordinated that they yield isomorphic models for the Dedekind forms. To believe that the existence of such an isomorphism between two entirely distinct classes of entities amounts to an ontological reduction is to confuse the relation of isomorphism with sameness. Or, if isomorphism and sameness are clearly distinguished, a peculiar notion of ontology must be involved.

There are times when Quine seems to have some doubts about his conception of ontology.* He holds, for example, that distinct domains of entities yield different models for arithmetic; and he points out that to identify, say, the progression of even numbers with the progression of odd numbers would contradict arithmetic.[3] Yet, he does not change his approach to ontology. He merely adds a pragmatic twist, as it were: "Any progression will serve as a version of number so long and only so

---

* Characteristically, Quine worries most about a technical objection to his conception of ontological reduction. According to the famous Loewenheim-Skolem theorem, a set of forms derived from any theory formulated in terms of the predicate calculus of first level has an arithmetic model. Given Quine's notion of ontological reduction, this could be understood to mean that only natural numbers exist. In order to avoid this *reductio* of his approach, Quine decrees that an ontological reduction is achieved only if the proxy function between the respective domains is actually specified.

long as we stick to one and the same progression."[4] Similar pragmatic pronouncements occur at other places. A few examples may give their general flavor. In *Set Theory and its Logic*, Quine says: "Any objects *will serve as numbers* so long as the arithmetical operations are defined for them and the laws of arithmetic are preserved."[5] On the same page he claims that *"We are free to take O as anything we like*, and construe *S* as any function we like, so long merely as the function is one that, when applied in iteration to O, yields something different on every further application." In another paper, Quine puts it this way: "Just so, we might say, Frege and von Neumann showed *how to skip the natural numbers and get by with* what we may for the moment call Frege classes and von Neumann classes." These classes, he continues, *"simulate the behavior* of the natural numbers to the point *where it is convenient* to call them natural numbers."[6]

Goodman, too, takes refuge in pragmatic musings when confronted with the question of whether or not two isomorphic models are the same. He readily admits that the construction of an isomorphic model does not decide the question of whether or not the correlated entities are the same.[7] But like Quine, he does not draw the obvious conclusion for ontology from this fact. He does not seem to see that the construction of isomorphic models does not even touch the ontological questions, say, of whether or not there are numbers and what they are. Instead, he talks about the purposes at hand and says that the reductionist proves that for the purposes at hand one need not assume that the entities of the original theory are anything other than the entities of the model.[8] His attitude is summed up by the following remark: "In other words, the reductive force of a constructional system consists not in showing that a given entity is identical with a complex of other entities but in showing that no commitment to the contrary is necessary."[9]

What are the "purposes at hand" when a philosopher asks whether or not numbers are, say, Frege classes? Surely, they do not consist in the construction of isomorphic models with entirely different domains. Moreover, what purpose could ever lead us to neglect deliberately the difference between two distinct models? Only one possibility comes to mind. If we do not care about the subject matter of the resulting axiom system, but only about turning the given forms into true axioms, then it does not matter which one of several satisfactory interpretations we pick. If our only purpose is to get true rather than false axioms, then any one of several models will do. But even from this point of view, it is not true that we need not commit ourselves to a difference among models. To say that any one of a number of different interpretations will do as long as it yields a true axiom system is not, indeed, to commit oneself to a specific model, but to commit oneself nevertheless to a difference among the given models.

Turning to Quine's justification, what could it possibly mean to say that we are free to take O as anything we like and to construe S as any function we like, as long as the repeated application of S on O yields a progression? We are free to consider any first element, it seems to me, and to pick any one of many possible functions, as long as we are not interested in the progression of natural numbers, but merely in *a* progression of whatever kind. Similarly, to say, as Quine does, that the progression of even numbers serves as a version of number can only mean that since even numbers and the natural numbers are both progressions, it does not matter which one we consider, so long as we are interested only in *a* progression, but do not care which. And to say that we can skip the natural numbers and get by with Zermelo classes can only mean that we can pick the progression of Zermelo classes rather than the progression of natural numbers, if we are interested only in considering *a* progression, but do not care which. In short, as long as we are not interested in a particular progression, but only in the feature of being a progression, any example of a progression will do for the purpose at hand, just as any human being will do as an example if we are merely interested in the property of being a human being. But just as there are many different human beings irrespective of which one we choose as our example, so there are many different progressions, irrespective of which one we consider. Both Zermelo classes and Frege classes form progressions. They are alike in this respect. This is the only sense in which the entities of the one domain "simulate" the behavior of the entities of the other domain. But there is no reason why we should confuse the one domain with the other. Zermelo is like Frege in that both are human beings and yet we do not for a moment think that this is a sufficient reason for confusing them with each other. Nor would it be convenient to call Zermelo 'Frege' or conversely. Why, then, should it ever be convenient to call Zermelo classes anything other than 'Zermelo classes' and to call natural numbers anything other than 'natural numbers'?

Natural numbers form a progression, and so do many other classes of entities. To believe that they can therefore be reduced ontologically to any other class of entities that form a progression is ultimately as absurd as to believe that Zermelo can be reduced to Frege just because they have in common that they are both human beings.

PART II

Properties and Classes

14 CONTEXTUAL DEFINITIONS

In connection with Quine's alleged definition of the property (or properties) F_i, I claimed that we cannot assume without further ado that the sign 'F_i' represents a property or properties (see chapter 13); and I also maintained at that point that the definiens of the proposed definition of F_i does not represent a property since it is a complex form. I shall defend these two assertions in the present chapter and the next one. For this purpose, we shall leave the problem of the ontological status of numbers, around which the discussion of ontological reduction has so far centered, and turn our attention to classes and properties. In particular, our observations about ontological analysis will be made for a while with an eye on the lessons of Russell's paradox and similar paradoxes.

Thinking of a certain property F, we may wish to know whether there is at least one entity with this property. Or we may inquire whether there is precisely one such entity. Of course, the mere fact that we can formulate indefinite and definite description expressions like 'an F' and 'the F' does not guarantee that the corresponding things exist. Consider now the expression 'the property f such that every property g has f if and only if g is not g'. Call this alleged property 'F'. Does the property F exist? No; for the assumption that it does yields the contradiction that F is F if and only if F is not F.[1] Or take the description expression 'the class of all classes,' and call this class 'S'. We can show that S does not exist.[2] According to Cantor's famous theorem, the power set of S must have a greater cardinality than S. However, since the power set of S is a subset of S, its cardinality cannot be greater than that of S. The assumption that the class S exists thus leads to a contradiction. What holds in these two instances, I submit, holds for all logical and semantical paradoxes: in each case, there is the presumption that a certain description is fulfilled and the subsequent startling discovery that this presumption leads to a contradiction.* It follows that the relevant descriptions are not fulfilled. The paradoxes thus teach us that certain entities do not exist. But this is merely their first and most obvious lesson.

Since the Russell paradox proves one and only one thing, namely, that there is no such property as F, what are we to make of the simple theory of types?[3] Do we have to reject Russell's view that individual things and properties (always including relations) form a hierarchy of different types of entities? Yes and no. We must reject his notion that expressions which violate the type rules are literally nonsense. Quite to the contrary, as I have already remarked in connection with ontologically impossible states of affairs, such expressions may be perfectly intelligible. They may even be true. The statement that the color green is green makes perfect sense, even though it is false (assuming, of course, that the descriptive expression 'the color green' describes the entity labeled as 'green'). Since it is false, it is true that green is not green. Equally true are such assertions as that properties do not exemplify individual things and that both the color green as well as the property of being a color are properties. There is indeed a hierarchy of types, but not as a matter of sense, if I may put it so, but as a matter of fact. There are, as a matter of fact, individual things. There are also, as a matter of fact, properties which are exemplified only by individual things. And there are, again as a matter of fact, properties which are exemplified only by the properties of individual things. Colors and shapes are exemplified only by individual things; the properties of being a color and of being a shape, only by properties of individual things. But these types of entity, starting with individual things and leading through properties of individual things to properties of properties of individual things, do not exhaust the realm of what exists. Not everything is either an individual thing or one of the properties of this

* From now on, when I speak of paradoxes, I shall always mean logical and semantical paradoxes.

hierarchy. There are, as we have seen earlier, also general quantifiers and numbers. And there are also, I submit, connectives, classes, and facts, to mention just a few additional categories. The properties of the type hierarchy do not even exhaust the realm of properties. There are properties which do not belong to any specific type. The property (category) of being a property is an example; another example would be the property F if there were such a thing.

The simple theory of types, when stripped of its claim to separate sense from nonsense and supplemented by the knowledge that there are entities—even properties—which do not belong to a specific type, constitutes a sound piece of ontology. But in this form the theory says nothing about the paradoxes. How, then, do we propose to deal with them?

Consider this description expression: 'The winged horse which sprang from Medusa at her death'. It is not hard to prove that this horse, Pegasus, does not exist; for the assumption that he does, in conjunction with certain laws of biology, leads to a contradiction. Have we then discovered a new paradox, the paradox of Pegasus? If not, what is the difference between the genuine paradoxes mentioned earlier and the nonexistence of Pegasus?

Genuine paradoxes, one may think, are "logical" in character, while the nonexistence of Pegasus is a mere biological fact. But this would be a mistake. Russell's paradox, it is true, arises as a matter of logic (property theory) pure and simple. But Cantor's paradox occurs in set theory and there are also the semantic paradoxes. That S does not exist cannot be deduced from logical premises alone. One also needs certain laws of set theory, such as Cantor's law about the cardinality of power sets. And similar considerations apply to the semantic paradoxes: here one needs certain semantic assumptions in order to arrive at a contradiction. The only difference between the case of Pegasus on the one hand and the Cantor paradox and similar paradoxes on the other is that in the first case certain biological laws lead to the contradiction, while in the latter cases the relevant laws belong to set theory and semantics. If Cantor's law did not hold, there would be no paradox of the class of all classes. If the laws of biology were different from what they actually are, the assumption that there is a winged horse would not yield a contradiction.

What is paradoxical about the nonexistence of F and S—and what is absent in the case of Pegasus—is our firm conviction that these entities must exist. We do not believe that Pegasus exists, and hence we are not at all surprised when confronted with a proof of his nonexistence. Nor do biologists imagine even for a moment that the very foundation of their science can be shaken by such a proof. But, turning to the paradoxes, we find that the situation is quite different. Since we cannot believe that certain descriptions are empty, we try to find fault with the reasoning that leads to the contradiction or with one or the other of the required premises. What distinguishes a genuine paradox from a mere empty description is that we firmly believe in the former case but not in the latter that the relevant description cannot but be fulfilled. If my analysis is correct, this belief must be abandoned. Such is, as I have said, the first lesson of paradox. But in order for the lesson to take, we must know in each case what it is that compels us to believe that the relevant description is fulfilled. Let us take a closer look at Russell's paradox.

Russell's paradox is often stated in the following way. (1) Starting with sentences like 'Green is not green,' one considers the form 'f is not f'. (2) Next one "defines" the crucial property F by the stipulation that 'f is F' shall be short for 'f is not f'. (3) This stipulation is thought to guarantee the truth of 'For all f, f is F if and only if f is not f'. The laws of logic then do the rest. If this were the correct way of setting up the paradox, its occurrence should indeed be baffling. The laws of logic needed for the deduction of the contradiction are above suspicion. We can hardly doubt, for example, that what holds for all properties f, holds for a particular property F. Furthermore, definitions (in the sense of abbreviations) are absolutely harmless. Nothing untoward can happen if we replace an expression by a shorter one. Hence we cannot find fault with step (2) of the derivation. Nor can the trouble lie with the third step. It follows from the very notion of an abbreviation that the abbreviation represents whatever the abbreviated expression represents. This leaves us with step (1), the bare form 'f is not f'. This seems to be the only step that could be wrong. Reasoning along these lines, one may arrive at the conclusion that the form 'f is not f' is to be blamed for the paradox. Hence one may try to avoid paradoxes by rejecting such forms as nonsense.[4] But this measure, as I pointed out earlier, would be a mistake. Expressions like 'There is an f such that f is not f are not only meaningful, they are even true. If so, then we must also accept step (1).

The existence of F is presumably guaranteed by step (2), and this step seems to involve nothing more than a harmless abbreviation proposal. But take a closer look. According to one version of step (2), the whole context 'f is F' is short for 'f is not f'. The second step, according to this formulation of the paradox, consists of a contextual definition. Does this contextual definition really assure the existence of F? I do not think so. That there is such a property as F does not follow from the acceptance of the proposal to write 'f is F' instead of 'f is not f'. We must not read into the abbreviation anything that cannot be gotten out of the abbreviated expression. In particular, we must not treat the sign 'F' of the abbreviation 'f is F' as if it were a constant representing a property.[5] Otherwise we may come to believe mistakenly that the contextual definition does not only introduce a certain completely arbitrary shape 'F,' but also a certain property F. If we treat 'F' not as a completely arbitrary new sign, but as a property constant, then we introduce covertly the entirely unjustified ontological assumption that there exists the property F.

It would be easy to avoid such hidden injections of ontological assumptions under the cover of mere abbreviations by choosing as parts of contextual abbreviations only expressions which have no prior meaning. But this elementary precaution, significantly enough, clashes in most cases with the very reason for using a contextual definition. In most cases, there is no point at all in proposing a contextual definition, unless certain ontological assumptions are smuggled in through the use of misleading expressions in the abbreviation. This should be obvious in the case of step (2). Had we abbreviated 'f is not f' by, say, 'X-f', no contradiction could be derived.

Another case in point is the contextual definition of class terms: 'e is a member of the class determined by the property F' is supposed to be just another expression—one can hardly call it an abbreviation—of 'e is F'.[6] If this purported definition were really a mere abbreviation proposal, no intelligible purpose could be served by using such expressions as 'class' and 'member'. These expressions should be avoided; for they only give the mistaken impression that one is talking about classes and their members when all one is talking about are properties and the things that have them. On the other hand, if the intention is to introduce classes and membership—as distinguished from properties and exemplification—then no mere abbreviation proposal could possibly turn the trick. The words 'class' and 'member' must then be used with their ordinary meaning. The proponents of contextual definitions cannot have their cake and eat it, too. Either the "shapes" 'class' and 'member' in the alleged abbreviation have no prior meaning of their own, or they mean here what they usually mean. In the first case, one merely creates unnecessary confusion by using them and hence should avoid them. In the second case, the contextual definition cannot really be a mere abbreviation proposal. It turns out to be a disguised equivalence statement to the effect that for all e and for all f, e is a member of the class determined by the property f *if and only if e* is f. This equivalence should never be called a definition. It is a bridge law connecting the theory of classes with the theory of properties. As such, it presupposes the existence of classes and of the membership nexus, just as much as the existence of properties and of exemplification. On closer inspection, almost all contextual definitions turn out to be disguised equivalence statements void of any reductive ontological power.

One more example. Recall our earlier discussion of the recursive description of addition. We noted a certain equivalence between the sum relation holding for three numbers and the zth iterate of the successor relation holding between two numbers. There is a further equivalence involving the sum relation: c is the sum of a and b *if and only if* any relation r which holds between O and a and which, if it holds between two numbers x and y also holds between the successor of x and y, holds between b and c.[7] One sometimes introduces the left side of this equivalence expression as an abbreviation for the right side, and one claims that this abbreviation proposal defines contextually the sum relation. Of course, there is nothing wrong with this particular abbreviation proposal as such. But I am criticizing the view that one can somehow show by means of contextual definitions that the entities apparently mentioned in the abbreviation do not really exist. To repeat, if it were not for the true equivalence about such entities as the sum relation and the successor relation, it would not occur to anyone to abbreviate the right side by just these particular shapes on the left side. And hence one has every reason to doubt that a genuine abbreviation proposal is here at work. In reality, the proponent of the contextual definition accepts the equivalence statement, a statement completely on a par with other true statements, but he tries to avoid the ontological consequences of this acceptance by pretending to introduce the left side of the equivalence expression as a mere abbreviation of the right side. That abbreviation is not really the name of the game is shown by the fact that he picks for the abbreviation not just any convenient shorter phrase, but the well-established phrase 'is the sum of'.

However, the proponent of contextual definitions need not insist that all he is about is mere abbreviation for the sake of brevity. He may concede the importance of the relevant equivalence. He could hold the following view about definitions.[8] There are two kinds of equivalences. Some equivalences fulfill the two conditions of eliminability and noncreativity; others do not. An equivalence is said to fulfill the first condition if and only if it follows from it that for every expression of the sort that occurs on the left side there is an equivalent expression of the kind that occurs on the right side. For example, the equivalence mentioned earlier guarantees that for every expression of the form 'sum (a, b, c)' there is an equivalent one that starts with 'for all relations r, if r holds between O and a'. Hence expressions of the form 'sum (a, b, c)' are said to be eliminable.[9] The above equivalence also fulfills the second condition, since there is no expression without the phrase 'is the sum of' which is not already derivable from the rest of arithmetic without the equivalence. Now, an equivalence is called a definition if and only if it fulfills the two conditions of eliminability and noncreativity.

The same holds true for identity statements. An identity statement is called a definition if and only if it fulfills the twin requirements of eliminability and noncreativity. Frege's so-called definition of the number of f's, for example, fulfills these conditions, because it fulfills the following "rule of definition": (a) the variables in the definiendum are distinct (there is only one in this case), (b) the definiens has no free variables other than those which occur in the definiendum, and (c) the only nonlogical constants in the definiens are primitive and previously defined expressions of the theory.

According to this conception, definitions are just certain kinds of equivalence and identity statements. One may object to this view on terminological grounds. Since the word 'definition' is often used either for an abbreviation proposal which is neither true nor false or for the trivially true identity statement that follows from the acceptance of such a proposal, it is quite misleading to call certain factual identities and equivalences "definitions." Frege's remark that "One must never present as a definition that which requires a proof or an intuition to establish its truth" is in the spirit of this criticism.[10] But in addition to this terminological consideration, there is the ontological point made earlier, namely, that eliminability—as understood in the present context—does not amount to ontological reducibility. The states of affairs represented by the definiendum in our example are said to be eliminable, since there are states of affairs which are equivalent to them. But equivalent states of affairs, even logically equivalent ones, are not necessarily the same. In particular, even though the equivalence under discussion fulfills the conditions of eliminability and non-creativity, it does not amount to an ontological reduction of the sum relation to some other entities. Thus our criticism of contextual definitions as a tool of ontology stands.

15 PROPERTY ABSTRACTION

The contextual definition of '$F(f)$', conceived of as a mere abbreviation, does not guarantee the existence of any property F. Hence we cannot use universal instantiation in order to derive the contradiction that F is F if and only if F is not F. There is no contradiction and hence no paradox. But this is not the only way of looking at step (2) of the proposed derivation of Russell's paradox.

Assume that we introduce 'F' as short for 'not-f'. In this case, '$F(f)$' will be short for 'not-$f(f)$,' just as intended. But before we apply universal instantiation, we must again be certain that 'F' represents a property, yet our abbreviation proposal tells us merely that 'F' represents whatever it is that 'not-f' represents. If we take it that 'F' represents a property, this belief must rest on the conviction that 'not-f' represents a property. Russell's contradiction, as I said earlier, acquires the appearance of paradox if and only if we are convinced that there is such a property as F. We are about to locate the basis for this conviction.

Behind most contextual definitions lurk true equivalences or, at least, equivalences that are thought to be true. The second step in the derivation of Russell's paradox is no exception. It consists of the equivalence: 'For all properties f, f is F *if and only if f is not f*. Why do we ordinarily accept this equivalence? What makes us believe that there is such a property as F? F's existence follows from the principle of property abstraction. According to this principle, there exists a property g which an entity e has *if and only if . . . e . . .* , where the dots indicate any well-formed propositional context.* Now, if this principle holds, then the important equivalence mentioned above follows, and we can then deduce the Russell contradiction. There is a paradox, because we can prove that F does not exist, even though F's existence follows from what seems to be a well-entrenched principle. I say *seems to be*, of course, because I think that Russell's contradiction shows that the principle of property abstraction is false. The paradox teaches us that not every well-formed propositional form represents a property. This is its second and most important lesson.

Why is the principle of property abstraction so uncritically accepted by many philosophers and, especially, by logicians? Let the propositional form be 'e is green and e is round'. According to the principle, there is a property, call it 'P,' such that an entity is P if and only if it is both green and round. But what property could that be? What further property is there that is common to all green and round things and only to such things? There is no plausible candidate. And this seems to show that we do not have sufficient reasons for accepting the principle of property abstraction in its full generality. Granted that entities have in many cases "additional" properties if and only if they have certain others, there seem to be quite a number of exceptions to this rule. At this point, however, the following idea is crucial. Even though there is no plausible candidate for the property P as long as we demand that P be a "third," quite different property, can we not fall back on the property of *being both green and round?* If we can, then there is after all no exception to the principle. There always exists at least the complex property represented by the relevant propositional form. The principle of property abstraction really reduces to the

* Everything I shall say about property abstraction also holds, of course, for forms which purport to represent relations.

principle that every well-formed propositional form represents a property. It is this idea, one may surmise, that convinces so many of the truth of the principle of property abstraction. Yet we should not be convinced. The briefest of reflections shows that this idea is not sound.

Assume that the individual thing A is both green and round; that it is a fact that A is green and round. Then A most certainly exists; and so do the two properties of being green and of being round. But there is no third property, no other entity belonging to the category of properties, that could be called the property of being green and round. I know of no argument that establishes the existence of such a third property. To the contrary, everything indicates that no propositional form whatsoever represents a property.* If it is a fact that A is identical with A, then there exists the entity A and also—at least in my view—the relation of identity. But there is no such thing as the property of being identical with A. If it is a fact that A is to the left of B, then the relation of being to the left of as well as A and B exist, but there is no such thing as the property of being to the left of B. To believe that there exist such entities as the property of being both green and round, the property of being identical with A, and the property of being to the left of B is sheer ontological superstition.

Consider the fact that A is to the left of B. If we accept the view that every well-formed propositional form represents a property (or relation), then we must hold that there are in this case the relation of being to the left of, the complex property of being to the left of B, and the complex property that A is to the left of something. Since these are different entities, there must also be three different facts into which these entities enter, namely, the fact that A stands to B in the relation of being to the left of, the fact that A has the property of being to the left of B, and the fact that B has the property that A is to the left of it.[1] Yet it is obvious that there is only one such fact, namely, that A is to the left of B. As Ramsey puts it, "So the theory of complex

---

* Not even the propositional form 'x is green' represents a property. The color is represented by 'green' (and described by 'the color green'), not by this form. Yet I shall continue to speak, say, of the property of *being green*. Grammar and/or style seem to require it or, at least, to invite it. But we must keep in mind that this is merely a figure of speech and that green is represented by 'green,' not by 'is green' or 'x is green'.

universals is responsible for an incomprehensible trinity, as senseless as that of theology."[2]

One can, of course, abbreviate the expression 'A is green and A is round' by saying 'A is ground'. But one must not conclude that 'ground' is here the name of a complex property. If it were the name of such a property, then '*A* is ground' could not possibly be an abbreviation for '*A* is green and *A* is round'; for then, as we just saw, '*A* is ground' would represent quite a different fact from '*A* is green and *A* is round,' since the former fact contains the property *ground*, while the latter does not. Thus if we assume that 'ground' represents a complex property, we cannot treat '*A* is ground' as a mere abbreviation of '*A* is green and *A* is round'. On the other hand, assume that 'ground' does not represent a complex property, and hence that in general no expression '*G*' which is introduced as part of an abbreviation in the manner indicated, represents the complex property under discussion. How, then, can we ever speak about this property, since no expression '*G*' will represent it? And what reason is there then to assume that such a complex property exists? Of course, we have the English phrase 'The property of being both green and round', and we can say that *A* is green-and-round. But is there the slightest reason to believe that '*A* is green-and-round' is anything but a shorter version of '*A* is green and *A* is round'? And if there is no such reason, what reason is there to believe that the complex property in question exists? This does not mean that we have to ban all expressions like 'the property of being both green and round' from ordinary discourse. For the sake of easy communication, we may very well wish to retain such phrases. However, we must realize whenever it matters that to say, for example, that *A* has the property of being both green and round is to say nothing more than that *A* is green and *A* is round.[3]

If *A* is green and round and *B* is also green and round, is there not something common to both *A* and *B*? And is that which is common to both *A* and *B* not a property, shared by both *A* and *B*? And what property could that be but the property of being both green and round? It is true that in a manner of speaking there is something common to both *A* and *B* in this example, but what is common is not a shared property. Rather, *A* and *B* are constituents of similar facts. The similarity between the fact that *A* is green and round and the fact that *B* is green and round does not consist in that both facts contain, in addition to different individual things, one and the same complex property, but rather in that both of them contain the same additional constituents (in the same order). Both facts contain the further constituents: *exemplification* (twice), *green, round,* and *and.* We may say that the structure of (the rest of) the two facts is exactly the same. And it is this identity of structure of the (rest of the) facts which is the common element in all those cases where one is tempted to speak of a shared complex property. In short, it is not *A* and *B* which have something in common, but rather the two facts. They have in common that they contain, with the exception of *A* and *B*, the same constituents (in the same order).[4]

If there are several things which are both green and round, then there exists the class of things which are green and round. But how could this class exist, unless the property of being green and round, which determines this class, existed? This objection assumes that, for every class, there is a property which determines this class, that is, that there is for every class a property such that an entity is a member of the class if and only if it has this property.* But this principle does not hold. There are numerous classes which are not determined by properties. For example, the intersection of any two classes exists, even if this intersection is not determined by a property; the power set of every class, which contains as elements all subsets of the class, exists, whether or not there is a corresponding property; for every class, there also exists the union class which contains as elements all elements of the elements of the original class; and this irrespective of whether or not there exists the determining property; and so on. In brief, starting with a collection of entities which are not classes (including individual things, properties, relations, connectives, quantifiers, etc.), there exists the class of all subsets of this collection. There exists, furthermore, the class of all subsets of this second class. And so on. Moreover, there also exists the union of all the classes of this hierarchy, and this union in turn has a power set.[5] And so on. All these classes exist quite independently of whether or not there are the corresponding prop-

---

* This property is sometimes thought of as the property *of being identical with A or with B or with C,* . . . , where *A, B, C,* . . . are the members of the class. But there is, of course, no such property either, if my argument is sound.

erties.* This view, I take it, agrees with the spirit of that type of axiomatized set theory which was first formulated by Zermelo.[6]

The fact that not every class is determined by a property is only one side of a coin. The other side consists of the fact that not every property determines a class. For example, the property of being a class does not determine a class. This second insight, of course, is the main lesson of the set-theoretical paradoxes. From one point of view, what the paradoxes of property theory and the paradoxes of set theory show is not at all that our intuitive ("naive") notions of property and of class were faulty, but rather that we accepted too thoughtlessly generalizations involving these notions. Observing quite correctly that some classes are determined by properties, we concluded too hastily that all properties determine classes. What is responsible for the two kinds of paradox is neither a defective notion of property nor a defective notion of class, but a wrong view about the relationship between these two kinds of entity. Properties and classes, if I may put it so, are not as intimately associated with each other as Frege, Russell, and others once thought. In particular, it turns out that there are classes without properties and properties without classes. Surely, this ought to be a powerful reason for keeping properties and classes apart in ontology and for distinguishing between property theory and set theory as two distinct disciplines.

To summarize, beginning with Russell's contradiction, I have argued that its paradoxical air derives from our mistaken belief that the principle of property abstraction holds. I traced this belief to the view that every propositional form represents a property. I claimed that Russell's paradox shows that this view is false. Then I argued, on independent grounds, that in fact no propositional form whatsoever represents a property, and I defended this assertion against some plausible objections. This defense made room for some rather sweeping observations about the relationship between properties and classes.

Let me conclude with a minor terminological point. One often speaks of the principle of property abstraction in analogy to the principle of class abstraction. But this terminology, as we now see, is

---

* Perhaps a less controversial example of a class without a determining property is the selection class which according to the axiom of choice, exists for any arbitrary class of classes.

rather misleading. If the principle of class abstraction states that every property determines a class, then the principle of property abstraction should state that every class determines a property, rather than what one usually understands by it, namely, that there exists a property f such that e is f if and only if . . . e . . . . If we revise the terminology accordingly, our results can be expressed as follows. First, no propositional form represents a property. Second, just as the set-theoretical paradoxes show that the principle of class abstraction is false, so the paradoxes of property theory show—though along more indirect lines—that the principle of property abstraction is false, that is, that there are classes which are not determined by properties.

16 SETS VERSUS CLASSES

The paradox of the class of all classes proves that such a class does not exist. Why then do we believe that there must be this class? Assuming that there are classes, we are convinced that there are entities which have the property of being a class. But if the property of being a class exists, we argue, then there must exist the class of all those entities which have this property. Hence there must exist the class of all classes. It is the second step of this argument which must be rejected. The principle of class abstraction, which states that every property determines a class, does not hold in general. This is the second lesson of all set-theoretical paradoxes.

There is a famous attempt to preserve the principle of class abstraction from which we can learn some ontological truths. This attempt rests on a distinction between two kinds of collections called *Sets* and *Classes.* In Cantor's view, for example, there are both Sets and Classes.[1] But Classes are distinguished from Sets by the fact that a contradiction follows from the assumption that all their elements form a unit, a finished entity.[2] The collection of all Sets is thus a Class rather than a Set. Now, it is not at all easy to clarify Cantor's ideas, because we do not know what to make of the notions of being united, of being together, of constituting a finished entity, when applied to the elements of a collection. One may be tempted to interpret Cantor to mean that some kinds of elements form a unit, while others do not. But according to this interpretation, the proper distinction would not be between two kinds of collections, but rather between two kinds of elements, namely, elements that form Sets and elements that do not; and it is only one step from this distinction to the view that some kinds of entities are such that they can form a unit, while others are not. Hence we are led back to the view that some properties determine classes, while others do not. The basic puzzle of Cantor's dichotomy is how elements which are not "united," which are not "together," which do not constitute a "finished entity," can possibly form a collection at all, irrespective of whether we agree to call the collection a Class rather than a Set. If certain elements form a collection, then they must in some sense be united, be together, constitute a finished entity; and how is this sense to be distinguished from the sense which Cantor has in mind when he maintains that the elements of a Class are not united, are not together, do not constitute a finished entity?

Fortunately, we need not linger with this puzzle. A recent version of Cantor's view explains the distinction between Sets and Classes in precise terms. What distinguishes Classes from Sets is the fact that the former are not elements of collections.[3] All those very big classes which, according to my understanding, do not exist, turn out to be (in Von Neumann's interpretation), on this view, existing Classes, but not Sets. For example, to the class of all classes there corresponds the Class of all Sets; to the class of all ordinal numbers corresponds the Class of ordinal numbers. In brief, the distinction between Sets and Classes is designed to assure the existence of certain "very large" collections and hence to save the principle of class abstraction.* But this is love's labor lost. From an ontological point of view, this response to the set-theoretical paradoxes is unacceptable.

* It must be emphasized, however, that there is another interpretation of the Class-Set distinction. According to this conception, Classes are properties (Zermelo's "definite Eigenschaften"), and while to every Set there corresponds such a Class, to some Classes there corresponds no Set. This view seems to coincide with our position that not every property determines a class (leaving aside the issue of whether or not every class is determined by a property). But this agreement is mere appearance; for the properties are "taken in extension," as the saying goes, and hence are really classes after all. Goedel and von Neumann can therefore identify (1) a Class for which there exists a Set with the same elements with (2) this Set, so that every Set is a Class, but not every Class is a Set.

One of the assumptions that leads eventually to Cantor's paradox of the class of all classes is that for every existing class, there exists its power class. If we drop this assumption, the contradiction cannot be derived. Now the existence of a power class *PC* of the class *C* implies that *C* is a member of *PC*. Consider, then, the class of all classes *S*. In order to avoid the contradiction, we may simply assert that *S* has no power class. Or we could maintain that *S* is not a member of any class and then conclude that therefore it has no power class. Taking the second way out, we arrive at the view that there is no such entity as the class of all classes, but that there is instead the Class of all Sets. The assumption that there exists this Class of all Sets does not lead to a contradiction because that Class has no power collection.

The situation is somewhat different when we turn to the Burali-Forti paradox.[4] This contradiction arises in the following way. We assume that the collection of all ordinal numbers is well-ordered. We further assume that every well-ordered collection has an ordinal number. It follows that the collection of all ordinal numbers has an ordinal number. Now this number would have to be both a member of the collection of all ordinal numbers and also larger than every member of this collection. But assume now that the collection of all ordinal numbers is a Class. Does this assumption suffice to avoid the paradox? My formulation of the derivation of the contradiction in terms of collections rather than classes shows clearly that it does not suffice. The distinction between Sets and Classes thus does not automatically eliminate all set-theoretical paradoxes. This fact is not too apparent, because ordinal numbers are usually "defined" as certain collections; and it is this kind of "definition" which, combined with the Set-Class distinction, helps to avoid the paradox. For example, the Burali-Forti paradox cannot arise if we assume that classes cannot be members of collections and if ordinal numbers are "defined" in the von Neumann fashion. According to this "definition," an *ordinal X* turns out to be the collection of all ordinals less than *X*. But such a collection is an ordinal number only if it is a Set. Now if we assume that the collection of all ordinal numbers is a Class rather than a Set, then we block the Burali-Forti contradiction; for if it is a Class, then it is an ordinal but not an ordinal number. Thus the "definition" of an ordinal number guarantees that certain collections have no ordinal number, because they *are* no ordinal numbers.

From our point of view, however, it cannot be taken for granted that ordinal numbers are certain kinds of collections. Perhaps they are properties of collections such that two collections share the same property if and only if they are isomorphic well-ordered collections.[5] What, then, are ordinal numbers? Indeed, are there such entities at all?

Consider two relations R_1 and R_2 and assume that there is a relation T such that the following four conditions are satisfied: (1) T is one-one; (2) the members of the field of R_1 are first-place members of T; (3) the members of the field of R_2 are second-place members of T; and (4) if any n members, say, a_1, a_2, . . . , a_n constitute an n-tuple satisfying R_1, then the members b_1, b_2, . . . , b_n related to them respectively by T constitute an n-tuple satisfying R_2, and conversely. If T fulfills these conditions, T is called a correlator between R_1 and R_2. If there exists a correlator between two relations R_1 and R_2, we shall say that R_1 and R_2 are isomorphic to each other. Instead of saying that two relations are isomorphic to each other, we shall also say that they have the same structure. Next, let us consider only a certain kind of relation, namely, well-ordering relations. We say that a relation is a well-ordering relation if it fulfills the following two conditions: (1) it is a simple ordering relation, and (2) every nonempty class of members of the field of the relation has at least one minimum with respect to the relation. To speak of a simple ordering relation and of the minimum of a class with respect to a relation are in turn short ways of saying more complicated things.[6] Finally, the structures of well-ordering relations are called ordinal numbers. Let us try to cut through this web of abbreviations to its ontological core.

First, notice that there may exist no relation T but only the corresponding class of ordered couples C_T. Hence we may have to reformulate the four conditions for the correlator so as to apply to this class of ordered couples.[7] This problem will recur throughout the next few paragraphs; in some cases when we speak about certain relations, only the corresponding classes may actually exist; and everything I say will have to be adjusted accordingly. Notice, too, that there is no such property as that of being a correlator (between R_1 and R_2). The form consisting of the conjunction of the four conditions for T does not represent a property. Finally, there exists no such relation as that of isomorphism between two relations. To say that R_1 and R_2 are isomorphic to each other is just a short way of saying that there exists a certain relation T (or class C_T). But notice also that if there were such a relation as isomorphism, this relation would be an equivalence relation; for if T is a correlator between R_1 and R_2, then the converse of T is a correlator between R_2 and R_1; and, furthermore, if T_1 is a correlator between R_1 and R_2 and T_2 is a correlator between R_2 and R_3, then the relative product of T_1 and T_2 is a correlator between R_1 and R_3. Last but not least, there is no such property as that of having the same structure. But there exist relations which are isomorphic to each other.*

Consider, for example, the series $< 0, 1, 2 >$, which is well-ordered by the smaller-than relation between natural numbers.† Compare this series with the series $< A_1, A_2, A_3 >$ consisting of squares which are well-ordered by the to-the-left-of-relation. There exists a correlator between these two well-ordered series; they are isomorphic to each other. Furthermore, any well-ordered series with three elements is isomorphic to $< 0, 1, 2 >$. Now assume that there exists the class of all such well-ordered series and call this class 'the ordinal number 3*'. It is clear that 3* is not the natural number 3; 3* is a class of well-ordered series, while 3 is not a class at all but a quantifier. Nor is 3* the same as the well-ordered series $< 0, 1, 2 >$; the latter is an element of the former. Nor, finally, does this series of numbers occupy a privileged position in regard to 3*; it is merely one member of 3* among many. Why, then, did we call the class of such series a number, an ordinal number, to be precise, and why did we use the numeral '3' as part of its name? Well, since every well-ordered series of whatever kind belongs to this class as long as it has precisely three elements, the number of the elements of a series in this class distinguishes it from all other equivalence classes of well-ordered series. Each one of these equivalence classes of finite series is characterized by the number of elements of the series which are members of the class. But this fact must not mislead us into thinking that our talk about ordinal numbers and the ordinal

* It will appear presently that the entities which are in reality isomorphic to each other are not *relations* but *structures*. Classical set-theory—as formulated, for example, in Cantor's "Beitraege zur Begruendung der transfiniten Mengenlehre"—deals not only with classes, but also with such structures, that is, with ordered classes.

† Series, as I shall explain in greater detail below, are neither properties nor classes, but belong to the main category of structures.

number 3* implies that there are two kinds of numbers, namely, cardinal numbers and ordinal numbers, as there are two kinds of quantifiers, namely, numerical and general quantifiers. In particular, our so-called ordinal numbers are not quantifiers at all. Ontologically speaking, they are as different from the natural numbers (cardinal numbers) as night is from day. They do not even belong, as we have seen, to the same ontological category. It will therefore be best if we henceforth drop our temporary convention and no longer talk of ordinal numbers in general and the ordinal number 3* in particular. In addition to the natural numbers, there are—among many other things—well-ordered series of entities, be these entities numbers, or squares, or classes, or what have you. And there may also exist a correlator for two series, so that it makes sense to say of two or more of these series that they are isomorphic to each other.*

If the difference between natural numbers and so-called ordinal numbers is all that great, why did anyone call these two entirely different categories of entity *number*? Obviously, because it was not realized that they are quite that different. Cantor, for example, thought of the power (*Maechtigkeit*) of a class as that general concept under which fall all and only those classes which are equivalent to the given one.[8] We may paraphrase, I think, and say that he conceived of the cardinal numbers as properties of classes. On the other hand, he thought of the ordinal number (*Anzahl* or *Ordnungszahl*) of a well-ordered class as that general concept under which fall all and only those well-ordered classes which are isomorphic to the given one. The ordinal numbers, according to this view, are properties of well-ordered classes. From Cantor's view, cardinal numbers and ordinal numbers are of the same cloth. They belong to the same category; both are properties. Moreover, they are both properties of classes—cardinal numbers, of classes proper, ordinal numbers, of well-ordered classes. Or consider Russell's view.[9] Cardinal numbers, in his opinion, are classes of equivalent classes; ordinal numbers are classes of isomorphic well-

---

* If we assume that there are infinite well-ordered series, as one usually does, then we can show that not all such series of the same cardinality are isomorphic to each other. This, of course, is the reason why ordinal numbers are distinguished from cardinal numbers even though finite ordinals are, as the saying goes, identified with the corresponding cardinals.

ordering relations. Again, cardinal and ordinal numbers belong to the same category; they are both classes.

I have assumed, for the sake of the argument, that there exists the class of all well-ordered series with three elements—what Russell calls the ordinal number 3. The purpose was to show that such classes, even if they existed, do not deserve to be called numbers, since they do not belong to the same main category as the natural numbers. But I hasten to add now that neither Cantor's properties of equivalent classes and of isomorphic well-ordered classes exist, nor do Russell's classes of all equivalent classes and classes of all isomorphic well-ordered relations. There are certain classes, and some of these classes are equivalent to each other; that is, there is a correlator for them. But we must not conclude from these facts either that therefore there exists the class of all those classes which are equivalent to each other or that therefore there exists a property which is shared by all and only those classes which are equivalent to each other. We saw earlier that the existence of a correlator between two classes or series does not imply the existence of a common property. In this particular case, moreover, no reason at all speaks for there being such a property. That no classes are determined by there being a correlator between certain classes or series follows from the fact that, if we assume the existence of these classes, we can derive a contradiction.

To return to the Class-Set distinction, the point is that this distinction blocks the Burali-Forti paradox only if ordinal numbers are conceived of as collections. To see this, assume for a moment that Cantor is right in holding that ordinal numbers are properties of well-ordered classes. If they are, then we are faced with the paradox even if we talk about collections in general, as I did earlier. Of course, we can now avoid the contradiction by rejecting some other premise, for example, the assumption that every well-ordered series has that particular property which is called the ordinal number of the series; and we may even agree to call collections which have no ordinal numbers *Classes*, and then distinguish them from Sets. But the point remains: the avoidance of the Burali-Forti paradox by means of the original Class-Set distinction rests on a specific conception of ordinal numbers. If we do not accept this view of ordinal numbers, we may have to revise our laws about classes in other ways, for example, by holding that not every class has an ordinal number.

Let us contemplate a similar method for Pegasus. Assume that people believe that there are winged horses as well as ordinary ones. Subsequently they discover that the assumption that there are winged horses leads to a contradiction. But these people are rather clever and realize that they can avoid this contradiction, and hence continue to believe in winged horses, if they proceed as follows. First, they distinguish between two kinds of (existing) horses: ordinary horses and winged horses. Second, assuming that they have axiomatized all laws about horses, they divide these axioms into two groups, axioms that hold for all horses and axioms that hold only for ordinary horses. This division is guided by the principle that the laws required for the derivation of a contradiction concerning winged horses belong to the second group; such laws are restricted to ordinary horses. By this method they can avoid the contradiction and thus allow for the existence of winged horses. In this manner, the difference between existents and nonexistents is magically transformed into a difference between two kinds of existents.

Nor do we have to stop this magic at winged horses. We can resurrect any nonexistent entity whatsoever. Consider the infamous round square. Assuming that it is a law of geometry that a round thing is not square, we can easily prove that there is no such entity as the round square; for if there were such an entity, it would have to be both square and not square.* But we know how to save the round square from the limbo of nonexistence. We merely have to maintain that certain laws of geometry—among them the one mentioned earlier—do not hold for round squares even though they hold for other kinds of squares. Then we can assert without contradiction that there are round squares as well as ordinary squares. In this fashion, one can avoid all contradictions arising from existence assumptions. Alas, all proofs of nonexistence—and hence ultimately all proofs of existence—would disappear.[10]

---

* I am assuming here that it is not a matter of abbreviation but a fact of geometry that round things are not square. But even if we assume that this is an abbreviational truth and hence an instance of a logical truth, the general principle of resurrection still applies: we must then exempt the round square, not from certain geometrical laws, but rather from certain logical laws in order to save its existence.

As a reward for a measure so drastic as the resurrection of nonexistent entities, we could at least expect that the principle of class abstraction continues to hold. But this reward is not forthcoming. Allowing for the Class-Set terminology, the principle of class abstraction reads: Every existing property determines a nonempty collection. If there are any entities that share a certain property, then there must be a collection of these entities. But consider now the property of being a Class. According to the view under consideration, there are Classes, that is, there are entities which have the property of being a Class. Hence, by the principle of class abstraction, there should exist a collection of all and only those entities which are Classes. But there is no such collection. The property of being a Class does not determine a collection. Thus the principle of class abstraction or, as we may now call it, the principle of collection abstraction does not hold for all properties. From an ontological point of view, nothing seems to be gained by substituting the puzzle of the nonexistence of the collection of all Classes for the puzzle of the nonexistence of the collection of all classes. To the contrary, in addition to the original problem, we now also have two kinds of entities, Classes and Sets, where formerly we only had classes.

17 IMPREDICATIVE DEFINITIONS

The semantical paradoxes are not essentially different from the logical and set-theoretical ones. Take, for example, the famous liar paradox. Assume that on page 5 of a certain book there occurs just one sentence: The statement on page 5 of this book is false. Now, if there existed such a statement, then it would be true if and only if it were false. Hence there is no such statement.* Yet we cling to the belief that there must be such a statement; for the expression on page 5 looks exactly like a (declarative) sentence. The liar paradox shows that not everything that looks like a (declarative) sentence expresses a statement. It reminds us that there are occasions when we must distinguish between sentences as marks and noises and statements expressed by such marks and

---

* Recall our earlier remark on the ontological status of statements.

noises.[1] The well-known Goedel sentence skirts the appearance of paradox, precisely because it presupposes this distinction. It does not state of itself that it is false, but merely that it is not provable. It merely states that a certain string of signs cannot be derived (in a certain system); and, as it turns out, this string of signs is just the one that expresses that statement.[2]

Or look at the Grelling paradox.[3] We agree to say that a predicate has the property of being heterological if and only if it does not have the property which it represents. What about the predicate 'heterological'? Is it heterological or not? If it is, then it represents a property which it does not have, and since it represents the property of being heterological, it is not heterological. But if it is not heterological, then it has the property which it represents, so that it is heterological. Thus the predicate is heterological if and only if it is not heterological. What this contradiction shows, I submit, is that there is no such property as that of being heterological. Why do we assume that there is? I suppose we do because we mistakenly believe that the form 'There is a property f which is represented by the predicate e and e is not f' represents a property, namely, the property represented by the abbreviation 'heterological'.

According to this point of view, the semantical paradoxes, too, teach us that certain entities do not exist, even though we believe we have the best of reasons for thinking that they do exist. As I have said, semantical paradoxes do not differ essentially from the logical and set-theoretical paradoxes. In particular, they do not necessitate the *ramified theory of types.* Russell, we remember, invoked at one point the vicious circle principle in order to deal with the paradoxes.[4] He noted that the paradoxes can be formulated in such a way that the important descriptions contain universal or existential quantifiers ranging over just the kind of entity to which the described entity belongs. For example, the description of F as formulated above contains a universal quantifier ranging over *all properties g.* Similarly, the following description of the class of all classes S contains a universal quantifier ranging over all classes: The class s such that all classes t are members of s. Descriptions of this type are called impredicative descriptions. Usually, one speaks of impredicative definitions rather than impredicative descriptions. But it will become clear presently, if it is not already, that this is a rather misleading terminology. At any rate, according to Russell's diagnosis, impredicative descriptions are to be blamed for the occurrence of paradoxes, because they contain a vicious circle. The cure, Russell believes, is to ban all impredicative descriptions. When imposed on a certain system, this ban results in the ramified theory of types.

The ramified theory of types—as distinct from the simple theory—was never widely accepted. Ramsey, following in Peano's footsteps, rejected the ramified theory as a logical system, because a simple theory of types presumably suffices to eliminate all the logical paradoxes, as distinguished from the semantical ones.[5] However, the main objection against the ramified theory (without the axiom of reducibility, of course) is that large parts of classical analysis have to be abandoned if impredicative descriptions are prohibited. For example, Dedekind's description of the square root of 2 as the least upper bound of the class of numbers whose square is at most 2 is impredicative by Russell's standards and hence inadmissible. Russell is able to retain certain parts of analysis only because he introduces the infamous axiom of reducibility. This axiom has been a center of controversy. Quine, for instance, pointed out that the axiom cancels, in a sense, the very ramification of propositional functions it was invented to cope with.[6] But be that as it may, it should be obvious in any case that the paradoxes cannot be blamed on impredicative descriptions; for, first, such paradoxes can also be derived from predicative descriptions, and, second, there are actually impredicative descriptions which are fulfilled. Cantor's paradox, for example, cannot be blamed on an impredicative description of the class S, because it appears also in connection with the description *the class of all entities which are classes*, which is as predicative as the description *the class of all entities which are green.* And there are also impredicative descriptions which do not lead to contradictions at all. Dedekind's description of the square root of 2, for example, does not, as far as we know, give rise to a contradiction. The description *the man who is as tall as or taller than any man in the room in which I type these lines* is impredicative; yet it is fulfilled and hence cannot possibly harbor a contradiction.[7]

Impredicative descriptions do not in general yield contradictions. Why, then, did Russell think at one time that they must be avoided, even at the price of having to accept the dubious axiom of reducibility? What made him, as well as some other philosophers, suspicious of impredicative descriptions? We do not get a clear answer from Russell himself. He seemed to believe that the very act of describing ("defining") an entity impredicatively somehow creates a new entity which does not belong to the totality of entities mentioned in the description expression ("definition"). According to Russell, "In each contradiction something is said about *all* cases of some kind, and from what is said a new case seems to be generated, which both is and is not of the same kind as the cases of which *all* were concerned in what was said."[8] A little later, he adds: "Thus all our contradictions have in common the assumption of a totality such that, if it were legitimate, it would at once be enlarged by new members defined in terms of itself."[9] However, in describing an entity, one obviously does not create it. Perhaps it may be said that we "create" a new description expression, but the entity described, provided that it exists, exists quite independently of our describing it. No new entity, no addition to the totality mentioned in the description expressions, is created by a description and so none is created which could enlarge that totality. When we describe the square root of 2 as the least upper bound of the numbers whose square is at most 2, we do not in any sense of the word "create" that number. The square root of 2 is one of the numbers whose square is at most 2; it is not *added* to these numbers by our describing it.*

Russell's main objection against impredicative descriptions, as far as I can make out, does not stand up. But there is another line of criticism, which I shall call Poincaré's objection. According to Poincaré, a definition is logically admissible only if it excludes all objects which are dependent on the notion to be defined.[10] A definition, in short, must not be circular. Impredicative definitions, according to Poincaré's objection, are circular and hence, like all such definitions, entirely worthless. Translated into our terminology, Poincaré's claim is that impredicative descriptions (of a previously specified entity) are faulty because they are circular.

Assume for a moment that Poincaré is right. Still, his objection does not shed any light on the sources of the paradoxes. Even if we

* Perhaps it is easier to believe that entities are created by definitions than that they are created by descriptions. If so, then the more common phrase 'impredicative definition' rather than my 'impredicative description' may be partially responsible for Russell's view.

assume that impredicative descriptions are worthless, our assumption does not explain why they lead to contradictions. If we believe that impredicative descriptions are circular and hence worthless, we have a good reason not to employ them. However, what we are after is not such a reason, but an explanation of why worthless descriptions give rise to contradictions.

But are impredicative descriptions really circular? Consider the proposition that the square root of 2 is the least upper bound of the numbers whose square is at most 2. This is a true identity statement with two descriptions. A certain number is described as the square root of 2 and also as the least upper bound of a certain class of numbers. One may put the matter this way: the notion of *being the square root of 2* and the notion of *being the least upper bound of the numbers whose square is at most 2*, though they are different notions, have the same extension. Obviously, all the different descriptions of a given entity are of this kind; they involve equivalent notions, that is, different notions with the same extension.* Now if an impredicative description is said to be circular because the specification of an entity and its subsequent alternative description involve equivalent notions, then all true identity statements with descriptions would have to be rejected as worthless. Zermelo thinks that this, indeed, is a consequence of Poincaré's criticism of impredicate descriptions. He concludes: "Strict observance of Poincaré's demand [to exclude all impredicative definitions] would make every definition, hence all of science, impossible."[11]

As I see it, though, the alleged circularity does not consist in the fact that the notion of *being the square root of 2* is equivalent to the notion *of being the least upper bound of the numbers whose square is at most 2*, but rather in the fact that the latter contains the notion of *being a number*.† As I interpret Poincaré, the notion of *the square root of 2* must be excluded from the notion of *all numbers* before the latter can be used in the "definition," because the notion of the square root of 2 is to be "defined" and hence must not be presupposed in the

---

* According to my view on descriptions and complex properties, the matter is more complicated. But the point I wish to make here does not require greater accuracy.

† It may contain this notion explicitly or merely implicitly through a restriction of the variable to numbers.

"defining" notion. According to this way of thinking, the notion of *all numbers* includes the notions of individual numbers. In order to have the notion of *all numbers*, one must already have the notion of *the square root of 2*. Hence, it would be circular to explain the latter in terms of the former. In a nutshell, circularity exists because what is to be "defined," the notion of *the square root of 2*, is already contained in one of the "defining" notions, namely, the notion of *all numbers*.

The class of all real numbers, I insisted earlier, includes the square root of 2. Does the notion of *all numbers* similarly include the notion of *the square root of 2*? I do not think so. We shall have to discuss in some of the next sections the various kinds of wholes and parts that play a role in ontological analysis. But at this point it should already be clear that there is no reasonable sense in which the notion of *the square root of 2* is a part of the notion of *all numbers*. Rather, taking for granted that 'all numbers' is merely short for 'all (existent) entities which are numbers,' this notion consists—in a sense that needs amplification—of such notions as *all, entity, exemplification,* and *number.* In order to have the notion of all numbers, one does not have to have the notion of each and every number taken distributively. Nor does one need to have the notion of a particular number, say, of the square root of 2. There may be numbers no one ever thought of; yet the notion of *all numbers* is perfectly clear and definite. And similar considerations hold for such notions as that of *all properties* and that of *all classes.* In these two cases, we need to have, in addition to the notions *all, entity,* and *exemplification*, the notion of *being a property* and the notion of *being a class*, respectively. But we need not have every or even any notion of every property and every or even any notion of every class taken distributively.

It may be objected that we cannot acquire the notion of *number* without having first acquired all the different notions of all individual numbers. But this kind of objection is so obviously mistaken, when applied to other cases, that there is no reason to believe that it works any better for numbers. For example, we come by the notion of, say *canary yellow* without having seen all canary yellow objects. How do we acquire it? The answer seems rather obvious. Some things have the property of being canary yellow, and on some occasion, when we see such a thing, we notice its color. We thus acquire the notion of *canary yellow* through a single perception that a certain object is canary yellow. Similarly, some entities are numbers; they have the property of being a number or, more precisely, they have the property of being a numerical quantifier. We acquire the notion of *being a number* through a single act of recognizing that a certain entity is a number. Of course, we may have to be confronted with a canary yellow object or a number of things on quite a number of occasions, before such acts of recognition occur. But this is an entirely different matter. We must not confuse the fact that it may take some time before a property is recognized with the entirely different fact that the property is recognized in its entirety in a single mental act.

This reply to the objection rests, of course, on the assumption that there are such properties as canary yellow and number. If we maintain instead that the word 'number' does not represent a common characteristic of individual numbers, but functions as a common name, then our reply to Poincaré will not do. According to the doctrine of common names, the word 'number'—if it represents anything— represents commonly or indifferently every individual number. And this may be taken to imply that one cannot fully know what the word represents until one has become acquainted with all individual numbers. It may be taken to mean, for example, that one cannot fully understand the word 'number' in the description of the square root of 2, unless one knows already the square root of 2. So, either one knows the square root of 2, in which case one need not further "define" it, or one does not know it, in which case one cannot "define" it in terms of the notion of *all numbers*; for one does not really have this latter notion.

I have argued elsewhere in some detail that the common name doctrine is unacceptable.[12] The very fact that we talk intelligibly about elephants, for example, without having seen all elephants seems to me to reduce this doctrine to absurdity.[13] Words like 'canary yellow,' 'number,' and 'elephant' do not each name many individual entities commonly, but each represents a single property properly. If so, then it is simply not true that impredicative descriptions are circular. Such descriptions cannot be charged with harboring paradoxes; nor can they be accused of involving circularity.

In closing, a note about (positive) real numbers is appropriate. I implied a few pages back that there exists the square root of 2. This was no ontological slip. According to my ontology, there are in addition to the natural numbers also (positive) rational numbers. It goes without saying that the (positive) rational numbers are not to be construed as classes of any kind but are, just like the natural numbers, quantifiers. The equation '1/2 = 2/4', according to this approach, is merely short for the sentence 'the number which stands in the relation of division to 1 and 2 is the same as the number which stands in this relation to 2 and 4,' and hence expresses a true identity statement with two descriptions. Irrational numbers, too, are quantifiers and not, say, classes of rational numbers. It was discovered rather early that some numbers, for example, the square root of 2, are not rational numbers. It was discovered in other words, that there are numbers other than natural and rational numbers. Dedekind, from this point of view, discovered, among other things, how irrational numbers can be described as determining certain classes of rational numbers.[14] The square root of 2, as a consequence, divides all real numbers into two classes, those that are smaller than it and those that are larger than it. This number can therefore be described either as the largest number of the former or as the smallest number of the latter class. I stress that the square root of 2 divides all real numbers into two classes, not only that it divides all *rationals* into two classes. There can be no talk about filling a "gap" between rational numbers by "postulating" the existence of the square root of 2. We do not, as Dedekind sometimes puts it, "create" the different kinds of numbers piecemeal by first "creating" the rational numbers out of the natural ones and then filling the "gaps" between the rational numbers. Rather, all of the (positive) real numbers exist, but we notice some kinds more than others, and we discover that these kinds can be described in various ways.

PART III

Individuals and Structures

18 WHOLES AND PARTS

There is no sense, I have said, in which the notion of *the square root of 2* is a part of the notion of *all numbers*. Talk about notions—or, as some prefer, concepts—comes quite naturally in this type of context, but is not essential for my point. So let us rephrase the point, for the sake of ontological clarity, and claim that what the expression 'the square root of 2' describes is in no sense a part of what the expression 'all numbers' or the expression 'number' represents. To substantiate this claim, we shall have to investigate in what different senses something can be a part of something else. We must turn to questions like these: What kinds of wholes and what kinds of parts are there? How many different part-whole relations are there, and what are they? In what ways can an entity be analyzed into its constituents? Is there such a thing as ontological analysis?

What kinds of wholes are there? First, an entity may be viewed as a whole consisting of all its properties. The properties of an entity may be said to be its parts.[1] The whole-part relation is then the nexus of exemplification. Notice that I speak of entities in general, not just of individual things, even though individuals are usually the only entities conceived of as wholes in this context. Notice also that if one thinks of an entity as a whole with its properties as parts, there arises the problem of how to accommodate the relations in which the entity stands to other entities. But the problem of the ontological status of relations does not arise only at this point, as Aristotelians often pretend. It lies much deeper; for the nexus of exemplification, the relation between an entity and its properties, is itself a relation among many; and there could be no talk about an entity's being a whole with its properties as parts, unless this particular whole-part relation existed.

Every existing entity exemplifies at least one property and every property is exemplified by at least one existing entity. Here we have a most conspicuous example of an ontological law. That every existing entity exemplifies at least one property may hardly be in doubt for "ordinary" entities. But what about such extraordinary entities as categorial properties? What, in particular, shall we say about the property of being an entity? Since everything is an entity, since everything has this property, the property of being an entity must be itself an entity. Hence it has the property of being an entity. Thus it, too, has a property.

The second conjunct of the ontological law appears far more doubtful; for it seems to be a widely accepted view that there are many properties which are not exemplified. One holds, for example, that there exists the property of being a winged horse, even though it is quite true that there are no winged horses, that is, even though nothing has this property. The properties which are claimed to exist even though they are not exemplified, it must be emphasized, are all complex properties. If there were such things, then they would all, in my view, be represented by complex propositional forms. Now I have already argued that such forms do not represent properties and hence, if my argument was sound, I have already shown that there can be no such complex properties. But we must be quite clear that what our opponent claims in regard to unexemplified properties is far more than merely that some complex propositional forms represent properties. To see this clearly, let us grant for the sake of the argument that there are indeed complex propositional forms which represent properties, namely, those forms which when completed in the appropriate manner yield true sentences. For example, the form 'x is green and x is round' is now assumed to represent a complex property, because there are things which are green and round. What is claimed is not only that forms of this kind represent properties, but that forms like 'x is a horse and x is winged' represent properties as well, even though there is nothing that is both a horse and winged.

We are really considering an extraordinary view, it seems, a view that stands in need of a rather strong argument. Yet the only argument we do find that has any chance of proving the point is the following.[2] It is maintained that the property of being a winged horse exists, because the two properties of being a horse and of having wings exist, and because the property of being a winged horse consists of these two existing properties and a certain logical relation in which they stand to each other. Now it is of course true that these two properties exist, but the question is precisely whether there also exists a further property consisting of these two properties in just this particular combination. Even if we assume, for the sake of the argument, that the two properties and the relation *and* between properties exist, we have no reason to conclude that therefore there exists a further property consisting of these two properties connected by *and*. There may or may not exist this particular complex entity. And when we compare it with, say, the property of being a horse *or* winged, we may very well conclude that while there is this latter property, there exists no such property as the property of being a horse and being winged.

The nexus of exemplification holds between an entity and one of its properties. However, exemplification is not itself and in turn related to the entity which exemplifies the respective property. This is the lasting lesson of Bradley's regress argument, which runs as follows.[3] Assume that A and B stand in the relation R to each other. Since R is connected with A, there must exist a second relation S between R and A. But this means that S is connected with R. Hence there must exist a third relation T which relates S and R. And so on. We seem to be forced to conclude that the existence of a relation R between two entities A and B implies the existence of an infinite number of further relations. But since there clearly do not exist all these further relations, we must conclude that A cannot really be related to B by means of a relation R.

This argument rests on a mistaken premise. It assumes that in order for any two entities to be related to each other, there must exist a relation between them. The argument does not show that A and B cannot be related by R, but rather that this assumption is false. It is not true that there must exist a relation between *any* two entities, if these entities are related to each other. What is true is merely that there must exist such a relation if neither of the two entities is itself a relation. What Bradley's argument shows is that there is one category, the category of relation, such that its members can relate without being related to what they relate.* It shows that there is a kind of entity

* There seem to be some exceptions to this ontological law. For example,

which is the glue that binds all other entities. Continuing the metaphor, we may say that just as glue does not need to be glued to what it holds together, so relations require no further relations in order to be connected to what they connect.

It may be objected that properties are "unsaturated" entities which can "connect" with objects without there being a relation. It is usually taken for granted that this objection derives what thrust it has from the soundness of Frege's distinction between unsaturated concepts (functions) and saturated objects. Quite so. But by the same token, it lacks, as does Frege's distinction, clarity and definite sense. There are a number of possible interpretations of Frege's notion of unsaturatedness.[4] But none of these interpretations furnishes any argument for the objection just raised, namely, that properties can be exemplified by entities without having to be related to them. After everything is said and done about Frege's distinction, the metaphor about the unsaturatedness of properties remains a metaphor, a fanciful way of saying, without argument, that properties need not be related to the entities which have them. Thus the common practice of referring to Frege is pointless; we must demand an argument.* Assume that A has the property F, while B has the property G. It seems obvious to me that in this case A is somehow related to the property F and B is in the same fashion related to G. To be sure, the fact that A "goes together" with F, while B "belongs together" with G can be depicted in many different ways. In English we have the common copula 'is' or the word 'has' in connection with 'property'; and we also have the extraordinary expressions which I just used. Furthermore, in a written artificial language, exemplification can be represented by juxtaposition or by any one of a number of spatial arrangements. But in some way or another we have to be able to express that A *has* the property F and that B *has* the property G. We have to be able to express the fact that there exists a relation between A and F which is distinct from other relations and which holds whenever an entity has a property.

---

negation, it seems, can "attach" to a state of affairs without there being a relation between it and the state of affairs. I say "seems," because I do not really know of an argument to this effect.

    * It is well to remember that Frege quite often talks about the falling-under relation.

So much about entities conceived of as wholes which consist of properties. Second, in a parallel vein classes may be thought of as wholes. Their members, then, are their parts, and the part-whole relation is that of class membership.

Third, numbers may be said to be wholes consisting of other numbers as their parts. For example, one can think of the number 5 as a whole consisting of the two numbers 3 and 2. It also consists, of course, of 4 and 1. Furthermore, since the number 2 consists, in the same sense of the term, of the number 1, and since 3 consists of 2 and 1, it may be said that 5 consists, but now in a slightly different sense, of 1s.* The way in which 5 consists of 2 and 3 is to be explicated, as is obvious, in terms of the sum relation. In our example, the sum relation is the whole-part relation. A number is called a whole insofar as it is the sum of two numbers; these two numbers are called its parts. This is all there is to this notion. A similar mode of expression may be adopted for other arithmetical relations among numbers. This part-whole conception of numbers is as commonsensical as it is philosophically harmless if it is properly explicated in terms of arithmetical relations.

Fourth, facts may be viewed as complex entities consisting of parts. I shall call the part-whole relation in which an entity stands to the fact of which it is a part *the relation of being a constituent of.* In this sense, numbers are constituents of facts, individuals are constituents of facts, quantifiers are constituents of facts, etc. Since there are complex facts, facts can be constituents of other facts. Moreover, it is clear that every existing entity is either a fact or a constituent of a fact. Hence, if we wish to know what kinds of entities there are, we must survey the constituents of facts and group these constituents from an ontological viewpoint. Ontological analysis consists in part, we may say, in the analysis of facts into their constituents according to categories.† We do not list helter-skelter all different constituents of all known facts, but try to discover interesting kinds, categories, of constituents. With the great variety of different constituents before us, we try to group these constituents into philosophically interesting classes. The

---

* This is an awkward way of putting it, but I do not think that one has to be misled into believing that there are literally several number 1s, several 2s, etc.

† In addition to listing all the categories and subcategories, we are, of course, also interested in discovering the laws which hold for these kinds of entities.

categories, then, are the most general properties of constituents of facts. In the search for categories, we are of course guided by the philosophical tradition. We are not tempted to divide the entities of the world into, say, entities which grow hair and entities which do not. There is nothing inherently wrong with such a division; it is simply not an interesting one, because it sheds no light on the traditional philosophical problems.

There is one traditional notion about ontology of which we must rid ourselves, no matter how firmly it is planted among our beliefs. I am talking about the notion that only simple entities exist or that, at any rate, ontology is interested only in what there is in the way of simple entities. Nothing could be further from the truth nor from the spirit of the ontological enterprise. Surely, classes exist just as much as their members, facts just as much as their constituents, and spatial structures just as much as their parts. What may be responsible for this idea that ontology is interested only in simple entities is a confused conception of ontological analysis derived from some unsatisfactory notion of definitional reduction.

Fifth, the paradigm of a whole, however, is neither that of an entity consisting of its properties, nor that of a class, a number, or a fact. There are, in addition to these kinds of entities, also what I shall call structures. The most obvious structures consist of spatial and/or temporal individuals. I shall therefore try to elucidate this most important notion of whole mainly by describing spatio-temporal entities.

What we ordinarily call individual things or individual objects are spatio-temporal structures consisting of spatio-temporal individuals. For example, a chessboard, a table, a ship, a mountain—these are all examples of spatio-temporal structures. There are also structures which consist of temporal individuals only. A melody is such a structure, for example. Consider the chessboard as our prime example. It consists of sixty-four (simple) squares. Each of these squares is a spatial part of the chessboard. There exists a relation, the relation of being a spatial part of, between each one of these squares and the whole chessboard. We might say that this is a relation between two individual things, the square and the chessboard, for we may call—for reasons which will become clear in a moment—a structure consisting of individuals an individual thing.

Each of the squares is a spatial part of the chessboard. The squares, however, are not parts of each other, but stand in different spatial relations to each other. The squares in this case are also contiguous to each other. But there are structures whose spatial parts are not contiguous; for example, five circles arranged at a certain distance from each other form a spatial structure. Nor are spatial relations all there is to space. There exist also spatial properties, namely, shapes and sizes. The chessboard does not only consist spatially of squares, it does not only stand in certain spatial relations to other spatial individuals, it has also a certain size.* What holds for the chessboard, holds for all spatial things. Indeed, to speak of a spatial thing is to speak of an entity which has spatial properties and stands in spatial relations to other things. Thus space is neither absolute nor is it wholly relative. It is not absolute in the sense that there are no individual places; properties and relations exhaust the spatial inventory. It is not wholly relative in the sense that there are, in addition to spatial relations, also spatial properties.

Similarly for time. There exist, in my view, no temporal individuals, no (absolute) moments. Time consists of temporal relations and temporal properties. A temporal individual does not only stand in certain temporal relations to other temporal things; it also has a duration. Just as two individuals may have the same shape, so two individuals may have the same duration. Time is therefore not purely relational. Furthermore, just as a spatial structure consists of spatial parts, so a temporal structure consists of temporal parts. The chessboard, for example, consists temporally of other temporal individuals; one of these temporal parts is, for instance, the chessboard before its black squares were repainted. This sounds awkward, but we have little choice in the matter, because the temporal parts of chessboards—unlike, for example, certain temporal parts of persons—have no particular names. We usually have to talk about the chessboard

* The spatial property of being square, for example, cannot be "defined" away in the familiar fashion by saying that a square is a rectangle with four equal sides. 'Square' is not an abbreviation for the longer expression. Rather, what is here, as usual, disguised as a definition is a geometrical truth, namely, the true equivalence that something is a square if and only if it is a plane figure bounded by four equal sides which stand at right angles to each other. As obvious as this equivalence may be, it is not an abbreviational truth.

before or after such and such happened to it. But the point should be clear: A temporal part of a temporal structure is in turn an individual thing, different from the individual of which it is a part, and yet a most intimate (temporal) part of the structure, because of the temporal part-whole relation in which it stands to the whole.

Just as the spatial parts of things can and do have properties which their wholes do not have, so temporal parts of individuals have properties which their temporal wholes do not have. Some of the squares of the chessboard are black, but the chessboard itself is not black. The black squares of the chessboard, before it was repainted, looked rather faded, but the same cannot be said of these black squares throughout their existence. To mention another example, the car that has been painted green after it had been blue is neither green nor blue. Rather, a certain temporal part of it is blue, another temporal part of it is green, and the former is earlier than the later.

If all structures were spatio-temporal in nature, we could simply distinguish between simple and complex individuals. A square of the chessboard, assuming that it is not further divided, would be a spatially simple individual; the chessboard, on the other hand, would be a spatially complex individual. This possibility arises, because all wholes which consist of spatio-temporal individuals are themselves spatio-temporal entities. These wholes, as well as their parts, have spatio-temporal characteristics. An individual, according to this possible explication, is a thing which has spatial and/or temporal characteristics, irrespective of whether or not it consists of further spatio-temporal entities. The notion of structure would then lose its importance; it would not have to be listed as a category side by side with individual, property, class, quantifier, etc. But there are also structures which do not consist of individual things. For example, numbers form such diverse structures as series, groups, rings, fields, and lattices. There are also structures consisting of properties; for example, the structure of the color solid arranged by hue, lightness, and saturation. Moreover, these structures do not have the same characteristics as their constituents. For example, the series of natural numbers does not stand in the sum relation to anything, and the color solid does not have a hue. These structures, unlike spatio-temporal ones, are entities of quite a different sort from their constituents. The series of natural numbers, for instance, is not itself a natural number. And this is the reason why the notion of structure acquires ontological importance, why it has to be ranked as one of the basic categories.

Structures, it is clear, resemble classes in that we can group them according to their nonrelational parts. Just as we can distinguish between classes of individuals, classes of properties, classes of quantifiers, etc., so we can distinguish between structures consisting of individuals, structures consisting of properties, structures consisting of quantifiers, etc. But structures differ from classes in that their parts stand in certain characteristic relations to each other. What distinguishes the series of natural numbers from the class of natural numbers, if I may so put it, is the relation of being smaller (or equal) between natural numbers. Of course, we must beware of identifying the series just mentioned with the class consisting of the natural numbers together with the relation of being smaller than, just as we must not confuse the chessboard with the class of its squares together with the relations between the squares. A list of the parts of any whole, be it a whole of properties, a class, a number, a fact, or a structure, is simply a class of entities. But this class must not be identified—except, of course, in the case where the whole is a class itself—with the whole of which its members are parts.

Let us return to the beginning. What motivated our inquiry into the nature of wholes and parts was the claim that there is no sense in which the square root of 2 is a part of all numbers. I hope to have made good this claim. More importantly, though, I hope to have shown that, among the various notions of whole, that of a structure is the most important, and that structures form an important category.

19   A   PROBLEM   OF   PERCEPTION

A structure is not identical with the class of its parts, not even if this class contains the relations between the parts. A spatial individual is not to be identified with the class of its spatial parts and spatial relations. To see this, one merely has to recognize the fact that such a spatial individual stands in spatial relations to other spatial entities, while a class—any class—is not a spatial entity at all. Classes have neither shape nor (spatial) size; and they do not stand in spatial relations to other entities.

In order to emphasize that structures are not classes of parts, a lesson from the theory of perception may not be out of place. Recall Husserl's much touted theory of *noemata* as profiles or aspects of perceptual objects.[1] Assume that there occurs a mental act of seeing whose intention is the state of affairs represented by the sentence 'This is an inkstand'. Assume, in other words, that you see that this is an inkstand (before you). According to Husserl's analysis, this single act of seeing presents you with only a certain aspect of the inkstand. What you really see in this situation is the front of the inkstand, one spatial part of it; its back and its side are hidden from you. However, from another standpoint, you may see, in another single act of perception, the rear of the inkstand. But now its front will be hidden from you. Even though you intend the same inkstand on both occasions, you see different aspects of it. No single perceptual act ever presents you with the whole perceptual object. You never see the inkstand as a whole.

The same view is expressed by G. E. Moore: "Nobody will suppose, for a moment, that when he judges such things as "This is a sofa," or "This is a tree," he is judging with regard to the presented object, about which his judgment plainly is, that it is a *whole* sofa or a *whole* tree: he can, at most, suppose that he is judging it to be *a part of the surface* of a sofa or *a part of the surface* of a tree."[2]

Are we then to believe Husserl and Moore, who claim that when we see that this is an inkstand, we are not seeing an inkstand but seeing a part of an inkstand instead? Surely, we do see an inkstand on such an occasion. Moore tries to overcome our reluctance to embrace his view by appealing to Russell's famous distinction between knowledge by acquaintance and knowledge by description. According to Moore, the inkstand is not known by acquaintance but rather by description. What one is literally acquainted with, what one sees in the literal sense, is a part of the inkstand. What one sees is not the state of affairs *This is an inkstand*, but rather the state of affairs *There is a thing which is an inkstand and of which this is a part*. In a sense, therefore, the perception is both a perception of an inkstand and a perception of a part of an inkstand. In this manner Moore tries to reassure us that we were partially right when we so stubbornly insisted that our perception is a perception of an inkstand. It is a perception of an inkstand, he maintains, but only *by means of* the perception of part of the inkstand. What one really and truly sees in the situation, what one is acquainted with, is still merely a part of the inkstand, not the whole inkstand. And Moore adds (a case of whistling in the dark, one suspects, for the champion of commonsense) that all this seems to him so clear that he wonders how anyone can deny it; and that perhaps nobody would.[3]

Husserl's and Moore's view comes down to this. First, when we think we perceive that this is an inkstand, we really perceive that this is part of something which is an inkstand. Second, we never, therefore, perceive the inkstand as such, but merely perceive parts of it. Third, what we therefore perceive, the *this*, is not an inkstand, but is part of an inkstand.

All three assertions, I think, are false. To start with the last point first, it seems quite absurd to maintain that we are literally mistaken when we see or say that *this* is an inkstand. It seems quite absurd to maintain that we mistake in such perceptions the front of the inkstand for the whole inkstand. We clearly do no such thing. We know very well the distinction between the whole inkstand and its front; and we do not see or judge that the front is an inkstand when we see or judge that this is an inkstand. When we truly see that that is the front of an inkstand, we are seeing quite a different thing from what we see when we see that *this* is an inkstand. Hence it is also not the case that whenever we presumably see that this is an inkstand, we see in reality something quite different, namely, that this is part of an inkstand. To see the one state of affairs is not to see the other; when we see the one, we do not see the other; we can see, on different occasions, both states of affairs; and we know which one it is we are seeing. Finally, since to perceive that this is an inkstand is not the same as to perceive that this is part of an inkstand, and since we are not mistaken in thinking that this is an inkstand, we do really and truly perceive inkstands, not just their parts.

Granted that Husserl's and Moore's position is untenable, are we not merely faced with the other horn of a dilemma? How can we possibly reconcile our assertion that we see perceptual objects and not just their parts with the plain fact that whenever we see a perceptual object, we do not see its rear, its inside, and so on? If it is unpalatable to hold with Husserl and Moore that we do not see perceptual objects, but only their parts, then it seems to be at least equally unpalatable to hold that we can see the whole perceptual object in one act of perception. But there is no dilemma. We do not have to choose. It is equally true, first, that we see perceptual objects and, second, that we do not see whole perceptual objects. Husserl and Moore mistakenly think that it follows from the fact that we cannot see the whole inkstand that we cannot see the inkstand. But this is not so; for to see the whole inkstand means in this context to see all the parts of the inkstand, and from the fact that we do not see all the parts of the inkstand in one act of perception, it does not follow that we do not see the inkstand in one act of perception. To see all the parts of the inkstand is not the same as to see that this is an inkstand, but rather to see first this side of it, then the back of it, then the inside of it, and so on; and we can see that this is an inkstand without first seeing this side of the inkstand, then the other side of the inkstand, then the inside of the inkstand, and so on. In brief, we can see the inkstand without having to see, first, all its parts.

But can we? The plain facts of perceptual experience show that we can. We see that this is an inkstand without having seen its back, without being able to tell what its rear looks like. Why would anyone think differently? Why would anyone brush the perceptual facts aside and conclude that we cannot see a perceptual object in a single act, since we cannot see all its parts in a single act? Well, if the perceptual object were nothing more than the sum total of its parts, then it would follow that one cannot see the object, unless one sees all its parts. The structural source of Husserl's and Moore's view, I submit, consists in their belief that a perceptual object is nothing but the class of all its parts, including the relational ones.

But the inkstand is a spatial structure. It is not a class, and in particular it is not the class of all the parts of the structure, including the relational ones. Hence, even if it is true—as I shall assume for the sake of the argument—that one cannot perceive a class of entities unless one perceives all the elements of the class, it does not follow that one cannot perceive the inkstand unless one perceives all of its parts.

A moment ago, I spoke of the *sum total* of the parts of the inkstand. Then I identified this sum total with a class. Could the expression mean anything else in this context and at the same time make sense? Of course, it could mean structure. To speak loosely about the sum total of certain parts would be, in more precise terminology, to speak about structures consisting of certain parts. If it does mean this, however, then there is no reason to assume that we cannot perceive a spatial structure unless we perceive all its parts, and all the perceptual facts, as I have tried to point out, speak actually against this assumption. What else could one mean by *'sum total'* and similar expressions? I can think of one more possibility. To say that the inkstand is nothing more than the sum total of its parts (always including the relational ones) may mean that it is identical with the thing which has such and such spatial parts standing in such and such relations to each other. One may mean to convey, in other words, that the inkstand is identical with something which is described in terms of its spatial parts and their mutual relations. But once more, from the fact that the inkstand is something which stands in the spatial whole-part relation to certain spatial entities which are spatially related to each other in certain ways, one cannot deduce that we cannot perceive the inkstand unless we perceive all of its parts. This follows as little from the description in spatial terms as it follows from a description in terms of properties that one cannot perceive a thing unless one perceives all of these properties. The opposite view arises, one may suspect, because the spatial part-whole relation is confused with some other kind of relation. Such confusion is of course invited by our ordinary way of talking about the inkstand as *consisting* of such and such parts, of *being made up* of these parts, etc.

This brief excursion was meant to underscore an ontological point. Structures in general and spatio-temporal structures in particular must under no circumstances be identified with classes, not even with classes that contain the relations holding between the parts of the structures. Structures and classes form two distinct categories.

20 BUNDLES OF PROPERTIES

Some structures consist of individuals. Such structures are then themselves spatial and/or temporal in character. We can therefore speak of simple and complex individuals. From now on, an individual is to be

understood as any spatial and/or temporal thing, regardless of whether
it is an individual proper or a structure consisting of proper individuals.

As so understood, individuals are different from classes, not only
from classes of spatio-temporal parts, but also from classes of
properties. The properties which an individual exemplifies are not
members or elements of it. To say that an individual consists of
properties or that properties are constituents of it can only mean that
the individual exemplifies these properties; under no circumstances
must it be taken to mean that the properties are members of the
individual, so that the individual turns out to be a class.[1] But if
individuals are not classes of properties, neither are they structures of
properties. The properties which an individual exemplifies are not parts
of it. An individual may have other individuals as parts; its properties,
though, are never parts of it. The relation which an individual has to its
properties is neither that of a class to its members nor that of a
structure to its parts. Unfortunately, though, these different whole-part
relations are often confused with each other, particularly when one
attempts to reduce individuals to bundles of properties.

Consider a square, A, a circle, B, and assume that A is red while B
is green. In this situation, there exist at least the following entities: two
individual things, namely, A and B; four properties of individuals,
namely, two colors and two shapes; the nexus of exemplification which
connects the individuals with their respective properties; various facts
like the fact that A is square, the fact that B is green, etc. I say that
there exist at least these entities, because there also exist others—like
the number 2 and the connective *and*—but I shall disregard all others
for the moment.

Recall now the classical argument against the existence of
material substances. Although it is directed against material substances,
it applies just as well to individual things, even though the individual
things of our ontology are not substances in the Aristotelian sense—
they have no natures, for example. Let us therefore pretend that
Berkeley meant to attack, not only material substances as understood
by him and his contemporaries, but also individual things in our sense.
Berkeley then contends that we are not acquainted with individual
things, that we never actually perceive an individual thing.[2] According
to him, we do indeed perceive properties like colors and shapes, but we

do not perceive the individual things in which these properties are said to inhere.* But this contention seems to be quite obviously false. It is true that we see colors and shapes, but it is equally true that we also see the things which have these properties. We do not merely see in our example, as Berkeley maintains, the colors red and green and the shapes square and circular, but we also see the two individuals, A and B, which have these properties. What makes Berkeley think otherwise?

We may speculate that he arrived at his position by focusing on Locke's notion of substance as the unknowable support of properties. Locke characterized substances as follows: "The idea then we have, to which we give the general name substance, being nothing but the supposed, but unknown, support of those qualities we find existing, which we imagine cannot subsist *sine re substante*, without something to support them, we call that support substantia; which, according to the true import of the word, is, in plain English, standing under or upholding."[3] Now, if substances were indeed unknowable, then they would justly be suspect; and Berkeley's attitude would be vindicated. But why does Locke believe that they are unknowable? Perhaps he reasoned that a substance, being that entity which has all its properties, can have no property by and of itself. We cannot possibly know a substance, according to this line of reasoning, since it is to be distinguished from everything that is knowable about it, namely, its properties.[4]

What does it mean to know something? If we can be said to know the entities with which we are acquainted, then I reassert that we know individual things. In this sense, I clearly know the square A, because I see it. And if to know something means to know something about the relevant entity, that is, to know that it has this or that property (or relation to other entities), then it is again true that we know individual things, for we know what properties they have. For example, I know the individual thing B, because I know that it is circular. I even know that it has the categorial property of being an individual. What kind of entity exemplifies such properties as colors, shapes, pitches, etc.? The

* Of course, Berkeley is also a nominalist, so that it is false to speak here of properties in our sense of the word. But I shall, for the sake of the present discussion, neglect this important side of the issue.

kind that shares the common categorial property of being an individual. Nor need we be ignorant about this category. We can discover laws that hold for individuals in general.

Locke compares us with an Indian who thinks that the world is supported by an elephant, the elephant by a tortoise, and the tortoise by something he knows not what. He believes that we do not know individual things any better than the Indian knows what supports the tortoise. But this comparison is all wrong, as we have just seen, if to know something means either to be acquainted with it or to know something about it. One suspects that Locke's view is the result of a rather peculiar notion of what it means to know something. According to this notion, when one knows that a certain entity has a certain property, one can only be said to know the property but not the entity which has the property. For example, to know that A is square is to know the property square but not the individual A. If we accept this peculiar notion, then it is of course as impossible to know an individual thing as it is to wash the fur without wetting it. But there is absolutely no reason why we should accept it.

Berkeley, however, accepts Locke's characterization of substance as the unknowable support of properties and relies on it in order to deny the existence of material substances. The square A of our paradigm, according to Berkeley, is not an individual thing but, rather, a collection of properties.[5] What is a collection?

The most obvious answer is that collections are classes. If so, then our individual things turn out to be classes of properties, according to Berkeley's ontology.[6] The two individuals of our example, A and B, are really the two classes [square, red] and [circular, green]. To say that A is red comes down to saying that red is an element of the class A^*, where 'A^*' is the name of the class [square, red]. Exemplification is supplanted by class membership.

But if this is Berkeley's view, why would he believe that the class A^* is any less "transcendental," or any more "knowable" than the individual thing A? The class A^* is one entity, its members—the various properties of A—are quite different entities. Presumably, one knows the properties of A, that is, a certain shape and a certain color. We do not know, according to Locke's and Berkeley's line of reasoning, anything else but the properties. Or do we? According to Locke, we may at least infer that there must be something else which supports these properties.

But if this inference is spurious, as Berkeley claims, why is it acceptable to infer instead that there must be a class to which these properties belong? The class A^* is in the same boat with the individual A if one accepts Locke's and Berkeley's controversial view that we know only the properties of things; and so, indeed, is any other type of entity whether we call it a "bundle" of properties, a "collection" of properties, an "aggregate" of properties, a "sum" of properties, or what have you. If we can know nothing but properties, then we cannot know bundles or collections of properties. And if we cannot infer that there must be something that supports these properties, then we cannot infer that there must be something of which these properties are elements or members.

This objection is directed against Berkeley's substitution of "unknowable" collections for "unknowable" individuals. But it is clear, at any rate, that individuals cannot be classes of properties; for not every such class "yields" an individual. Since there exist, in our example, the color green and the color red, there also exists the class consisting of these two colors. Yet there exists no corresponding individual. Again, there exists the class consisting of the color red and the shape circular, but there exists, by hypothesis, no red circle. The ontological reduction of individuals to classes of properties fails for this reason alone.

What happens if we add a relation of association to the ontological inventory and identify an ordinary object with the structure consisting of its properties and the relation of association between these properties? The structure consisting of the two properties square and red and the relation of association between them would then be said to form the object A. On the other hand, the two properties red and green do not form an object, because they are not associated with each other. This gambit, however, does not only add a new and fundamental relation to the ontological list, it also introduces a new category, namely, that of structure. Since this kind of structure consists not of spatio-temporal individuals but, rather, of the properties of a thing, I shall call it a bundle from now on. Another way, then, of looking at Berkeley's proposed substitution of collections of properties for material substances is to think of it as a substitution of bundles for such substances. Since we have agreed to conceive of substances in the present context as individuals in our sense, we can also put it this way:

Berkeley's move may be construed as an attempt to substitute bundles, that is, structures of properties, for complex individuals, that is, structures of spatio-temporal individuals. At any rate, it is obvious that the substitution of bundles for individuals neither reduces one's ontology nor dissolves the alleged mystery of how one can be acquainted with anything else but properties. And Berkeley seems to have thought that by denying material substances and affirming the existence of collections of properties he had achieved a great ontological feat!

Thus far we have discussed the attempt to reduce individual things to bundles of properties in connection with Berkeley's criticism of material substances. Let us now turn to a modern version of this ontological approach. I have in mind Goodman's construction of individuals out of properties.[7]

Goodman's endeavor is motivated by a rejection of individuals as well as an aversion to classes. The basis for his rejection of individuals is as follows: "Since a realistic system treats all individuals as made up of qualities, it might be regarded as founded upon the principle that all differences are intensive. The principle is not peculiar to the realistic approach, for the notion of sheer undifferentiated quantity seems hardly intelligible from any point of view."[8] What does Goodman mean by this rather cryptic remark? Perhaps he means to say that any two individuals differ in some property (including relations) or another? If so, then I fail to see how this fact, assuming that it is a fact, shows that there are no individuals in addition to properties or that the notion of an individual is unintelligible. Quite to the contrary, this very fact presupposes the existence of individuals. Or, perhaps, Goodman has some kind of Lockean argument in mind according to which individuals are unknowable when they are thought of as stripped of all their properties. Be that as it may, Goodman's reason for declaring classes incomprehensible is much clearer.

Consider again our paradigm of a spatial whole, the earlier mentioned chessboard consisting of sixty-four squares. This chessboard consists also of sixteen blocks of four squares each. Each of these blocks, as I shall call them, is as truly a spatial part of the board as each square is. Each block in turn is a spatial structure; it, too, consists of squares. Notice now the following differences between classes and membership, on the one hand, and spatial structures and the spatial part relationship, on the other. (1) The class of sixty-four squares has as its elements the squares. It does not consist, for example, of the sixteen blocks mentioned earlier. But, of course, there is also a different class, the class of all blocks, which consists of these blocks. The spatial structure, on the other hand, has as its spatial parts not only the squares, but also the blocks. The entity formed by the squares is the very same spatial structure as the entity formed by the blocks.* (2) A member of the class of squares is not itself a class. An element of a class need not be a class. Of course, there are also classes of classes, but the elements of the class of squares are individual things. On the other hand, a spatial part of a spatial structure may itself be a spatial structure. For example, each block is a spatial structure consisting of spatial parts. (3) Finally, compare the class of sixty-four squares with the class whose elements are the sixteen classes each of which consists of four squares forming a block. These are two different classes. Yet the "ultimate" elements of the two classes are the same. On the other hand, the spatial structure consisting of the sixty-four squares and the spatial structure consisting of the sixteen blocks each of four squares are one and the same entity.

Goodman cannot endure classes. "In the nominalist's world," he says, "if we start from any two distinct entities and break each of them down as far as we like (by taking parts, parts of parts, and so on), we always arrive at some entity that is contained in one but not the other of our two original entities. In the platonist's world, on the contrary, there are at least two different entities that we can so break down (by taking members, members of members, and so on) as to arrive at exactly the same entities."[9] In brief, Goodman objects that classes, in distinction to spatial wholes, could differ even though they have the same "ultimate content," and that such entities are unintelligible.

Goodman's aversion seems to stem from his vague notions of content, of breaking an entity down, of what an entity is made up of, etc. It is quite true that if we start with two different spatial structures and analyze them into spatial parts, we will eventually find a spatial entity which is a spatial part of one structure but not of the other. But

---

* This is to say that the following identity statement is true: The spatial structure which has the sixty-four squares as parts is the same as the structure which has the sixteen blocks as parts.

the same does not hold true for an entirely and radically different kind of whole, namely, classes. If we analyze two distinct classes into their "ultimate" members, we may discover that these members are the same. Nor should this difference come as a surprise; for the notion of analysis is quite different in these two cases. Classes have no spatial parts and cannot therefore be spatially analyzed; spatial individuals, on the other hand, have no members and cannot therefore be analyzed into elements. Goodman, it seems, starts out with some rather vague but very general notions of whole, part, and analysis, but implicitly or explicitly fastens onto the spatial meanings of these terms and decides that they are the only intelligible ones. Consequently, he finds it incomprehensible that classes should behave differently from spatial wholes. I find it, though not incomprehensible, at least hard to believe that classes should behave exactly like spatial structures. I find it hard to believe that the two classes mentioned earlier, the class of sixty-four squares and the class whose members are the class of four squares each, could differ in an "ultimate" member. If we take our cue from the behavior of classes, we may just as well argue that there are no spatial structures; for, since it is obvious that two classes may differ without difference in their ultimate content, it must be false that there are wholes which cannot differ unless there is a difference in ultimate content. From the many different kinds of wholes and corresponding part-whole relations, Goodman selects the spatial case and proclaims that it is the only intelligible one. More precisely, he insists that there is only one "generating relation" and that this relation must resemble the spatial part-whole relation rather than, say, the (ancestral of the) membership relation.

So much about Goodman's argument against the existence of classes. What does he propose to put in their stead? In particular, since an individual cannot be the class of its properties if there are no classes, how does he conceive of an individual? All technical details aside, and disregarding some of Goodman's more idiosyncratic appraisals of his own method and commitments, individual things turn out to be bundles of properties. Goodman's ontology, whether he thinks so or not, comprises, in addition to properties, structures consisting of properties. Hence it also contains—again whether he admits it or not—a characteristic part-structure relation and a relation of association between properties. Since we admit—indeed, insist—that there are structures, why do we reject Goodman's ontological analysis of individual things?

First, Goodman's solution to the problem of individuation turns out to be unsatisfactory. Consider the red square A. According to Goodman, A consists not only of the two properties red and square, but it contains also a place and moment. Every spatio-temporal individual, in his view, contains in addition to certain other properties a spatial property, a place, and a temporal property, a moment. Let us neglect the temporal aspect for the sake of simplicity and discuss only places. Goodman's analysis fails because these places are supposed to be properties. Yet it is, presumably, ontologically impossible for two individuals to contain the same place. But anything which has this characteristic ought to be excluded from the category of property; for properties are such—ontologically speaking—that they can be exemplified by more than one individual. Thus, if there are places, they cannot possibly be properties, but must belong to a different category. Of course, we would categorize them as individuals, but that would be incompatible with the spirit of Goodman's analysis. Aside from the fact that places would have to be individuals rather than properties, there is the decisive fact that places simply do not exist. Nobody, I am convinced, is ever acquainted with a mere place, a mere spatial individual. We perceive spatial relations and we perceive such spatial properties as shapes and sizes, but we do not perceive, in addition, spatial individuals.

Second, there exists no such relation as the relation of association between properties of the same individual. This is not to deny that properties may form structures by virtue of standing in certain relations to each other. I mentioned earlier the color solid as an example of a structure of colors. The parts of this structure form a whole because they stand in certain relations to each other. There is, for example, such a relation as that of *being lighter than* among colors. But there is no relation of association between the properties of an individual. Of course, red and square are both exemplified by A, as we would say, but there is no relation between red and square of the assumed kind. What suggests the existence of such a relation is the mistaken view that the expression 'being jointly exemplified by A' represents a relation. Red is indeed exemplified by A, and so is square, but there does not exist, in addition, the relation between red and square of being jointly exemplified by A. Similarly, even if red were a part of the bundle A and square were a part of this bundle, there would not necessarily exist, in addition to the relation of being a part of a bundle, also the relation of being jointly parts of the same bundle. In brief, neither direct acquaintance nor argument shows that the properties of an entity are connected with each other by a unique relation of association.

For these two main reasons, we consider the ontological assay of individual things as bundles of properties mistaken.

21 SPATIAL VERSUS ONTOLOGICAL ANALYSIS

Spatial analysis, it is obvious, must not be confused with ontological analysis. The chessboard we talked about is a structure consisting of spatial parts which stand in certain spatial relations to each other. Some of these parts—rows and blocks of squares, for example—are themselves spatial structures. Other parts, the sixty-four squares, are spatial individuals. Therefore, all the spatial parts of the chessboard consist ultimately of spatial individuals. If one of the sixty-four squares is divided into four even smaller squares, then it is again a structure that consists of individuals. And so on. Every spatial structure, in short, is ultimately composed of spatial individuals which stand in spatial relations to each other, so that, no matter how far we proceed with a spatial analysis, we shall never discover anything else but (a) spatial structures, (b) spatial individuals, and (c) spatial relations. There are no other subcategories involved. Thus all the ontological simples, all the subcategories, involved in a spatial object can already be discovered in connection with the chessboard. We need go no further in our ontological analysis. Spatial division will yield smaller and smaller spatial individuals, but it will not yield simpler and simpler ontological kinds. It will not yield new categories. Yet so pervasive is the notion of spatial analysis that it has at times been confused with ontological analysis. Wittgenstein is a case in point. This section is about his unsuccessful search for ontological simples and his eventual rejection of the very idea of the search itself.

Wittgenstein, in his later philosophy, seems to hold the view that there is no such thing as ontological analysis and that there are no such things as ontological simples.[1] It is commonly claimed that he shows in the *Investigations* that there is no such thing as absolute complexity and absolute simplicity.[2] Something may be called simple or complex only relative to a certain purpose, a certain point of view, or in regard to a certain comparison. Whether something is simple or complex depends entirely on the context in which it is considered.[3] This later rejection of absolute complexity and absolute simplicity is at the same time interpreted as a rejection of the program of the *Tractatus* and Wittgenstein's earlier writings in which he tried to discover what he then called the simple objects of logic and what I shall call the ontological simples.* But Wittgenstein's later attitude may also be viewed as a direct consequence of his inability to find the logical simples he was looking for. And this inability, as I shall briefly show, is due in part to his confusing spatial with ontological analysis.

What are the ontological simples? This is one of the main questions of Wittgenstein's *Notebooks*.[4] In his characteristic manner, he tries out a whole series of answers. His starting point, his paradigm of a complex entity, could well be our chessboard; for he speaks of parts of his visual field, and it is quite clear that he has spatial parts in mind. His examples of simple entities are spatial points (of the visual field).[5] With this notion of what it means to be complex and what it means to be simple, he immediately runs into all sorts of problems in his quest to discover what he calls the logical simples. Small wonder; for spatial simplicity just is not the same as ontological simplicity. Or is it?

The main problem which he observes is this. The chessboard as a paradigm of complexity cannot only be analyzed into the various white and black squares, but these entities can presumably be further analyzed into smaller and smaller spatial parts, until we arrive at points.[6] But if the chessboard consists of points, then there may be

---

* In general, the philosophy of *logical* atomism might as well be called the philosophy of *ontological* atomism.

infinitely many such points and it may become impossible to give a complete analysis of the chessboard.[7] Furthermore, since we do not literally see these ultimate points, how can we be sure that it really does consist of such points?

Wittgenstein is firmly convinced that such entities as a chessboard, a pencil stroke, and a steamship are paradigms of the kind of logical complexity he is after. Such is the hold of the mistaken notion that analysis must be spatial analysis. On the other hand, he also notices that such things are not commonly treated as logical complexes.[8] It does not seem to be a mere trick of language that we can refer to such things by means of simple names.[9] Perhaps, Wittgenstein muses, a square of the chessboard is a simple entity insofar as we do not perceive any single point of it separately.[10] At any rate, he is also inclined to believe that the fact that we can represent spatial things by simple names speaks against their being complex. This second theme in his deliberations clashes with his identification of analysis with spatial analysis.

Wittgenstein tries to resolve this conflict in various ways. He suggests at one point that the whole question of whether or not there are simple entities is nonsense.[11] In another place he considers the possibility that simplicity is a relative notion, thus anticipating his later view.[12] But he really seems to favor the following view. The quest for analysis makes sense, even though we are not acquainted with simple entities in perception; for we are acquainted with complex entities—for example, chessboards—and we are also acquainted with simpler parts of such entities—for instance, squares of chessboards. Thus we can know simple objects "by description," as it were, as the end product of analysis.[13] The idea of a simple entity, in other words, is somehow contained in the two ideas of a complex entity and of analysis.[14] Of course, this leaves the question open whether there really are simple entities. Perhaps there is no limit to analysis. Wittgenstein rejects this possibility on the ground that if there were no simple entities, then the world would have to be indefinite and could not have the specific structure which it has.[15] At other places he argues that if there were no simple entities, then sentences about things could not have a definite sense.[16] But these reasons remain rather obscure, as obscure as his argument in the *Tractatus* for the existence of simple entities in terms of the unalterable form of the world.[17]

Thus even though Wittgenstein realizes dimly that a chessboard, a steamship, a pencil stroke are "logical" simples, namely, structures, his tendency to think of ontological analysis in analogy to spatial analysis wins out in the end. But it occurs to him that this identification may be a mistake after all, for he asks: "Is spatial complexity also logical complexity?"[18] When he raises this question, he is not certain about the correct answer: "It seems to be yes." But then he succeeds in convincing himself that the answer must be affirmative. He even finds an argument to this effect: "The complexity of spatial objects is a logical complexity, for to say that one thing is part of another is always a tautology."[19] Alas, he never tells us why he believes that statements about spatial relations among spatial entities are tautologies. The follower of the later Wittgenstein, however, may not be at a loss for an answer. Such statements, he is prone to claim, are tautologies, because their truth follows from the "logic of spatial relation terms."

As a consequence of his identification of spatial with ontological analysis, Wittgenstein is unable to give examples of logical simples; for spatial analysis does not seem to yield spatial simples, at least not of the perceptual kind. In this connection, it is interesting to note that his reason for rejecting shades of colors as examples of logical simples rests, similarly, on his belief that certain statements are tautologies. Wittgenstein holds that it is tautologous to assert that no surface can be both red and green all over at the same time.[20] If this statement is a tautology, then it follows from his explication of the notion of tautology in terms of truth-tables that either red, or green, or both properties, cannot be simple properties. And if shades of colors are not examples of simple properties, what properties could be?

In the *Tractatus*, as many recent commentators have noted, Wittgenstein talks about simple objects but does not give a single example of such an object. This omission, together with the fact that his remarks about objects are rather obscure, has provided fuel for the controversy as to whether or not he was a nominalist when he wrote the *Tractatus*.[21] There is no easy resolution of this issue. One thing is certain: since Wittgenstein mistakes certain statements about the spatial composition of spatial entities and certain statements about the incompatibility of properties for tautologies, he is unable to give examples of simple individuals and of simple properties. Perhaps, he meant to leave open what particular individuals and properties have to be regarded as simple, insisting, however, that there must be simples of these two kinds. Or, perhaps he meant to imply that our inability to point out simple individuals and simple properties means that the required simple objects must be of an entirely different kind, that they must be neither individuals nor properties. Or, perhaps, he could not make up his mind about these two possibilities. It is not even entirely unlikely that he continued to think of the simple objects of his ontology more often than not as spatial individuals while he was elaborating the thoughts of the *Notebooks* and writing the *Tractatus*.

As I mentioned at the beginning, it is usually said that Wittgenstein rejected in his later philosophy the notion of absolute simplicity and, hence, also the search for simple entities as it occurs in the *Notebooks* and the *Tractatus*. Now, it is quite true, for example, that the elements of chemistry are different from the elementary particles of physics. It is, furthermore, true that it is not always clear what kind of analysis and what kind of simple entity someone has in mind when he talks about these things. But these facts have not the slightest tendency to discredit the program of the *Notebooks* and the *Tractatus*. There can be little doubt that Wittgenstein is after ontological simples in these books. He tries to make out the ontological building blocks of the world, not the chemical or physical ones. There exists in these works a definite frame of reference for the questions of whether or not there are simple entities and what they are. Thus it is not true at all that Wittgenstein's search in his earlier books depends on an absolute notion of simplicity, whatever that may be. Rather, it rests on the notion of an *ontological kind*, the notion of a *category*. I have argued that Wittgenstein does indeed confuse spatial with ontological analysis, but he confuses these two things with each other, not because he thinks in terms of absolute simplicity, but because he mistakenly believes that certain statements about spatial relations among things are tautologies.

The real question, then, is not whether there is such a thing as absolute simplicity, whatever that may be, but rather whether there is ontological simplicity. Wittgenstein in his later philosophy, and indeed most of his followers, seem to confuse these two quite different issues with each other. They seem to reason that, since there is no absolute simplicity, there is no ontological simplicity. Since there is no ontological simplicity, a search for ontological simples is pointless.

Since such a search is pointless, there is really no such enterprise as ontology or metaphysics. One sees how this line of reasoning can lead directly from a rejection of the bogus notion of absolute simplicity to a rejection of ontology or metaphysics as a whole.

Be that as it may, even in *The Philosophical Investigations*, Wittgenstein talks about spatial simplicity in order to make the point that things are only relatively simple.[22] A white square of a chessboard, he claims, is relatively simple when compared with the whole board. It is not absolutely simple, he seems to imply, because it can be divided into smaller parts. But is not the shade of white of this small square at least a simple entity? According to Wittgenstein, one may consider it to be simple, but one may also think of it as composed of pure white and pure yellow. This answer shows that the idea of ontological analysis continues to elude him. Granted that a shade of white may be thought of as "composed" of pure white and pure yellow, this does not show that it is not, ontologically speaking, simple. It does not show that this shade cannot belong to an ultimate category. The shade of white is a property and so are the two colors of which it is assumed to be "composed." By "decomposing" the shade into pure white and pure yellow, we merely get further examples of the category *property*. This fact, if it has any bearing on the search for the basic categories, may reinforce a philosopher's conviction that properties form a category.

22 EMERGENT PROPERTIES

If one attempts to discover the ontological categories by a spatial analysis of wholes into smaller and smaller parts, in the spirit of the early Wittgenstein, one is at once confronted with the possibility that this analysis has no obvious end. Wittgenstein, as we saw, was deeply disturbed by this fact. But this is not the only feature of spatial analysis that may be thought to raise ontological problems. If we analyze a spatial object far enough into its spatial parts, we arrive eventually at elementary particles, certain types of things studied by the physicist. These elementary particles have certain properties and lack others, as the physicists have discovered in investigations. Now, it seems that to the best of the physicist's present knowledge, the particles of which spatial objects consist do not share with these objects all their properties. Particles have properties which the perceptual objects do not have, and conversely. For example, while some perceptual objects are colored, the particles of which they consist are not colored. This fact has led some philosophers to conclude that a perceptual object cannot really be one and the same thing as the structure of the particles which are its parts. Presumably, this conclusion follows from a straightforward application of Leibniz's principle. It leads to the kind of view most forcefully expressed in Eddington's claim that there are really two tables, with one of which, the "perceptual table," he has been familiar from earliest years, with the other of which, the "physical table," he has more recently become acquainted.[1]

Others react to the physicist's facts by denying either the existence of the "perceptual table" or the existence of the "physical table." According to the former view, physics has the last word when it is a question of what there is; and since physics clearly shows that particles have no colors, we are allegedly forced to conclude that there are no perceptual objects. They are merely "appearances" to human observers of systems of imperceptible particles. According to the latter view, common sense has the last word when it comes to the question of what exists; and since there are clearly tables, and since they are equally clearly colored, there can be no such things as particles. Particles, in the spirit of this approach, are merely "logical constructions."

There are other ways out. It may be argued that what the facts of physics show is, not that there is no perceptual table, but that it is not, contrary to all appearances, colored. Or one may claim that since the perceptual table is clearly colored, the physicist must be wrong when he maintains that particles are not colored. Or it may be said that the perceptual table is in one sense the same as the physical table, but that in another sense they are not the same.[2] At any rate, we do not have to choose among these equally preposterous alternatives, and I shall show why.

I take it that there are perceptual objects and that some of them are colored. I also believe that a table consists of particles and that these particles are not colored. But it does not follow that there must be two tables, as Eddington claims. A table consists spatially of particles; entities of a certain kind, which have certain properties and which stand in certain relations to each other, are the ultimate spatial parts of the table. This does not mean, of course, that the table is identical either with any one of these particles or with the class of all these particles. A single particle is not a table; nor is a class of particles a table. What is identical with the table is a certain structure, in our technical sense of the term, of certain particles. The chessboard, similarly, is not identical with any one of its squares, nor is it the class of squares. It is identical, though, with the (spatial) structure of sixty-four squares. Just as the chessboard is that structure, so the table is the structure of its elementary particles. So much in disagreement with Eddington's claim that there are two tables.

Are we, then, implying that Leibniz's principle does not hold? Are we asserting that one and the same object, the table, can both be colored and also not colored? Of course not. The physicist does not tell us that those structures which are tables are not colored. He merely maintains that certain parts of these structures, elementary particles, are not colored. He claims to have discovered that certain very small spatial parts of tables do not have the same properties as the tables themselves. But this should not come as a philosophical shock to anyone. We do not have to consider such esoteric entities as elementary particles to see that the spatial parts of an object do not have to have the same properties as the object of which they are parts. For example, a certain square of the chessboard is white, but the chessboard itself is not white. Only parts of it are white. Or imagine a square A whose diagonals have been drawn, so that it consists of four triangles. A has the property of being square, but none of its four spatial parts has this property. On the other hand, every one of these four parts of A is triangular, even though A itself is square. To sum up, if we acknowledge that the spatial parts of perceptual objects may have properties other than those which the whole perceptual object has, none of the unsatisfactory positions mentioned above is forced upon us. We do not have to accept Eddington's duplication of objects. Nor do we have to choose between perceptual objects and elementary particles.

Tables are colored, elementary particles are not. But the former consist of the latter. There is no puzzle. No drastic revision of our common-sense beliefs, including those of the scientist, is necessary. Why, then, is there all the fuss? I shall venture a guess. Our defense of common sense must have clashed with some kind of basic philosophical dogma. Let us see.

Sellars, who has discussed this matter more thoroughly and more astutely than most contemporary philosophers, argues that we have to choose, as I have put it, between perceptual objects and physical objects, between the manifest image, as he puts it, and the scientific image.[3] He believes that a perceptual object cannot be identical with a structure of particles "in that simple sense in which a forest is identical with a number of trees."[4] Thus he disagrees with our view. But he concedes that "there is nothing immediately paradoxical about the view that an object can be both a perceptible object with perceptible qualities *and* a system of imperceptible objects, none of which has perceptible qualities. Cannot systems have properties which their parts do not have?"[5] Indeed, cannot the table have properties that the particles of which it consists do not have? According to Sellars, the answer is affirmative as long as we have certain properties in mind, but it is negative if we think of the colors of perceptual objects. What are these two kinds of properties for which Sellars claims different answers?

Sellars's answer is not as straightforward as one would wish.[6] A system of pieces of wood, according to Sellars, can have the property of being a ladder, even though none of its parts has this property. What holds for this property holds presumably for many others. What all these properties have in common is, in Sellars's words, that "these properties are a matter of the parts having such and such qualities and being related in such and such ways."[7] The color of a pink ice cube, on the other hand, is in Sellars's view a property of a different kind. Presumably, one cannot plausibly maintain that the color of this ice cube is a matter of its parts (particles) having such and such imperceptible qualities and standing in such and such imperceptible relations to each other. Sellars puts it this way: "*Pink* does not seem to be made up of imperceptible qualities in the way in which being a ladder is made up of being cylindrical (the rungs), rectangular (the frame), wooden, etc." The underlying principle of this division of properties of perceptual objects into those that are merely a matter of the parts having certain properties and standing in certain relations and those that are not, is as follows: "If an object is *in a strict sense* a system of objects, then every property of the object must consist in the fact that its constituents have such and such qualities and stand in such and such relations, or, roughly, every property of a system of objects consists of properties of, and relations between, its constituents."[8]

What Sellars has in mind, I think, is this.[9] The colors of perceptual objects are simple properties. If one holds that a perceptual object is a structure of elementary particles, however, then no property of such a structure could be simple. Hence one cannot hold both that the colors of perceptual objects are simple and that these perceptual objects are structures of particles. In terms of Sellars's distinction between two kinds of properties, his main contention is that all the properties of a structure must be "complex." Structures cannot have simple properties. What properties they do have are "definable" or "reducible" to the properties of their ingredients and the relations among these ingredients.[10] In one sentence, there are no emergent properties.

The property of being a ladder is cited as an example of a "reducible" property; it is listed as an example of a property that can be "defined" in terms of the properties of and the relations among the parts of the object which is a ladder. The color pink, on the other hand, can, allegedly, not be so "defined." If my earlier arguments have been sound, then there are no such things as complex properties. But Sellars's distinction can nevertheless be explicated within our framework. The expression 'A is a ladder,' we may say, is merely short for a longer expression of the following sort: 'A consists spatially of such and such pieces of wood of such and such shapes which stand in such and such relations to each other'. The idea is, of course, that the longer sentence mentions only properties of and relations among spatial parts of A. When we say that A is pink, on the other hand, we are not abbreviating in a similar fashion a longer statement about the properties of and relations among parts of A. Let us grant, for the sake of argument, these two assertions about the predicates 'ladder' and 'pink'. We can now reformulate Sellars's principle like this: All statements which attribute properties to perceptual objects are mere abbreviations of longer statements which attribute properties to and relations among parts of the perceptual objects. His argument comes down to this: If a perceptual object were a structure of elementary particles, then all its properties would have to be reducible in the precise sense just explicated. But the perceptual object has a color and this color is not so reducible. Hence, a perceptual object cannot be identical with a structure of particles.

Since I agree with Sellars that colors are simple properties of perceptual objects, but since I nevertheless claim that a perceptual object is a structure of particles, I must reject Sellars's principle of reduction. Structures can have "simple" properties; they can have properties which are not "reducible" to the properties of and relations among their parts. That this is so, and hence that the principle of reduction is false, seems rather obvious. There are many examples of simple properties of structures, so that one cannot help but wonder why the principle of reduction has been so widely accepted.[11] First of all, there are the colors of perceptual objects. But we do not have to conceive of perceptual objects as structures of esoteric particles in order to see that the principle of reduction is violated. Consider again the square A with its diagonals drawn. It consists of four triangles which stand in certain spatial relations to each other. A has the simple property of being square, even though none of its four spatial parts has this property. Nor can it be an abbreviation to say that A is square; for there are squares which do not consist of four triangles but consist, for example, of sixty-four smaller squares; and there are even squares which do not have any perceptible spatial parts, like one of the small squares of the chessboard. In general, shape is an "*emergent*" property which is not "*reducible*" to the properties of and relations among the parts of the shaped entity.

Of course, not all properties of structures "emerge" in this sense. I granted earlier, for the sake of the argument, that being a ladder is not a simple property in the sense discussed. Perhaps, it isn't. But take the "property" of the series of natural numbers of having a first but no last element. To say this of the series, I am fairly sure, is merely short for saying that there is an element such that all other elements of the series are larger than it, while there is no element which is the largest. The thesis, then, is not that all supposed properties of structures emerge, but merely that there are such properties and, specifically, that colors and shapes are among the emergent properties of spatial structures. In particular, we are not committed to accept as emergent such suspect properties as "the will of the people," "the mood of the crowd," and the like.[12] It is not to be decided by "a priori argument" whether there can or cannot be emergent properties of structures. This is a factual matter. Some properties of some structures appear quite obviously to be emergent; others seem quite clearly to be "reducible"; still other properties may be in doubt. But we insist on two essential points in regard to the holism-individualism controversy, namely, first, that there are "irreducible" structures and, second, that there are "emergent" properties.

We can now appreciate the force of Sellars's argument. Nothing less is at stake than the existence of emergent properties. Sellars is basing his argument against the identity of perceptual objects with structures of particles on the commonly accepted dogma that there are no emergent properties. As much as I admire some of the incisive criticism which earlier philosophers of science advanced against vitalists, holists, and Gestalt theoreticians of various persuasions, I can only disagree with the general thesis of reduction.

Sellars mentions a further objection which is of interest here to the view I have defended.[13] He argues, if I understand him correctly, that in order to show that, say, brown can be predicated of a structure, one must show that some statement of the form 'brown (. . .)' is true, where the expression filling the blank belongs "to the conceptual space of a set of elements, and has the appropriate logical form for referring to an aggregate of the elements."[14] It will not do, according to Sellars, to fill the blank with an expression for a perceptual object, say, the description 'the table before me'; for the "problem of *in what sense* tables are "in fact" aggregates is left completely unilluminated."[15] He may mean to say that I assume what I am supposed to show when I (a) point out that I can say that the table before me is brown, that this is an appropriate statement, and (b) conclude that, therefore, brown can be a property of aggregates; for then we simply take for granted, of course, that the table is an aggregate, without explaining in what sense and how it is one. If this is what Sellars has in mind, let us rephrase the relevant statement and say: The structure which consists of such and such particles in such and such relations is brown, where the blanks have to be filled in by the physicist, so that we get a rather detailed description of the structure under consideration in terms of its physical constituents and their relations to each other. But I have the impression that Sellars would still not be satisfied; for what he is driving at in this

passage is, it seems, that if we fill the blank in 'brown (. . .)' with an
expression that really and truly has the appropriate logical form for
referring to an aggregate, we will get "a number of subjects" for the
property *brown*, so that this property will have to be relational in
character. We will get something of the form 'brown $(x_1, x_2, \ldots)$,'
where brown turns out to be some kind of relation among x_1, x_2, etc.
But since it is clearly not a relation, as is agreed by all parties to the
dispute, this will not do. In short, Sellars argues that, if we try to give a
detailed analysis of the perceptual structure and do not just presuppose
that the perceptual object is a structure, we will inevitably arrive at a
statement in which brown is attributed, not just to one subject, but to
several such subjects; and, hence, we shall have to give up the view that
brown is a property rather than a relation.

But the statement with the detailed description mentioned earlier
shows clearly that this consequence is not forthcoming. The phrase 'the
structure which consists of such and such particles in such and such
relations to each other' describes a single entity, not a multitude of
entities. To say that this structure is brown is, therefore, to predicate
the color brown of a single thing. Brown does not turn into a relation
among particles, but remains a monadic property of perceptual objects.
The description of such an object, it is true, is in terms of a multitude
of its parts, but it is not a description of these parts. What can fill the
blank in 'brown (. . .)' and be, at the same time, informative about the
structure of the perceptual object is a description of this object in terms
of the properties of and relations among its parts. Analogously, being
square does not have to be conceived of as a relation if we say that the
object before us consisting of the four triangles *a, b, c,* and *d* which
stand in such and such spatial relations to each other is square. The
property of being square is predicated of a single thing *A*—consisting of
other things—not of the four triangles of which *A* consists. This reply to
Sellars assumes, of course, that what he calls an "expression belonging
to the conceptual space of a set of elements, and having the appropriate
logical form for referring to an aggregate of these elements" can be a
description of a single entity in terms of the entities of which it consists
and their properties and relations. Every entity of whatever kind can in
my opinion be both labeled as well as described. A mere label for the
perceptual object is in our case excluded by Sellars's insistence—
justified or not—that the sense in which a perceptual object is a

structure of particles must be illuminated. This leaves us only descriptions. But certain descriptions, as I have tried to show, will do nicely.

Sellars may have been misled by the common practice of referring to a class by an expression of the form '$(a, b, c \ldots)$'. If we put a predicate in front of such an expression, we get an expression that seems to represent relational predication; a relation seems to be predicated of the entities $a, b, c,$ etc. But we must not be misled by this superficial similarity. In reality, the expression '$(a, b, c, \ldots)$' means something quite different when it is used to represent a class and when it is used to represent the entities among which a certain relation holds. In the first case '$(a, b, c, \ldots)$' is just another expression for what the expression 'the class consisting of $a, b, c, \ldots$' describes.

Let me summarize the most important results of our discussion of structures. We distinguished at the beginning between five different kinds of wholes. Correspondingly, there are five different notions of *analysis*. An entity may be said to be analyzed if one has listed all of its properties. If one believes that the properties of an object can be divided into important and unimportant ones, into essential and inessential properties, one may wish to speak of true analysis only in those cases where all the essential properties have been listed. Furthermore, if to analyze an entity in this manner is to define it, then it turns out that the definition of an object consists in a list of its essential properties. What comes to mind in this connection is the possibility of thinking of the essential properties of an entity as its categorial properties. To define an entity, according to this possibility, is to categorize it.

Classes may be said to be analyzable into their elements, and numbers may be said to be analyzable into other numbers. More important, philosophically speaking, is the fourth notion of analysis according to which facts can be analyzed into their constituents. The ontological enterprise, as we have seen, rests on this possibility. It consists partly in the analysis of facts and the subsequent categorization of their constituents.

But the most important idea of analysis for ordinary purposes is the one according to which structures can be analyzed into their parts; and among structures, spatio-temporal structures—ordinary perceptual objects—are the most obvious and interesting examples. In regard to such complex individuals, we noted that they can be perceived in single mental acts of perception, contrary to a widespread view embraced, for example, by Husserl and Moore. We compared individuals with bundles of properties and criticized both Berkeley's as well as Goodman's attempts to reduce the former to the latter. Important as the spatial analysis of a (spatial) thing, or individual, is for certain purposes, one must not confuse it with ontology. This point was emphasized in connection with the discussion of some of Wittgenstein's earlier ideas about the nature of the search for logical simples. We noted, incidentally, a connection between Wittgenstein's early conception of ontological analysis and his later rejection of the whole metaphysical enterprise. Last but not least, we pointed out that spatio-temporal structures have emergent properties, and that colors are among these properties. Since perceptual objects have such properties, one of the most profound reasons for denying that they are structures consisting of colorless elementary particles disappears.

CONCLUSION

A List of Categories

At this point, the presentation of an ontological inventory is appropriate. What follows is a tentative list of categories. This list is supposed to be complete as far as the main categories are concerned.

The most general category is that of being an *entity*. Everything is an entity. Even states of affairs which do not obtain—which are merely imagined or thought of—have this property of being an entity. Being an entity is thus *summum genus*. Or, we may wish to say, drawing on a scholastic proposition, that the property of being an entity is not really a genus since it transcends all genera. We could call it a transcendental property in order to emphasize its special status among the categories. But we must not be misled by this similarity between the scholastic view about the place of the category entity and our view. All the nonexistent entities of our ontology are states of affairs. They belong therefore to a category which is completely neglected by scholastic philosophers. It is not the case, as most scholastic philosophers maintain, that something can be a thing and yet not exist. There are no nonexistent things. Nevertheless, according to our use of the word 'entity,' something can be an entity even if it has no ontological status. But all the entities without ontological status belong to the category of state of affairs.

Entities divide into things and states of affairs. Of course, this is not the only possible division of all entities into two mutually exclusive classes. One could, for example, divide all entities into those which are relations and those which are not relations. But two considerations seem to speak strongly for the dichotomy here proposed. First, the difference between things and states of affairs seems to be more fundamental than any other difference between two categories. States of affairs are the only entities which can have properties and stand in relations to other entities even if they do not exist (or obtain). Things, on the other hand, cannot have properties and cannot stand in relations, unless they exist. In brief, the distinction between things and states of affairs corresponds to what appears to be a very profound distinction between entities that cannot have properties and cannot stand in relations unless they exist and entities which can have properties and can stand in relations even though they do not exist (or obtain). Second, the division of all entities into things and states of affairs yields automatically a subdivision of states of affairs based on the kinds of things there are; for states of affairs are to be distinguished in terms of their constituents.

Nothing can have the property of being a thing unless it exists. But an entity can be a state of affairs and yet have no existential status whatsoever. This, as I said, is a fundamental difference between things and states of affairs. Is there also a corresponding difference between the kind of being which a thing has when it exists and the kind of being which a state of affairs has when it obtains? Are there two modes of being, one for things and one for states of affairs? I do not know. I have usually said that things exist, while states of affairs obtain, but I do not know whether or not there really is a difference between the being of things and the being of states of affairs. I am inclined to believe that there is no difference. 'Existence,' I tend to think, is univocal. Of one thing, though, I am quite certain. If there are two modes of being, one for things and one for states of affairs, then neither one of these two modes is more exalted than the other. It may turn out to be the case that states of affairs are not "there" in the very same sense in which things are "there," but in whatever sense states of affairs may turn out to be "there," they will not be condemned to an inferior, less perfect, kind of existence. Note, particularly, that I have expressed no doubts about existence and the nature of existence, but only about the existence of a second sort of being which would be peculiar to states of affairs. It is not a question of being uncertain as to whether or not there is the category of existence.

Let us assume from now on that there is only one mode of being, namely, existence. This category is not coextensive with the category of entity. Not every entity exists. Nor is it coextensive with the category state of affairs. Not every state of affairs exists. Nor, finally, is it coextensive with the category of thing; for some existents are not things. But every thing, at least, is an existent. Does this mean that existence is a property of all things and of certain states of affairs? There are two kinds of properties: properties which are exemplified only by existents and properties which are exemplified by nonexistent entities as well. It is clear that existence cannot be a property of the second kind; for existence never belongs to an entity which does not exist. But it is also clear that existence cannot be a property of the first kind. Given any existent, such a property may or may not be exemplified by it. Such a property has the characteristic that it divides all existents into two exclusive classes, into those existents that have the property and those that do not. Existence, on the other hand, does not share this feature. Existence is not something which an existent may or may not have. It is not something which may or may not be "added on" to an existent. Put differently, while any property—even the queer properties of being an entity and of being a state of affairs—stands in the relation of exemplification to an entity, existence is not exemplified at all. Existence belongs to an entity much more intimately. This does not mean that the existent entity and existence are one and the same. How could they be the same, since existence belongs also to many other entities? Does an existent stand in some other kind of relation to existence? Again, I must confess that I do not know what to say. But I am drawn toward the view that there is no relation whatsoever between an existent entity and existence. Be that as it may, existence is not a property of entities.

There are, therefore, categories which are not properties. Existence is not the only such category, for that matter; negation, too, is a category, but not a property. Hence there are three kinds of categories. First, there are categorial properties which can be exemplified by nonexistent entities. As examples we have the category of entity and the category of state of affairs. Second, there are categorial properties which can be exemplified only by existents. The category of a thing, the category of a relation, and the category of a class may serve as examples. Third, there are categories which are not properties at all, neither properties of the first kind nor properties of the second kind. Existence and negation are of this sort.

There are eight kinds of *things:* (1) existence, (2) negation, (3) property, (4) relation, (5) class, (6) quantifier, (7) structure, and (8) individual.

Since we have already said the most important things about *existence,* let us turn immediately to *negation.* Negation forms its own category, as it were. It attaches itself only to states of affairs. There are no negative properties. Nor is there, according to our ontological assay, a relation of negative exemplification, that is, a relation which holds between an entity and a property whenever the entity does not have the property. In regard to negation, I am drawn to a view similar to the one just mentioned in connection with existence, namely, that there is no relation between negation and the state of affairs which is negated. Just as existence may turn out to be *in* a thing without being related to it, so negation may turn out to be *attached* to a state of affairs without being related to it.

Negation, it is obvious, attaches only to nonexistent states of affairs. The state of affairs represented by 'Not-*P*' exists only if the state of affairs represented by '*P*' does not exist. In this respect, negation resembles those properties and relations which can connect with nonexistents. But there is also a difference. Most of these properties and relations do not connect solely with nonexistents. Negation does. The property of being an entity, for example, is exemplified by existents as well as nonexistents; the relation *or* connects two existents as well as an existent and a nonexistent. Negation is the only category which never attaches itself to an existent.

There are many kinds of *properties.* We have repeatedly mentioned the very fundamental distinction between properties that can be exemplified by nonexistent entities and properties that cannot be exemplified by such entities. Properties can also be classified according to their generality. The most general properties are, of course, the categorial ones.

Some categories of entities show a marked and surprising lack of properties; others have a wealth of properties. Existence and negation, for example, are entities and things, but they do not seem to have any other properties. States of affairs and numbers, too, seem to have no properties other than categorial ones. But they, in distinction to existence and negation, stand in a number of characteristic relations.

States of affairs are related to each other by connectives, they are related to mental acts through the nexus of intentionality, and they have various entities as constituents. Numbers stand in arithmetical relations to each other. To say that the number 2 is even is not to say, according to our analysis, that the number 2 has the property of being even. Rather, what we mean is that the number 2 is divisible by 2; and that turns out to be a statement about a certain arithmetical relation among three numbers. Even quantifiers, classes, and relations show this property of properties. As it turns out, individuals and certain kinds of structures are the main bearers of properties. Property theory, as it turns out, deals in the main with the properties of individuals and structures.

Individuals are characterized by the properties from the sensory dimensions. Among these properties, the spatial and temporal ones occupy an ontologically privileged position. Every individual, to begin with, is a temporal entity. Moreover, even some nonindividuals, certain structures, have temporal properties. Thus the "property" of having a duration is, in a sense, wider than that of being an individual. One could, therefore, speak of a category of temporal entities, entities with properties which are durations. Similarly for space. Even though not all individuals are spatial, those that have properties which are shapes and sizes form a distinct group, comprising not only individuals but also certain structures. These features are responsible for the generally felt ontological eminence of space and, especially, of time. They may lead a philosopher to make his foremost categorial distinction between entities that are in space and/or time and entities that are not.

I have no doubt whatsoever that there are properties of properties. Being a duration, for example, is a property of properties; and so is being a color. To say of something that it is colored is to say that it has a color. And to say that an individual has a color is to say that it has a property which is a color. There exists no such property of individuals as that of being colored. It must be admitted, though, that some philosophers cannot be convinced of this fact. They insist that it is just the other way around: to say of an individual that it has a property which is a color is, according to them, just a clumsy way of saying that the individual is colored.

Even though we have acknowledged the existence of a great variety of properties—for example, properties of properties, categorial properties, etc.—there are limits to our ontological generosity. Onto-logical realism, needless to say, is what we call our attitude. First, there are no relational properties. There are only relational predicates, that is, expressions which are carved out of sentences and which represent relations together with at least one of their terms. Second, there are no complex properties. Complex propositional forms do not represent entities belonging to the category of property.

There are *relations* that relate only existents and relations that hold even if one or more of their terms do not exist. All relations between things are of the first kind. Only relations involving states of affairs are of the second kind. In particular, the connective *or* can relate an existent to a nonexistent state of affairs; and the connective *neither-nor* always obtains between two nonexistent states of affairs. The intentional nexus connects a mental act with a state of affairs, even if the state of affairs does not exist. A thing may be a constituent of a state of affairs, even if the state of affairs does not exist. For example, red is a constituent of the *state of affairs* that A is red, even if A is not red. One can tell what constituents a nonexistent state of affairs has. Finally, states of affairs can exemplify the two properties of being an entity and of being a state of affairs, even if they do not exist. Thus there are at least four kinds of relations of the second type, namely, connections, intentionality, being a constituent of (a state of affairs), and exemplification.

Another important ontological division separates relations that can bridge main categories from those that cannot. Let us call each relation of the first sort a *nexus*; let us call relations of the second kind *connections*.

There are at least six groups of nexus. (1) Exemplification can hold between a property and an entity which is not a property. For example, individuals exemplify properties but are not themselves properties. (2) The membership relation holds not only between classes and other classes, but also between individuals, properties, numbers, etc., on the one hand, and classes, on the other. (3) The parts of a structure need not be structures. The natural numbers, for instance, are not structures even though they are parts of the series of natural numbers. (4) Some constituents of states of affairs are not themselves states of affairs. (5) The relation of intentionality, according to a view here presupposed but not explained, holds between a certain property of a mental act—a property which is sometimes called the content of the act—and a state of affairs. It holds therefore always between two entities which belong to different categories. (6) Last but not least, spatial and temporal relations can obtain between structures, on the one hand, and individuals, on the other. For example, the spatial relation of being a spatial part of may hold between a spatial structure and an individual which is a simple part of the structure. Hence, spatial and temporal relations can bridge categories, at least, according to our separation of structures from individual things.

Connections divide into at least three groups. (1) There are relations which hold only between properties. To this group belong, for example, relations between pitches. (2) Arithmetical relations are connections among quantifiers. (3) The connectives relate states of affairs with states of affairs and never cross from one category to another.

The most common division of relations divides them into such kinds as asymmetrical relations, transitive relations, reflexive relations, etc. Just as there are no such properties of relations as being a nexus and being a connection, there are no such properties as being asymmetrical and being transitive. To say of a relation that it is symmetrical, for example, is just another way of saying that, if the relation holds between two entities e_1 and e_2, then it holds also between e_2 and e_1.

The two relations of identity and diversity are in a class all by themselves. Their ontological importance cannot be overemphasized. Identity holds between everything and itself. Its field is as large as that of the category of entity. Diversity, too, has this extreme generality. Every entity is different from every other entity. We could, therefore, assign identity to the class of connections and diversity to the class of nexus. But it may be better to distinguish identity and diversity from all other relations whether they are nexus or connections.

Identity and diversity, I just said, hold between entities in general. Not only existents stand in these two relations to each other. Of course, if it were not for the fact that some nonexistent entities are states of affairs, the problem of the identity and diversity of nonexistent entities would not arise. As it is, the problem narrows down to this: Under what conditions is a nonexistent state of affairs P identical with a state of affairs Q, and under what conditions is P

different from Q? Recall our earlier discussion of the identity of states of affairs. What we said there holds generally, even for nonexistent states of affairs. Two states of affairs are the same if and only if they have the same constituents, in the same order, the same number of times. Even if P is a nonexistent state of affairs, we can still make out its constituents, and hence we can still compare it with another state of affairs by comparing the constituents, their order, and their number in the two states of affairs. Since identity and diversity can obtain between nonexistent entities, they belong together with such relations as the connectives, the intentional nexus, being a constituent of, and exemplification.

Relations are different from most other kinds of entities in the following important respect. Almost all nonrelational entities require relations in order to form wholes. Two individuals, for example, cannot be related to each other, unless there exists a relation between them. An individual and a property, to give another example, cannot form a state of affairs, unless the nexus of exemplification holds between them. And so on. But this is not the case for relations themselves. A relation R is not related to its two terms A and B by a second relation, say, S. Rather, R "attaches" to A and B directly. Relations furnish so to speak the glue of the world, while nonrelations are comparable to wooden boards. Two wooden boards will not stick together without glue, but the glue sticks to a wooden board without having to be glued to it by means of some second kind of glue. This characteristic of relations, that they relate nonrelations without being related to them, is called to our attention by Bradley's famous argument. What this argument proves is, not that there are no relations, but rather that one of the premises of the argument is false, namely, the assumption that a relation is always related to its terms by another relation.

I said cautiously that relations differ in this respect from most other entities. The exceptions I had in mind are existence, negation, and the quantifiers. These three kinds of entities, one may hold, can "attach" to their respective entities without being related to them by a separate relation. Negation, as I remarked before, seems to attach directly to states of affairs; it is neither exemplified by a state of affairs nor in any other familiar sense related to it. Similar considerations hold for existence. Existence seems to belong to an entity in a completely unique way, a way which does not involve a relation. Finally, quantifiers seem to be attached to the category *entity* without being related to it. Now, I do not know whether this hunch will stand up under philosophical probing. But I am fairly sure that if negation, existence, and the quantifiers are related to their respective entities, then there must be three different relations, one for each of these three cases. Negation must be related to a state of affairs quite differently from the manner in which existence belongs to an entity; and both of these relations must differ from the one that then presumably connects a quantifier with the category of entity. In short, if negation, existence, and the quantifiers are not exceptions to the rule that all nonrelations require relations in order to be related to each other, then we must acknowledge the existence of a relation of *attaching* between negation and states of affairs, the existence of a relation of *belonging* between existence and entities, and a relation of *being tied to* between the quantifiers and the category of entity.

Next, we shall consider *classes*. Classes, one may wish to hold, are either finite or infinite. Of course, this distinction makes sense only if there are indeed infinite classes. Are there infinite classes and, hence, infinite numbers? Once again, I must admit that I do not know the answer. But I am, once more, relatively sure of something else. There is no sound argument, to the best of my knowledge, which proves that there are infinite classes. On the other hand, the assumption—the axiom, if you prefer—that there are infinitely many entities is perfectly compatible with the rest of our ontology. Hence I shall continue to assume that there are indeed infinitely many entities, so that the distinction between finite and infinite classes remains significant.

One can also distinguish between classes of classes and classes which consist of other kinds of entities. There are, surely, both kinds of classes. I do not share Goodman's inability to comprehend how different classes can consist of the same ultimate elements. We could further distinguish between homogeneous and inhomogeneous classes. A homogeneous class consists of members which belong to the same category; an inhomogeneous class contains members from different categories. For example, a class of individuals is a homogeneous class, while a class containing both individuals and properties is an inhomo-geneous class. Finally, and most importantly, classes can be grouped according to the kinds of entities which they contain as members. There are, for example, classes of natural numbers, classes of colors, classes of human beings, and so on.

I shall be brief about *quantifiers*, since we have discussed them so extensively earlier in this book. Quantifiers can be divided into two large groups, namely, into numbers on the one hand, and what I shall call, for want of a better term, general quantifiers, on the other. There are a great many numbers, but only a few general quantifiers. Usually, one thinks only of *all* and *some* as belonging to the class of general quantifiers. But it seems to me that there also exist at least the two quantifiers *no* (as in 'No entities which are properties are such that') and *the* (as in 'The entity which is an individual and which has the property P such that'). There may or may not be infinitely many numerical quantifiers. A moment ago, we decided to assume that there are infinitely many. But be that as it may, the numerical quantifiers which quite obviously exist can be further divided in a familiar fashion into natural numbers, rational numbers, irrational numbers, etc.

Quantifiers are tied to only one entity, namely, the category entity. But this does not mean, of course, that they cannot quantify many different kinds of entities. But a so-called quantification over individuals, would be most conspicuously expressed by 'All entities which are individuals are such that'; a quantification over properties, by 'All entities which are properties are such that'; and so on. Since the quantifiers are tied to entity, they range over nonexistents as well as over existents.

Structures, like classes, are to be grouped according to their parts. We must distinguish between the proper parts and the parts of a structure. The proper parts comprise all parts of a structure with the exception of the characteristic relation or relations of the structure. The parts of a structure, on the other hand, include these characteristic relations. Some structures contain only one characteristic relation; so, for example, the series of natural numbers ordered by the relation of being greater than or equal to. Other structures have several characteristic relations. A spatial structure like the chessboard we talked about, for example, contains a large number of spatial relations. The proper parts of the series of natural numbers are, of course, the natural numbers; the ultimate proper parts of the chessboard are spatial individuals.

Among structures, the spatial and/or temporal ones stand out. Notice that a spatial structure need not form a "continous object"; its spatial parts need not lie adjacent to each other. Sixty-four squares in a row with a space between each square and the next one form just as much a spatial structure as the sixty-four squares of the chessboard. Similarly, a series of temporal individuals with temporal "gaps" between them form just as much a temporal structure as a continuous sequence of temporal individuals. What we ordinarily call a perceptual object, such as a table, is a spatially and temporally continuous structure. It is a structure whose spatial and temporal parts are spatially and temporally contigous to each other.

Perceptual objects change. Does this mean that we have to add a category of change to our ontological inventory? Or does change, perhaps, occur under one of the categories we have already acknowledged? The answers to both questions are negative. To say of a perceptual object that it has changed properties is to say, according to our analysis, that it has temporal parts with different properties. Assuming, for example, that a certain object A has changed from being red to being blue, we would say that A has two temporal parts, b and c, such that b is red, c is blue, and b is earlier than c. A similar analysis would be given of relational change, that is, of cases where individuals stand (at different times) in different relations to other individuals. In short, while it is of course true to say that there is change and that things change, there does not exist an entity called change. Rather, what exists are the various temporal parts of individuals and of structures with their sometimes quite different properties. Needless to say, events do not play a role in our ontology either, as long as one does not mean by 'event' a state of affairs or some other kind of entity listed in our ontological table.

It should be obvious, but apparently is not, that isomorphic structures are not necessarily the same. Two structures are the same if and only if they have the same proper parts and these proper parts stand in the same relations to each other.

Individuals fall into two main groups, namely, temporal individuals and spatio-temporal individuals. We have already alluded to the almost categorial significance of time, and the somewhat lesser ontological importance of space.

Generally speaking, individuals are to be divided according to the properties they have and the relations in which they stand. Some individuals have spatial properties and stand in spatial relations to other things; these individuals also have temporal properties, various durations, and stand in temporal relations to other entities. Similarly, some individuals have colors and can be classified by this fact; others have pitches and can be characterized by this feature. We also noted earlier that there are dependencies between certain properties of individuals, so that the same class of individuals may be determined by two different properties. For example, it is presumably a fact—puzzling to many philosophers—that all extended individuals have colors and that all colored objects are extended. The sum total of such laws, laws which connect the different members of a sense dimension or establish relations between sense dimensions, constitutes the area of synthetic a priori knowledge.

There is one division of individuals which we have so far neglected, although it has created a great amount of philosophical controversy. Some individuals are commonly said to be mental; others are said to be physical. Since this is not the proper place for an explication of the cluster of problems which constitutes the mind-body issue, two brief comments must suffice.

According to one idea, forever associated with Brentano's philosophy, all mental entities are mental acts. The division between the mental and the physical coincides with the division between mental acts and all other things. Mental acts are characterized by the feature of intentionality. In order to understand the nature of mental things it becomes, therefore, necessary to illuminate the nature of intentionality. Brentano's students—especially Meinong and Husserl—devote many pages to this task. We should note one peculiar feature of Brentano's dichotomy. Sense impressions, for example, turn out to be "physical" things, since they are not intentional and hence are not mental acts. If one thinks of sense impressions as paradigms of mental things, then one cannot follow in Brentano's footsteps. Intentionality cannot be the essential feature of all mental things.

At any rate, any division of individuals into mental and nonmental things rests on a division of properties and/or relations into mental and nonmental things, since individuals are classified by means of the properties which they have and the relations in which they stand to other things. Mental acts, for example, can be distinguished from other individuals by virtue of the fact that they are the only things which have two properties, namely, a property that determines the quality of the act and a property that determines the content of the act. Furthermore, it has been held—in the spirit of the Brentano tradition—that the contents of mental acts are those things which stand in the intentional nexus to the objects of acts. What sets mental acts apart from other individuals are, therefore, the following facts: first, that there are two groups of special properties which only mental acts have and, second, that there is a unique relation which holds always between a property from one of these two kinds and something else.

So much for the eight main categories of things. *States of affairs*, as we saw earlier, can be classified in regard to their constituents. Here are some of the more important ontological distinctions.

First, states of affairs divide into states of affairs which are quantified and states of affairs which are not quantified. Quantified states of affairs, in turn, can be grouped according to the kinds of quantification they contain and the order in which these quantifiers occur. Recall, for instance, the importance of the Skolem normal form for property theory.

Second, states of affairs can be divided into atomic and molecular states of affairs. An atomic state of affairs is a nonquantified state of affairs without negation and connectives. A molecular state of affairs is a nonquantified state of affairs which contains negation and/or at least one connective.

Third, states of affairs can be grouped into a number of classes according to the entities, other than quantifiers and connectives, which they contain. This is the most common distinction. It separates ontological states of affairs from logical states of affairs, arithmetic from set theory, geometry from chemistry, and so on.

Certain traditional distinctions between kinds of states of affairs (or propositions, or statements) do not occur in our ontology. We do not think that these distinctions reflect ontological differences. For example, the well-known distinction between lawful and accidental generalities has in our view no basis in ontological fact. Very roughly, a general state of affairs is classified by us as being accidental rather than lawful whenever we can see no connection between this state of affairs and what we consider to be a more or less well-established body of laws. Similarly, necessary states of affairs do not contain a characteristic constituent which could be identified with necessity. They do not contain a "modal operator," nor do they contain some special kind of necessary exemplification. Rather, they are thought of as necessary, because we see that they follow logically from what we consider to be well-established laws. Or they are considered to be necessary, because we cannot imagine circumstances under which they would not obtain.

To some philosophers, this ontological list will appear to teem with unnecessary entities. To others, it may appear impoverished and incomplete. Not all the future criticism of our ontology, however, will flow from thoughtful argument. In matters ontological, philosophical temperament is, alas, a powerful motive. The ontological miser will continue to define away all kinds of entities, no matter how thoroughly his so-called definitions have been discredited as ontological tools. The ontological spendthrift, on the other hand, will still insist on ever finer distinctions and ever more modes of being. Their attitudes differ greatly from the spirit in which this book was written. An inquiry into the categorial structure of the world should be undertaken with the expectation that the world may turn out to be more complicated than expected, but without the unending yearning for a richness that is not there.

NOTES

Introduction: A Principle of Acquaintance
1 Perceiving and Sensing

1 Gottlob Frege, *The Foundations of Arithmetic*, 2d rev. ed. (Evanston, 1968), p. 32.

2 I refer the reader to Reinhardt Grossmann, *The Structure of Mind* (Madison and Milwaukee, 1965).

3 Frege, *Foundations*, p. 31.

4 Ibid., pp. 29, 36.

5 Cf. Reinhardt Grossmann, *Reflections on Frege's Philosophy* (Evanston, 1969), pp. 43-46.

6 See Gustav Bergmann, "Intentionality," in *Meaning and Existence* (Madison, 1960); and Grossmann, *The Structure of Mind*.

2 Intuition and Judgment

1 Compare the following explanation from Kant's *Logik*: "Ein Urtheil ist die Vorstellung der Einheit des Bewusstseins verschiedener Vorstellungen oder die Vorstellung des Verhaeltnisses derselben, sofern sie einen Begriff ausmachen." *Akademie Edition* (Berlin, 1968), 9:101.

2 See, for example, Franz Brentano, *Psychologie vom empirischen Standpunkt* (Leipzig, 1925), vol. 2.

3 See Gottlob Frege, "On Concept and Object," "Function and Concept," and "On Sense and Reference," in *Translations from the Philosophical Writings of Gottlob Frege*, eds. Peter Geach and Max Black (Oxford, 1952).

4 See A. Meinong, *Ueber Annahmen*, 2d ed. (Leipzig, 1910).

5 See Reinhardt Grossmann, "Sensory Intuition and the Dogma of Localization," in *Essays in Ontology* [by] Edwin B. Allaire [and others], (The Hague, 1963).

6 See Edmund Husserl, *Logische Untersuchungen*, 2d ed., vol. 2, pt. 2 (Halle, 1913).

7 For a more extended criticism of perfect particulars, see Edwin B. Allaire [and others], *Essays in Ontology* (The Hague, 1963). For specific criticism of this feature of Husserl's philosophy, see Gustav Bergmann, "The Ontology of Edmund Husserl," in *Logic and Reality* (Madison, 1964).

8 Gottlob Frege, *The Foundations of Arithmetic*, 2d rev. ed. (Evanston, 1968), p. xxii.

9 Ibid.

10 Ibid., p. 116.

3 Atomic and Molecular Facts

1 Ludwig Wittgenstein, *Tractatus Logico-Philosophicus* (London, 1961), p. 88.

2 Cf. H. Hochberg, "Negation and Generality," *Nous* 3 (1969): 325-43.

3 Bertrand Russell, "On Propositions: What They Are and How They Mean," in *Logic and Knowledge*, ed. R. C. Marsh (London, 1956), p. 287.

4 Raphael Demos, "A Discussion of a Certain Type of Negative Proposition," *Mind* 102 (1917): 188-96.

5 See Russell's criticism of Demo's article in "On Propositions."

6 Gustav Bergmann, "Generality and Existence," in *Logic and Reality* (Madison, 1964).

Part I: Numbers and Quantifiers
4 Abbreviations

1 Cf. Gottlob Frege, *Die Grundlagen der Arithmetik* (Breslau, 1884) and his *Die Grundgesetze der Arithmetik*, (Jena, 1893-1903) vols. 1 and 2. I shall quote from J. L. Austin's translation of *Die Grundlagen: The Foundations of Arithmetic*, 2d rev. ed. (Evanston, 1968). For Frege's place in the history of logic, see William and Martha Kneale, *The Development of Logic* (Oxford, 1962).

2 I shall speak of classes rather than extensions and I shall disregard all complications introduced by Frege's notion of a value-range. On this matter see R. Wells, "Frege's Ontology," *The Review of Metaphysics* 4 (1951): 537-73; Montgomery Furth, trans., Introduction to *Grundgesetze: The Basic Laws of Arithmetic* (Berkeley and Los Angeles, 1964); and Th. Simpson, "Dos problemas en la doctrina de Frege," *Critica* 1 (1967): 110-11.

3 See, for example, Gottlob Frege, *The Foundations of Arithmetic*, 2d rev. ed. (Evanston, 1968), p. 78.

4 See especially the metaphorical description of definitions on pp. 100-01 of the *Foundations*.

5 Gottlob Frege, *Zeitschrift fuer Philosophie und philosophische Kritik* 103 (1894): 320. It is not hard to understand why the notion of definition is obscure in the *Foundations*; for Frege also lacks a clear understanding of informative identity statements. His program of reduction raises two important questions which are not answered in the *Foundations*. First, are "reductive" definitions informative identity statements? Second, how are informative identity statements possible? Frege answers the second question to his own satisfaction in the famous paper "Ueber Sinn und Bedeutung." But his most penetrating description of definitions occurs in an unpublished manuscript called "Ueber Logik in der Mathematik," which was apparently written in 1914 and is kept at the University of Muenster. For a discussion of this paper see my *Reflections on Frege's Philosophy* (Evanston, 1969), pp. 248-53.

6 Cf. Frege's unpublished paper "Ueber Logik in der Mathematik."

7 For further remarks on the nature of definite descriptions, see Chapter 6.

8 Cf. Frege, *Foundations*, p. 78, and Frege's review of Husserl's *Philosophie der Arithmetik*.

9 Cf. Fred Wilson, "Definition and Discovery," *The British Journal for the Philosophy of Science* 18 (1967): 287-303 and 19 (1967): 43-56.

5 Identity and Equivalence

1 I shall continue to speak of sentences and statements for stylistic reasons. But there is no category of statements in my ontology. Very roughly, the relevant entities are (mental) thoughts, (perceptual) signs and noises, and states of affairs. Cf. Reinhardt Grossmann, *The Structure of Mind* (Madison and Milwaukee, 1965). For a discussion of some confusions surrounding the notions of statement, assertion, etc., see Herbert Hochberg, "On Referring and Asserting," *Philosophical Studies* 20 (1969): 81-88.

2 Cf. Bertrand Russell, *Principles of Mathematics*, 2d. ed. (New York, 1964), pp. 95-96.

3 See Gottlob Frege, "Die Verneinung," *Beitraege zur Philosophie des deutschen Idealismus* 1 (1919): 143-57; translated in

Translations from the Philosophical Writings of Gottlob Frege, eds. Peter Geach and Max Black (Oxford, 1960). Frege seems to hold a similar view at least in regard to negation.

4 On this point, cf. Reinhardt Grossmann, *Reflections on Frege's Philosophy* (Evanston, 1969), and Reinhardt Grossmann, "Non-existent Objects," *American Philosophical Quarterly* 6 (1969): 17-32.

6 Descriptions and Leibniz's Law

1 Gottlob Frege, *The Foundations of Arithmetic*, 2d rev. ed. (Evanston, 1968), pp. 76-77.

2 But we must remember that earlier, Frege distinguished not between sense and reference, but rather between an entity and the way in which this entity is determined. For a detailed discussion of Frege's sense-reference distinction, see Reinhardt Grossmann, *Reflections on Frege's Philosophy* (Evanston, 1969), pp. 154-224.

3 This is, I think, the most important part of Russell's analysis of definite descriptions. For a discussion of his analysis see Grossmann, *Reflections on Frege's Philosophy*, pp. 167-77.

4 See Chapter 15 for a discussion of the existence of complex properties including relational properties.

7 Recursive Definitions

1 Bertrand Russell, *Principles of Mathematics*, 2d ed. (New York, 1964), p. 119. Russell does not merely claim that arithmetical relations can be "reduced" to relations among classes, but also that the latter can be reduced to logical relations, that is, connectives.

2 Russell formulates this "definition" only for the sum of $1 + 1$; I have taken the liberty of generalizing it. But on p. 118 of *Principles of Mathematics*, he gives a general definition which agrees with my version (R).

3 See, for example, Richard Dedekind, *Was sind und was sollen die Zahlen* in *Gesammelte mathematische Werke*, (Braunschweig, 1932), vol. 3.

4 For a description of recursive functions, see Kurt Goedel, "Ueber formal unentscheidbare Saetze der *Principia Mathematica* und verwandter Systeme I," *Monatshefte fuer Mathematik und Physik* 38 (1931): 173-98; English translation in Jean van Heijenoort, *From Frege to Goedel* (Cambridge, Mass., 1967), pp. 596-616.

5 See, for example, Alfred North Whitehead and Bertrand

Russell, *Principia Mathematica*, (Cambridge, 1910), vol. 1. But we must keep in mind Russell's fondness for the term 'propositional function'.

6 See Willard Van Orman Quine, *Set Theory and Its Logic* (Cambridge, Mass., 1963), pp. 79-80.

8 Definition by Abstraction

1 Gottlob Frege, *The Foundations of Arithmetic*, 2d rev. ed. (Evanston, 1968), p. 80, footnote.

2 The classic work on definition by abstraction is by H. Scholz and H. Schweitzer, *Die sogenannten Definitionen durch Abstraktion*, vol. 3 of *Forschungen zur Logistik und zur Grundlegung der exakten Wissenschaften* (Leipzig, 1935). In addition to the passages from Frege and Russell cited below, cf. Giuseppe Peano, "Le Definizioni Per Astrazione," in *Opere Scelte*, (Rome, 1958), 2: 402-16.

3 Frege, *Foundations*, pp. 74-79.

4 Ibid., p. 78.

5 Cf. Rudolf Carnap, *Introduction to Symbolic Logic and Its Applications* (New York, 1958).

6 Cf. Bertrand Russell, *Principles of Mathematics*, 2d ed. (New York, 1964), pp. 114-15, and also a later remark by Frege in *Grundgesetze der Arithmetik*, (Jena, 1903), 2: 70-71, footnote.

7 Frege was well aware of this objection. He claims that it can be met, but does not explain how. See *Foundations*, p. 80, footnote.

8 Cantor seems to have held this latter view. He conceives of a number as a general concept (*Allgemeinbegriff*) under which all (well-ordered) classes fall that are similar to each other, and under which only these classes fall. See his review of Frege's *Foundations* in *Gesammelte Abhandlungen* (Berlin, 1932), pp. 440-41.

9 See *Foundations*, pp. 68-69. Frege makes this point repeatedly. But then he goes on to argue that numbers are objects rather than concepts.

9 Existence and the Quantifiers

1 Gottlob Frege, "Ueber Begriff und Gegenstand," *Vierteljahrsschrift fuer wissenschaftliche Philosophie* 16 (1892): 192-205; translated in *Translations from the Philosophical Writings of Gottlob Frege*, eds. Peter Geach and Max Black (Oxford, 1952).

2 Geach and Black, eds., *Translations*, p. 49.

3 Ibid., p. 50.

4 Bertrand Russell, "The Philosophy of Logical Atomism," in *Logic and Knowledge*, ed. Robert C. Marsh (London, 1956), p. 252.

5 Cf. Russell's remark: "You see, therefore, that this proposition 'Romulus existed' or 'Romulus did not exist' does introduce a propositional function, because the name 'Romulus' is not really a name but a sort of truncated description. It stands for a person who did such-and-such things, who killed Remus, and founded Rome, and so on. It is short for that description; if you like, it is short for 'the person who was called "Romulus" '." *Logic and Knowledge*, p. 243.

6 Ibid. Cf. Frege's remark quoted on p. 76.

7 Gottlob Frege, "Kritische Beleuchtung einiger Puntke, in Ernst Schroeder's, *Vorlesungen ueber die Algebra der Logik*," *Archiv fuer systematische Philosophie* 1 (1895): 433-56; Geach and Black, eds., *Translations*, p. 104.

8 Nor are Kantians the only ones who fall into this trap. Witness Franz Brentano's transformation of '*A* is green' into 'green *A* is (exists)' in his *Psychologie vom empirischen Standpunkt*, (Leipzig, 1925), vol. 2; see also the passage translated by D. B. Terrell in *Realism and the Background of Phenomenology*, ed. R. M. Chisholm (New York, 1960), pp. 62-70.

9 G. E. Moore, *Philosophical Studies* (London, 1922), pp. 212-13.

10 Cf. Jaako Hintikka, "Studies in the Logic of Existence and Necessity," *The Monist* 50 (1966): 55-76.

11 It is true, of course, that a thing exists if and only if it is self-identical; for the relation of self-identity holds only if the respective thing exists. But this is not an abbreviational equivalence, and hence there is no ontological reduction of existence to identity. For an attempt to "define" existence in this fashion, see, for example, George Nakhnikian and Wesley Salmon, " 'Exists' as a Predicate," *The Philosophical Review* 66 (1957): 535-42.

10 Necessity

1 On this characterization, cf. Gustav Bergmann, "Synthetic A Priori," in *Logic and Reality* (Madison, 1964).

2 Cf. Roderick M. Chisholm, *Theory of Knowledge* (Englewood Cliffs, 1966), pp. 70-90.

3 Gottlob Frege, *Begriffsschrift* (Halle, 1879), §4.

4 Ibid.

5 For this Humean answer, see, for example, Gustav Bergmann,

"Comments on Professor Hempel's 'The Concept of Cognitive Significance'," in *The Metaphysics of Logical Positivism* (New York, 1954);
and Willard Van Orman Quine, "Necessary Truth," in *The Ways of
Paradox* (New York, 1966).

6 The ontological reduction of dispositional properties to laws
involving nondispositional properties proceeds along similar lines. For
details see F. Wilson, "Dispositions: Defined or Reduced," *Australasian
Journal of Philosophy* 47 (1969): 184-204; H. Hochberg, "Dispositional Properties," *Philosophy of Science* 34 (1967): 10-17; and Gustav
Bergmann, "Dispositional Properties and Dispositions," *Philosophical
Studies* 6 (1955): 57-60.

11 Possible Entities

1 Cf. Nino B. Cocchiarella, "Existence Entailing Attributes,
Modes of Copulation and Modes of Being in Second Order Logic,"
Nous 3 (1969): 33-48.

12 Implicit Definitions

1 Richard Dedekind, "Was sind und was sollen die Zahlen," in
Gesammelte mathematische Werke, (Braunschweig, 1932), 3: 335-90.

2 Ibid., p. 360.

3 Ibid.

4 See Bertrand Russell's criticism of Dedekind's "definition" in
Principles of Mathematics, 2d ed. (New York, 1964), pp. 248-49.

5 Ibid., p. 249.

6 Cf. Gottlob Frege's criticism of "definitional abstraction" in
The Foundations of Arithmetic, 2d rev. ed. (Evanston, 1968), p. 45.

7 See David Hilbert, *Grundlagen der Geometrie* (Leipzig, 1899).

8 Gottlob Frege, "Ueber die Grundlagen der Geometrie,"
Jahresberichte der deutschen Mathematiker-Vereinigung, vol. 12
(1903): I: 319-24, II: 368-75; vol. 15 (1906): I: 293-309, II: 377-403,
III: 423-30.

9 Reduction sentences are, incidentally, implicit definitions and
hence, according to our analysis, not really definitions at all. They do
not ontologically reduce the dispositional properties to other properties, but introduce them as irreducible entities. See on this point Fred
Wilson's essay, "The Notion of Logical Necessity in the Later
Philosophy of Rudolf Carnap" in A. Hausman and F. Wilson, *Carnap
and Goodman: Two Formalists* (The Hague, 1967).

10 Willard Van Orman Quine, "Implicit Definition Sustained," *Journal of Philosophy* 61 (1964): 71-74.

11 Cf. David Hilbert and Paul Bernays, *Grundlagen der Mathematik*, (Berlin, 1939), 2: 253.

12 Cf. David Hilbert and Wilhelm Ackermann, *Principles of Mathematical Logic* (New York, 1950), p. 115.

13 See Chapter 14 on contextual definitions.

14 See Chapter 15 on property abstraction.

15 On this and some of the following points compare Fred Wilson, "Implicit Definitions Once Again," *Journal of Philosophy* 59 (1965): 364-74.

13 Constructional Definitions

1 See Nelson Goodman, "Constructional Definitions," in *The Structure of Appearance* (Cambridge, Mass., 1951); see also Willard Van Orman Quine, "Ontological Reduction and the World of Numbers," *Journal of Philosophy* 61 (1964): 209-16, and "Ontological Relativity: The Dewey Lectures 1968," Ibid. 65 (1968): 185-212. Both of these articles have been reprinted in Quine's *The Ways of Paradox* (New York, 1966).

2 Ernst Zermelo, "Ueber die Grundlagen der Arithmetik," *Atti del IV Congresso internazionale dei matematici*, Roma, April 1908, vol. 2 (*Accademia dei Lincei*, Rome, 1909), pp. 8-11; John von Neumann, "Zur Einfuehrung der transfiniten Zahlen," *Acta litterarum ac scientiarum Regiae Universitatis Hungaricae Francisco-Josephinae, Sectio scientiarum mathematicarum* vol. 1, (1923) pp. 199-208. This article is translated in Jean van Heijenoort, *From Frege to Goedel* (Cambridge, Mass., 1967), pp. 346-54.

3 Quine, *"Ontological Relativity,"* p. 198.

4 Ibid. The italics in this quotation and the following ones are mine.

5 Quine, *Set Theory and Its Logic* (Cambridge, Mass., 1963), p. 81.

6 Quine, *The Ways of Paradox*, p. 200.

7 Goodman, *The Structure of Appearance*, p. 28.

8 Ibid.

9 Ibid., p. 29.

Part II: 14 Contextual Definitions

1 See Russell to Frege, 16 June 1902, in Jean van Heijenoort, *From Frege to Goedel* (Cambridge, Mass., 1967), pp. 124-25.

2 See Cantor to Dedekind, 31 August 1899, in Georg Cantor, *Gesammelte Abhandlungen*, ed. Ernst Zermelo (Berlin, 1932), p. 448.

3 See Bertrand Russell, *The Principles of Mathematics* (Cambridge, 1903), Appendix B; and Russell's paper "Mathematical logic as based on the theory of types," *American Journal of Mathematics* 30 (1908): 222-62, reprinted in *From Frege to Goedel*, pp. 152-82.

4 Similar considerations may have led Russell to accept the simple theory of types. But we must not forget that he also proposed other solutions to the paradoxes, among them the view that the paradoxes merely prove that certain entities like the class of all classes do not exist. See, for example, Bertrand Russell, "On some difficulties in the theory of transfinite numbers and order types," *Proceedings of the London Mathematical Society*, 2d series, 4 (1907): 29-53.

5 This point has often been noted. See, for example, Alonzo Church, *Introduction to Mathematical Logic* (Princeton, 1956), p. 323.

6 Cf. Willard Van Orman Quine's theory of virtual classes in his *Set Theory and Its Logic* (Cambridge, Mass., 1963). Quine, of course, treats 'F' as a schematic letter rather than a quantifiable variable, but this makes no difference in my criticism of the illicit use of contextual definitions. To use class terminology when one does not really mean it, as Quine does, serves no philosophical purpose. To pretend that one is talking about classes by using class terminology when one really is not, or to pretend that one is not when one really is, or even to do both of these things in the same context, is merely hocus-pocus and has no bearing on ontology.

7 See David Hilbert and Paul Bernays, *Grundlagen der Mathematik*, (Berlin, 1939), vol. 2, Supplement IV G; and also L. Kalmar, "On the possibility of definition by recursion," *Acta Scientiarum Mathematicarum*, vol. 9 (1940), pp. 227-32; and E. Landau, *Grundlagen der Analysis* (Leipzig, 1930).

8 Cf. Hilbert and Bernays, *Grundlagen der Mathematik*, (Berlin, 1934), 1: 292-93, 391-92; and Patrick Suppes, *Introduction to Logic* (Princeton, 1957), pp. 152-63. This conception of definitions and the requirements for rules of definition can be traced back to Stanislaw Leśniewski.

9 Heinrich Behmann claims that the contextual definition: " '$F(f)$' is short for 'not-$f(f)$' " does not allow the elimination of the defined expression from the formula '$F(F)$'. He maintains "that there is

no expression free from abbreviations of which '$F(F)$' would be an abbreviation." And he comes to the conclusion that "what is responsible for the occurrence of the set-theoretical contradictions is neither the naive concept of a set nor the concept of infinity, but essentially the characterized misuse of abbreviations or variables." H. Behmann, "Zu den Widerspruechen der Logik und der Mengenlehre," *Jahresbericht der deutschen Mathematiker-Vereinigung* 40 (1931): 37-48.

10 See Frege's review of Hilbert's *Die Grundlagen der Geometrie* translated as "On the Foundations of Geometry," *The Philosophical Review* 69 (1960): 3-17; see p. 5 in particular.

15 Property Abstraction

1 See F. P. Ramsey, *The Foundations of Mathematics and Other Logical Essays* (New York and London, 1931), pp. 112-34. This argument and the following one are essentially Ramsey's. He argues, just as I do here, that there are no complex properties. But his real objective is to shed some light on the difference or lack of difference between particulars (individual things) and universals (properties and relations).

2 Ibid., p. 118.

3 What holds for 'ground,' holds ipso facto for 'grue'. There simply is no such property as *grue,* because there is no such property as the property of being green if examined before time t, and otherwise being blue. Since there is no such property, Goodman's new riddle of induction disappears. See N. Goodman, *Fact, Fiction, and Forecast* (Cambridge, Mass., 1955).

4 Compare this view with Ramsey's, according to which 'A has all the complex properties of B' is to be interpreted as the joint assertion of all propositions of the form 'If $F(A)$, then $F(B)$'. *The Foundations of Mathematics*, pp. 119-20.

5 As Goedel points out, this view about the existence of classes has never led to a paradox. See his "What is Cantor's Continuum Problem?", in Paul Benacerraf and Hilary Putnam, *Philosophy of Mathematics* (Englewood Cliffs, 1964), pp. 258-73.

6 See Ernst Zermelo, "Untersuchungen ueber die Grundlagen der Mengenlehre I," *Mathematische Annalen* 65 (1908): 261-81; translated in Jean van Heijenoort, *From Frege to Goedel* (Cambridge, Mass., 1967), pp. 199-215. For a more recent version, see Paul Bernays, *Axiomatic Set Theory* (Amsterdam, 1958).

16 Sets versus Classes

1 Cantor to Dedekind, in Georg Cantor, *Gesammelte Abhandlungen*, ed. Ernst Zermelo (Berlin, 1932), p. 448.

2 Ibid., pp. 447-48; translated in Jean van Heijenoort, *From Frege to Goedel* (Cambridge, Mass., 1967), pp. 113-17. Cf. J. Koenig, "Ueber die Grundlagen der Mengenlehre und das Kontinuumproblem," *Mathematische Annalen* 61 (1905): 156-60; translated in *From Frege to Goedel*, pp. 143-49.

3 See, for example, John von Neumann, "Eine Axiomatisierung der Mengenlehre," *Journal fuer die reine und angewandte Mathematik* 154 (1925): 219-40; translated in *From Frege to Goedel*, pp. 394-413; and also Kurt Goedel, *The Consistency of the Continuum Hypothesis* (Princeton, 1940).

4 Cesare Burali-Forti, "Una questione sui numeri transfiniti," *Rendiconti del Circolo matematico di Palermo* 11 (1897): 154-64; translated in *From Frege to Goedel*, pp. 105-12.

5 This seems to have been Cantor's view. See *Gesammelte Abhandlungen*, pp. 441, 444.

6 For the details of this traditional construction, see Rudolf Carnap, *Introduction to Symbolic Logic and Its Applications* (New York, 1958).

7 This consideration takes care, I think, of W. Kneale's objection to Frege's definition of similarity between concepts (classes). See William and Martha Kneale, *The Development of Logic* (Oxford, 1962), pp. 461-62.

8 Cantor, *Gesammelte Abhandlungen*, p. 441.

9 See Bertrand Russell, *Introduction to Mathematical Philosophy* (London, 1919).

10 Compare Zermelo's criticism of attempts by Bernstein and Schoenflies to save the class of all ordinal numbers in his "Neuer Beweis fuer die Moeglichkeit einer Wohlordnung," *Mathematische Annalen* 65 (1908): 107-28; translated in *From Frege to Goedel*, pp. 183-98.

17 Impredicative Definitions

1 Cf. Paul Finsler, "Gibt es unentscheidbare Saetze?", *Commentarii mathematici helvetici* 16 (1944): 310-20.

2 See Kurt Goedel, "Ueber formal unentscheidbare Saetze der *Principia Mathematica* und verwandter Systeme I," *Monatshefte fuer Mathematik und Physik* 38 (1931): 173-98; translated in Jean van

Heijenoort, *From Frege to Goedel* (Cambridge, Mass., 1967), pp. 596-616.

3 Kurt Grelling and Leonard Nelson, "Bemerkungen zu den Paradoxien von Russell und Burali-Forti," in *Abhandlungen der Friesschen Schule,* n.s. (1907-08), 2: 300-24.

4 Bertrand Russell, "Mathematical logic based on the theory of types," *American Journal of Mathematics* 30 (1908): 222-62.

5 See F. P. Ramsey, *The Foundations of Mathematics and Other Logical Essays* (New York and London, 1931).

6 Willard Van Orman Quine, "On the Axiom of Reducibility," *Mind* 45 (1936): 498-500.

7 Cf. Ramsey, *The Foundations of Mathematics,* p. 41.

8 Russell, "Mathematical logic as based on the theory of types," in *From Frege to Goedel,* p. 154.

9 Ibid., p. 155.

10 Henri Poincaré, "Les mathématiques et la logique," *Revue de métaphysique et de morale* 14 (1906): 294-317.

11 Ernst Zermelo, "Neuer Beweis fuer die Moeglichkeit einer Wohlordnung," *Mathematische Annalen* 65 (1908), 107-28; translated in *From Frege to Goedel,* p. 191. Compare also Peano's interpretation of Poincaré's objection in *Opere Scelte,* vol. 1 (Rome, 1957), pp. 344-58.

12 See Reinhardt Grossmann, "Common Names," in *Essays in Ontology* [by] Edwin B. Allaire [and others] (The Hague, 1963), pp. 64-75. The common name doctrine has a contemporary version. It is now fashionable among some philosophers to say such things as that 'green' is true of *A* instead of that *A* is green. For a criticism of this nominalistic gambit see Herbert Hochberg, "Nominalism, Platonism, and "Being True of"," *Nous* 1 (1967): 413-19.

13 Cf. Frege's criticism of common names, for example, in his review of Husserl's *Philosophie der Arithmetik* in the *Zeitschrift fuer Philosophie und philosophische Kritik* 53 (1894): 313-32.

14 Richard Dedekind, *Stetigkeit und irrationale Zahlen,* in *Gesammelte mathematische Werke* (Braunschweig, 1932), 3: 315-34.

Part III: 18 Wholes and Parts

1 This is a favorite idea of Brentano's students, as a glance at Meinong, Husserl, and others shows. For the flavor of the idea, see Kurt Twardowski, *Zur Lehre vom Inhalt und Gegenstand der Vorstellungen* (Vienna, 1894).

2 See, for example, Rudolf Carnap, *Meaning and Necessity*, 2d ed. (Chicago, 1956), pp. 20-21, 30-31.

3 F. H. Bradley, *Appearance and Reality* (Oxford, 1930), p. 18.

4 See Reinhardt Grossmann, *Reflections on Frege's Philosophy* (Evanston, 1969), pp. 50-83.

19 A Problem of Perception

1 Edmund Husserl, *Ideas. General Introduction to Pure Phenomenology* (London, 1931).

2 G. E. Moore, "Some Judgments of Perception," in *Philosophical Studies* (London, 1922), p. 230. (The italics are mine.) I shall completely neglect two important features of Moore's analysis, because they are not essential for my discussion. First, Moore speaks of judgments where I shall speak of perceptions or acts of seeing. Second, and more importantly, Moore identifies the perceived parts of perceptual objects with sense impressions. I shall not.

3 Ibid., p. 234.

20 Bundles of Properties

1 Nor are properties constituents of individuals in the sense in which something is a constituent of a fact. Philosophers who speak, say, of the color red as a constituent of a perceptual object may be misled into believing that such perceptual objects are not individuals, but are facts (states of affairs) instead. A case in point is Bergmann's claim that an ordinary object is a state of affairs. See Gustav Bergmann, *Realism. A Critique of Brentano and Meinong* (Madison and Milwaukee, 1967). See also Edwin B. Allaire, "Bare Particulars," in *Essays in Ontology*, [by] Edwin B. Allaire [and others] (The Hague, 1963), and "Another Look at Bare Particulars," *Philosophical Studies* 16 (1965): 16-21.

2 George Berkeley, *The Works of George Berkeley*, eds. A. A. Luce and T. E. Jessop, (London, 1948-57), 9 vols.; *Three Dialogues*, 2: 231-32; and *Principles*, sec. 49.

3 John Locke, *An Essay Concerning Human Understanding*, Book II, xxiii, sec. 2. Cf. Edwin B. Allaire, "The Attack on Substance: Descartes to Hume," *Dialogue* 3 (1965): 284-87.

4 Compare Leibniz's remark: "In distinguishing two things in substance, the attributes or predicates, and the common subject of these predicates, it is no wonder that we can conceive nothing particular in this subject. It must be so, indeed, since we have already

separated from it all the attributes in which we could conceive any detail." *New Essays*, II, xxiii, sec. 2.

5 Berkeley, *Principles*, sec. 1.

6 Just as I neglect Berkeley's nominalism by talking freely about collections of properties, so I shall neglect his idealism by avoiding the identification of properties with ideas. For a discussion of the connection between Berkeley's rejection of material substances and his idealism, see Edwin B. Allaire, "Berkeley's Idealism," in *Essays in Ontology*, pp. 92-105, and Jonathan Bennett, "Substance, Reality, and Primary Qualities," *American Philosophical Quarterly* 2 (1965): 1-17.

7 See N. Goodman, *The Structure of Appearance* (Cambridge, Mass., 1951). For a criticism of Goodman's ontology, see Alan Hausman, "Goodman's Ontology," in A. Hausman and F. Wilson, *Carnap and Goodman: Two Formalists* (The Hague, 1967).

8 Goodman, *The Structure of Appearance*, p. 156.

9 N. Goodman, "A World of Individuals," in *The Problem of Universals* (Notre Dame, 1956), p. 19.

21 Spatial versus Ontological Analysis

1 See Ludwig Wittgenstein, *Philosophical Investigations* (Oxford, 1953).

2 See, for example, George Pitcher, *The Philosophy of Wittgenstein* (Englewood Cliffs, 1964).

3 Wittgenstein, *Philosophical Investigations*, § 47.

4 Ludwig Wittgenstein, *Notebooks* 1914-1916, eds. G. H. Wright and G. E. M. Anscombe (New York, 1961).

5 Ibid., pp. 45, 67.

6 Ibid., pp. 45, 51.

7 Ibid., p. 62.

8 Ibid., pp. 43, 53, 69.

9 Ibid., pp. 47, 60, 67.

10 Ibid., p. 64.

11 Ibid., p. 45.

12 Ibid., p. 70.

13 Ibid., pp. 46, 50.

14 Ibid., p. 60.

15 Ibid., p. 62.

16 Ibid., pp. 46, 63, 64.

17 Ludwig Wittgenstein, *Tractatus Logico-Philosophicus*, trans. D. F. Pears and B. F. McGuiness (New York, 1961), entries 2.02, 2.021,

2.0211, 2.0212, 2.026, and 3.23. For an attempt to explicate these remarks, see Julius R. Weinberg, "Are There Ultimate Simples?" *Philosophy of Science* 2 (1935): 387-99.

18 Wittgenstein, *Notebooks*, p. 45.

19 Ibid., p. 62.

20 Wittgenstein, *Tractatus*, entry 6.3751. See also his "Remarks on Logical Form," *Aristotelian Society*, (1929), supp. vol. 9, pp. 162-71.

21 See a number of articles by I. M. Copi, E. B. Allaire, E. Stenius, and others in *Essays on Wittgenstein's Tractatus*, eds. I. M. Copi and R. W. Beard (New York, 1966).

22 Wittgenstein, *Philosophical Investigations*, Sections 47-49.

22 Emergent Properties

1 Arthur Eddington, *The Nature of the Physical World* (Cambridge, 1928), pp. xi-xii.

2 See May Brodbeck, "Mental and Physical: Identity vs. Sameness," in *Mind, Matter, and Method*, eds. P. K. Feyerabend and G. Maxwell (Minneapolis, 1966), pp. 40-58.

3 See Wilfrid Sellars, *Science, Perception, and Reality* (London, 1963).

4 Ibid., p. 26.

5 Ibid.

6 The passage under study here contains the makings for a second argument—the so-called grain argument—which I shall not discuss, mainly because I think that it is unsound, but also because it is rather shallow. See on this matter especially W. Sellars, "Philosophy and the Scientific Image of Man," in *Frontiers of Science and Philosophy*, ed. R. G. Colodny (Pittsburgh, 1963), pp. 37-38, and some criticism of this argument by Bruce Aune in his comments on a paper by Sellars in *Intentionality, Mind, and Perception*, ed. Hector-Neri Castañeda (Detroit, 1967), pp. 283-84.

7 Sellars, *Science, Perception, and Reality.*

8 Ibid., p. 27.

9 Cf. W. Sellars, "Phenomenalism," in *Intentionality, Minds, and Perception.*

10 Sellars calls this the principle of reducibility. See *Science, Perception, and Reality*, p. 35.

11 On emergent properties see the classical article by K. Grelling and Paul Oppenheim, "Der Gestaltbegriff im Lichte der neuen Logik,"

Erkenntnis 7 (1937-38): 211-24. On emergence in explanation see Carl G. Hempel and Paul Oppenheim, "The Logic of Explanation," *Philosophy of Science* 15 (1948): 135-75.

12 On different kinds of emergence in the social sciences, see the papers by Gellner, Watkins, Brodbeck, McCiver, and Addis in *Readings in the Philosophy of the Social Sciences*, ed. M. Brodbeck (New York, 1968).

13 See Sellar's rejoinder to Aune's comments in *Intentionality, Minds, and Perception*, especially pp. 299-300.

14 Ibid., p. 300.

15 Ibid.

INDEX

Abbreviations: and Leibniz's law, 48; and logical truths, 38-39; and perception, 16

Abstract entities, and sensible entities, 10

Abstraction, numbers as products of, 95

Ackermann, W., 198n

Acquaintance: and existence, 3; and knowledge, 155-57; consists of mental acts, 4; explication of, 4; with constituents of states of affairs, 9-10; with individual things, 155-58

Addis, L., 206n

Allaire, E. B., 191n, 192n, 202n, 203n, 204n, 205n

Analysis: and spatial points, 163-64; according to Wittgenstein, 164-65; kinds of, 174; spatial vs. ontological, 162-67

Analyticity: and certainty, 88-89; and definitions, 100; and logical laws, 88; and necessity, 87-89; and sameness of meaning, 47; as a matter of use, 89

Anscombe, G. E. M., 204n

Aristotle, and acquaintance with numbers, 5n

Arithmetic statements, nature of, 29-30

Arithmetic relations, as part-whole relations, 145

Aune, B., 205n, 206n

Austin, J. L., 192n

Axioms: and analyticity, 100; and definitions, 96-101; compared with forms, 94; of choice, 121; of infinity, 185; of reducibility, 132

Beard, R. W., 205n

Behmann, H., 200n

Being, modes of, 178

Benacerraf, P., 200n

Bennet, J., 204n

Bergmann, G., 50n, 191n, 192n, 196n, 197n, 203n

Berkeley, 203n, 204n; and individual things, 156-57; and material substances, 154-58

Bernays, P., 198n, 199n, 201n

Bernstein, F., 201n

Black, M., 191n, 194n, 195n, 196n

Bradley, F. H., 201n; and relations, 184; his regress, 143-44

Bretano, F., 191n, 196n, 203n; on judgments, 10; on mental acts,

188; on nonexistent entities, 90; on relations, 92; on sense-impressions, 188

Bridge laws: and modalities, 87; and ontological dependency, 85-86; between mental and physiological states, 86; between property theory and set theory, 86-87; explicated, 47

Brodbeck, M., 205n, 206n

Burali-Forti, C., 201n, 202n; his paradox, 124, 128

Cantor, G., 64n, 195n, 199n, 200n, 201n; and the distinction between sets and classes, 122-23, and impredicative descriptions, 132; his paradox, 111, 124; his theroem, 109-10; on ordinal numbers, 127-28

Carnap, R., 195n, 197n, 201n, 203n, 204n

Castaneda, H. N., 205n

Categorial properties, 142

Categories: and constituents of states of affairs, 144-45; and mental acts, 13; and the *Tractatus,* 166; of connective, 18; of entity, 177; of existence, 78, 179; of quantifier, 18; of structure, 148-49; which are not properties, 179

Change, not a category, 187

Chisholm, R. M., 196n

Church, A., 199n

Classes: and successor relation, 61; as related to properties, 121; compared with numbers, 53-54; compared with ordered couples, 40n; compared with spatial wholes, 158-59; expressions for, 175; Goodman's rejection of, 158-60; homogeneous vs. nonhomogeneous, 185; identity of, 40; infinite,

185; kinds of, 185-86; not spatial, 149-50

Class-membership, as part-whole relation, 145

Cocchiarella, N., 197n

Colodny, R. G., 205n

Colors: and eidetic intuition, 12; and elementary particles, 168-75; and sensory intuition, 13; according to Sellars, 170-75; are sensible entities, 6, 11

Common names, and vicious circle principle, 136-37

Communication, and abbreviations, 31

Conception: vs. imagination, 82-83; vs. intuition and judgment, 10

Concepts, conceived of as nonsensible, 5-6

Confirmation, paradox of, 41n

Connections: distinguished from nexus, 182; kinds of, 183

Connectives: and nonexistent states of affairs, 44, 91; and syncategorematic expressions, 38; are connections, 183; as kinds of relations, 182; not characteristic of logic, 45; reduction of, 17-18

Copi, I. M., 205n

Criterion: of equivalence, 39-40; of identity, 39-41

Dedekind, R., 57n, 194n, 197n, 199n, 201n, 202n; and abstraction, 95-97; and definition of number, 94-95; and irrational numbers, 132, 137; his axioms, 94; on addition, 57-58

Definite descriptions: and existence of individuals, 74-75; and identity statements, 32-35; and Leibniz's law, 50-51; and recursive definitions, 58-59; and states of affairs, 52-53; as impredicative, 132-33; as recursive, 58-60; nature of, 33; of perceptual objects, 173-74; vs. lables, 32n; vs. logical proper names, 74-75; what they describe vs. what they represent, 52-53

Demos, R., 192n; on negative facts, 22

Descartes, 204n

Dewey, J., 198n

Diversity, nature of, 183-84

Dunn, M., 2

Eddington, A., 205n; on perceptual objects, 168

Eidetic intuition, compared with sensory intuition, 12

Eisenberg, P., 2

Elementary particles: according to Sellars, 170-75; and emergent properties, 167-75; and spatial analysis, 167-75

Entities: actual vs. possible, 79; and modes of being, 78; divided into things and states of affairs, 177-78; analysis of, 175; as property of everything, 142; as most general category, 177; attached to quantifiers, 73, 186; complex vs. simple, 163-67

Equivalence: and contextual definitions, 113-17; and definitions by abstraction, 65-66; and Leibniz's law, 48; and sameness of meaning, 37; criterion of, 39-40; of states of affairs, 18-19; vs. identity, 38

Equivalence classes, and definition by abstraction, 63-65

Events, do not form a category, 187

Exemplification: and Bradley's regress, 143-44; and existence, 76; and part-whole relation, 141-45, 154; and property theory, 45; as a nexus, 182; compared with association among properties, 161; nature of, 143-44

Existence: and acquaintance, 3; and entities, 184; and exemplification, 76; and existence-properties, 92; and logical proper names, 74-75; as a category, 78, 179; as a mode of being, 178; as univocal, 178; compared with negation, 180; compared with mode of obtaining, 39n; compared with quantifiers, 75-78; definitions of, 92; Moore on, 76-77; not a property, 78, 179; of atomic facts, 17; of functions, 56-57; of individual things, 74-77; of molecular facts, 17

Existential quantifier: and definitions of existence, 78; compared with property of properties, 70-71; compared with relational property, 71-72; Frege's notion of, 70-71

Factual truths: and Frege's definition of number, 36; vs. abbreviational truths, 35-36

Feyerabend, P. K., 205n

Finsler, P., 201n

Forms: and properties, 142, 117-21; compared with axioms, 94; conceived of as implicit definitions, 96-97

Frege, G., 191n, 192n, 193n, 194n, 195n, 196n, 197n, 198n, 199n, 200n, 201n, 202n; and acquaintance with numbers, 5-6; and categorical statements, 53, 53n; and existence of individual things, 73-77; and informative identity statements, 33; and Leibniz's law, 48; and notion of thought, 71; and numbers as properties, 61; and objective entities, 14-16; and philosophy of arithmetic, 29-30; and quantifiers, 69-71; and sense-impressions, 6-10; and the sense of definite descriptions, 51-52; and sensible entities, 14-16; and subjective entities, 14-16; his definition of numbers, 30, 36-37, 47, 54; his explication of necessity, 83-84; on definitions, 30-31, 116; on definition by abstraction, 62-63; on the existence of functions, 57; on implicit definitions, 96-97; on judgments, 10-11, 15-16; on model construction, 94; on numbers, 14-16; on sense-impressions, 7n; on sense-impressions vs. concepts, 14; on unsaturatedness, 144

Functions, existence of, 56-57

Furth, M., 192n

Geach, P., 191n, 194n, 195n, 196n

Gellner, E., 206n

Goedel, K., 194n, 198n, 199n, 200n, 201n, 202n; his distinction between classes and sets, 123n

Goodman, N., 197n, 198n, 200n, 204n; and isomorphic models, 103; and the existence of classes, 158-60, 185; his analysis of individuals, 158-162; on individuation, 161

Grelling, K., 202n, 206n; his paradox, 131

Grossmann, R., 191n, 193n, 194n, 202n, 203n

Hausman, A., 197n, 204n

Heijenoort, J. van, 194n, 198n, 199n, 201n, 202n

Hempel, C. G., 197n, 206n

Hilbert, D., 197n, 198n, 199n, 200n; on axioms as implicit definitions, 96-97

Hintikka, J., 196n

Hochberg, H., 192n, 193n, 197n, 202n

Hume, 204n

Husserl, E., 31, 191n, 192n, 193n, 202n, 203n; and acquaintance with properties, 12-13; and eidetic intuition, 14; and mental acts, 188; and noemata, 150-52; and nonexistent things, 90n

Identity: as a symmetric relation, 41; criterion of 39-41; degrees of, 49; nature of, 183-84; of classes, 40; of descriptions, 51; of nonexistent states of affairs, 183-84; of states of affairs, 21, 39-41; vs. equivalence, 38; vs. isomorphism, 187

Identity statements: and abbreviations, 33-35; and definitions, 30-36, 115-16

Imagination: and induction, 82; and necessity, 79-83; vs. conception, 82-83

Individual things: according to Goodman, 158-62; and acquaintance, 154-58; and intuition, 11; and sensory dimensions, 181; are not classes of properties, 157; as spatiotemporal structures, 146-48, 181; compared with substances, 154; existence of, 74-77; explained, 154-56; kinds of, 187-88; mental vs. physical, 188-89; perception of, 150-53; simple, 165-66; vs. classes of properties, 154; vs. structures of properties, 154

Induction: and imagination, 82; and perception of molecular facts, 24-25; and synthetic apriori, 81-82; explication of, 81-82n

Informative identity statements, 32-34

Intentionality, as characteristic of the mental, 188

Intentional nexus, and non-existent states of affairs, 91-92

Irrational numbers, not classes of rational numbers, 137

Isomorphism: and models, 101; and ontological reduction, 102-105; of progressions, 61; of relations, 125-27; vs. identity, 102, 187

Jessop, T. E., 201n

Judgment: and negative facts, 22-25; and perception, 16; and seeing, 23-25

Kalmar, L., 199n

Kant, 191n; on judgments, 10

Kneale, W. and M., 192n, 201n

Knowledge: and acquaintance, 155-58; of individuals, 154-58; of substances, 154-58

Koenig, J., 201n

Labels, vs. definite descriptions, 32n

Landau, E., 199n

Laws: and accidental generalities, 87; and necessity, 87

Leibniz, 204n

Leibniz's law, 40-41, 62; and alleged exceptions, 49-51; and Frege, 48; and the color of perceptual objects, 168-69

Lesniewski, St., 199n

Localization, dogma of, 12-13, 17

Locke, 204n; and knowledge of substance, 155-56

Loewenheim-Skolem theorem, 102n

Logic, explication of, 43-46

Logical equivalence, explained in terms of material equivalence, 38-39, 42

Logical laws, as factual truths, 35-36; see also logical truths

Logical proper names, vs. descriptions, 74-75

Logical truths: and abbreviations, 38-39; and definitions, 39; and Leibniz's law, 48

Logical words, 21; and truth tables, 19; conceived of as syncategorematic, 18-19

Luce, A. A., 201n

MacIver, A. M., 204n

Marsh, R. C., 11n, 192n, 196n

Material equivalence, vs. logical equivalence, 38-39, 42

Maxwell, G., 205n

McGuinness, B. F., 205n

Meinong, A., 191n, 203n; on judgments, 11; on mental acts, 188; on nonexistent things, 90n

Membership relation, is a nexus, 182

Mental acts: and acquaintance, 4; and individuals, 188; are propositional, 8-9, 13; described, 188-89; intend states of affairs, 9; kinds of, 13; of conception, 10; of intuition, 10-11; of judgment, 10-11; of sensing, 8

Modalities: and quantifiers, 79;

are not part of the furniture of
the world, 79, 189-90; de dicto
vs. de re, 51n
Modal properties, 51n
Models: and ontological reduction, 103; for forms, 101
Modes of being, 78, 90
Moore, G. E., 196n, 203n; on
existence, 76-77; on perception
of wholes, 150-52

Nakhnikian, G., 196n
Necessity: and analyticity, 87-89;
and bridge laws, 87; and imagination, 79-83, 189-90; and
lawfulness, 83-87, 189-90; and
synthetic apriori, 80-82; kinds
of 79-80, 84-85
Negation: and existence, 180; and
states of affairs, 184; as a
category, 179-80; attached to
states of affairs, 180
Negative facts, perception of,
21-24
Nelson, L., 202n
Neumann, J. von, 198n, 201n; his
definition of ordinal numbers,
124; his distinction between
sets and classes, 123, 123n;
progressions, 101
Nexus: distinguished from
connections, 182; kinds of,
182-83
Numbers: and merely possible
states of affairs, 78-79; and
objects of intuition, 11-12; and
perception, 4-10; and theory of
types, 67-68; as quantifiers, 69,
93, 186; as sensible entities, 8;
conceived of as classes, 36,
53-54; conceived of as properties, 61, 67-69; conceived of
as relational properties, 66-67;
conceived of as wholes, 145;
Frege's definition of, 30

Objects, of sense vs. objects of
reason, 10
Ontological laws, and factual
truths, 35-36
Ontology, and logic, 43
Oppenheim, P., 206n
Ordinal numbers: as defined by
von Neumann, 124; conceived
of as numbers, 127; explicated,
125-28

Paradox: and empty description,
112; and existence assumptions, 129; of confirmation,
41n; nature of, 109-37;
Poincaré's view, 133-36; semantical, 130-37
Peano, G., 195n, 202n; and the
ramified theory of types, 132
Pears, D. G., 205n
Perception: of atomic states of
affairs, 17; of colors, 4; of
molecular states of affairs, 17,
21; of negative facts, 21-24; of
numbers, 4-10; of quantified
facts, 24-25; of spatial points,
164; of spatial wholes, 150-53;
vs. judgment, 16
Perceptual acts: as irreducible, 9;
as propositional, 16
Perceptual objects: and spatial
parts, 152; as consisting of
elementary particles, 168-75
Pitcher, G., 204n
Places: do not exist, 161; cannot
be properties, 161
Poincaré, H., 202n; and impredicative descriptions, 133-36
Possibility: explicated, 84-85, 89;
kinds of, 84-85
Possible entities, vs. actual
entities, 79
Possible things: and being, 90;
have no properties, 90-91
Properties: and localization, 12;

and numbers, 67-69; and structures, 157-58; and unsaturatedness, 144; are always exemplified, 142-43; as categorial, 180;
as constituents of states of
affairs, 13; as defined by abstraction, 61-65; as parts of
entities, 141; as sensible, 11;
emergent, 148; general theory
of, 43-46; instances of, 12-14;
intentional, 49-50; modal,
49-50; no complex ones,
118-21, 181-82; no negative
ones, 180; no relational ones,
182; not determined by forms,
117-21; of nonexistent states
of affairs, 91; of properties,
181; of spatial parts, 167; of
structures, 171-73; recognition
of, 135-36; reducible vs. irreducible, 171-72; simple vs. complex, 165-66; two kinds of,
180-81
Property theory: and nonexistent
properties, 46; and quantification theory, 46; and type
theory, 46
Propositions: and logic, 43-44; vs.
states of affairs, 43-44
Putnam, H., 200n

Quantified facts, perception of,
24-25
Quantifiers: and entities, 73; and
general theory of states of
affairs, 44-45; and impredicative descriptions, 131; and
logic, 44-45; and merely possible states of affairs, 93; and
modalities, 79; and numbers,
69; and states of affairs, 77-78;
as parts of any theory, 45;
distinguished from existence,
75-77; Frege's conception of,
69-71; kinds of, 186; not

characteristic of logic, 45;
Russell's conception of, 70;
tied to variable entity, 186
Quine, W. V. O., 195n, 197n,
198n, 199n, 202n; and isomorphic models, 101; on axiom of
reducibility, 132; on implicity
definitions, 97-101; on ontological reduction, 101-105

Ramified theory of types, and
semantical paradoxes, 131-37
Ramsey, F. P., 200n, 202n; and
ramified theory of types, 132;
on complex properties, 118-19
Rational numbers, are not classes
of natural numbers, 137
Recursive descriptions, and contextual definitions, 114-15
Relational properties: and classes,
54; and numbers, 54; and
quantifiers, 71-73
Relations: and arithmetic, 55; and
being a spatial part, 146-47;
and being a temporal part,
147-48; and Bradley's argument, 184; and successor,
57-61; and diversity, 183-84;
and equivalence, 63-65; and
identity, 183-84; and inclusion
and exclusion among pro-
perties, 81; and the intentional
nexus, 182; and isomorphisms,
125-27; and well-ordering,
125-27; among nonexistent
states of affairs, 91-92; among
nonexistent terms, 182; among
numbers, 180; among things,
182; as constituents of states
of affairs, 13; general theory
of, 43-45; kinds of, 92, 182-85;
nexus vs. connections, 182-83;
sense of a relation, 40-41
Russell, B., 192n, 193n, 194n,
195n, 196n, 197n, 199n, 201n,

202n; and existence of individual things, 73-77; and definition of arithmetical relations, 60; and definition of definite descriptions, 51n; and impredicative descriptions, 132-33; and knowledge, 150; and quantifiers, 70; and states of affairs, 11n; and vicious circle principle, 131-33; and watered-down existence, 90; on Dedekind's notion of number, 95; on existence of functions, 57; on negative facts, 21-22; on ordinal numbers, 127-28

Russell's paradox: 109-22; and contextual definitions, 113

Salmon, W., 196n
Schoenflies, A., 201n
Scholz, H., 195n
Schroeder, E., 196n
Schweitzer, H., 195n
Seeing: as irreducible mental act, 16; of negative facts, 22; vs. judging, 9, 23-25
Sellars, W., 205n, 206n; and the principle of reduction, 171-72; on colors of perceptual objects, 170-75; on perceptual vs. physical objects, 170-75
Semantical paradoxes: and ramified theory of types, 131-37; and vicious circle principle, 131-37
Sense-impressions: and numbers, 4-8; and perceptual objects, 7-9; as mental things, 188; of colors, 4-5; vs. concepts, 7
Sensible entities: and abstract entities, 10; and intuitions, 11; as individuals, 11; explication of, 9-10; Frege's view on, 14-16
Sensing, vs. seeing, 9

Sensory dimensions, and individual things, 181
Sensory intuition, of property items, 12-13
Simpson, Th., 192n
Skolem normal form, 189
Space: and the senses, 14; as characteristic of individuals, 181; as form of intuition, 12-13; and spatial relations and properties, 147; does not consist of places, 161; is not absolute, 147; is not wholly relational, 147
Spatial analysis, 158-60
States of affairs: acquaintance with, 9-10; and being, 178; and laws, 189; and ontological analysis, 145-46; and quantifiers, 78-79; and the constituent relation, 145-46; and things, 39n, 177-78; as wholes, 145-46; atomic vs. molecular, 189; category of, 11; equivalence of, 18-19, 37-38; general theory of, 43-46; identity of, 39-41, 183-84; intended by mental acts, 9; kinds of, 189-90; merely possible, 89, 91; possible vs. actual, 77; presented in perception, 16; quantified vs. nonquantified, 189; vs. propositions, 43-44; which do not obtain, 44
Stenius, E., 205n
Structures: and characteristic relations, 186; and elementary particles, 167; and space and time, 146-48, 187; as wholes, 146-49; compared with classes, 149; kinds of, 186-89; not consisting of individuals, 148-49; of properties, 157-58; parts of vs. proper parts of, 186; their properties, 171-73

Substance, knowledge of, 154-58
Substitution, and Leibniz's law, 51
Suppes, P., 199n
Syncategorematic expressions: and connectives, 38; and ontological reduction, 19; as mere artifacts of language, 21
Synthetic apriori: and induction, 81-82; and general facts, 81-82; and necessity, 80-82; and sensible dimensions, 80-81; explicated, 80-81

Terrell, D. B., 196n
Things: and existents, 74n; contrasted with states of affairs, 177-78; kinds of, 180
Time: and sense-experience, 14; as characteristic of individual things, 181; as form of intuition, 12-13; consists of relations and durations, 147-148; does not consist of moments, 147
Truth-tables, are not definitions, 19
Truth-values: and logic, 43-44; vs. states of affairs, 43

Types: and numbers, 67-68; and Russell's paradox, 110-11; and sense vs. nonsense, 110-11
Twardowski, K., 203n

Vicious circle principle, and common names, 136-37

Watkins, J. W. N., 206n
Weinberg, J., 205n
Wells, R., 192n
Whitehead, A. N., 194n
Wiener-Kuratowski device, 40n
Wilson, F., 193n, 197n, 198n, 204n
Wittgenstein, L., 192n, 204n, 205n; on molecular facts, 18-19; on negation, 18; on ontological analysis, 163-67; on simplicity and complexity, 163-67
Wright, G. H., 204n

Zermelo, E., 198n, 199n, 200n, 201n, 202n; and axiomatized set theory, 121; on impredicative descriptions, 134; his "definite Eigenschaften," 123n; progressions, 101, 104